Qatar Communication Strategies

From Managing a Crisis To Creating a Successful National Brand

QATAR COMMUNICATION STRATEGIES

From Managing a Crisis To Creating a Successful National Brand

Dr. Salim Zakhour   Dr. Nadine Mounzer Karam

Hamad Bin Khalifa University Press
P.O. Box 5825
Doha, Qatar

www.hbkupress.com

All rights reserved.

No part of this publication may be reproduced or transmitted in any form or by any means, electronic or mechanical, including photocopying, recording, or any information storage or retrieval system, without prior permission in writing from the publishers.

No responsibility for loss caused to any individual or organization acting on or refraining from action as a result of the material in this publication can be accepted by HBKU Press or the author.

The opinions expressed in this book do not necessarily reflect the opinion of Hamad Bin Khalifa University Press.

First English edition in 2022
ISBN: 9789927161476

Printed in Beirut-Lebanon

Qatar National Library Cataloging-in-Publication (CIP)

Zakhour, Salim, author.

Qatar communication strategies : from managing a crisis to creating a successful national brand / Dr. Salim Zakhour, Dr. Nadine Mounzer Karam. - First English edition. - Doha, Qatar : Hamad Bin Khalifa University Press, 2022.

272 pages ; 24 cm

ISBN 978-992-716-147-6

Includes bibliographical references.

1. Communication policy -- Qatar. 2. Branding (Marketing) -- Qatar. 3. Artificial intelligence -- Marketing applications -- Qatar. 4. Qatar -- Foreign relations -- 21st century. I. Karam, Nadine Mounzer, author. II. Title.

P95.82.Q2 Z35 2021
302.2095363– dc 23   20222854626x

Contents

CHAPTER ONE: COMMUNICATION STRATEGIES ADAPTING TO TECHNOLOGICAL DEVELOPMENT 17

TECHNOLOGY'S IMPACT ON COMMUNICATION 17
How has technology changed the world? 18
   Media & Communications.. 18
   Global Village: The Rise of Social Networks 23
   Communications Innovations in Politics 24
   Technology servicing Modern Democracy................................. 25
   American Election 2008: A Shift in Political
   Social Media Campaigns 27
   Information Technology in the Arab World............................ 30
   ICT and the Arab Spring 31
   Digital transformation in Qatar.. 33
   Qatar's Digital Vision... 35
   Steps towards a digitalized future 38

REFERENCES...40

CHAPTER TWO: ARTIFICIAL INTELLIGENCE REVOLUTIONIZING COMMUNICATIONS TOOLS AND PRACTICES 43

What is Artificial Intelligence?... 43
   Linguistic Definitions 44
   Scientific Definitions... 45
   Who is controlling what? 48
   The Extents of AI... 48
   Setting a framework for AI 50
   New and ethical concerns on Artificial Intelligence,
   and human values.. 54

Responsible AI 54
Achieving Ethical AI 56
Artificial Intelligence techniques in communications 58
Best Artificial Intelligence Practice from
a communications perspective 63
How could the State of Qatar implement AI effectively 68

REFERENCES 72

CHAPTER THREE: QATAR BLOCKADE HISTORY AND CRISIS MANAGEMENT 77

QATAR: A QUICK LOOK 77
THE CRISIS: 5 JUNE 2017 80
    The Demands 81
    Reasons given for the blockade 83
QATAR'S RESPONSE: ABSORB, SAFEGUARD, PREVENT 84
    Official Statements 85
    Government's Information Strategy 87
    International Lobbying 88
    Qatar's Economic & Social Strategy 90
    Diplomacy Outcome 92
H.H. THE AMIR'S SPEECH: A TURNING POINT 94
    H.H. the Amir's Legacy 94
    Audience 94
    View on Terrorism 96
    Qatar's Future 97
    Speech Reactions 98
COMMUNICATION OUTLETS 98
    MEDIA 99
    Social media 103
HOW DID QATAR OVERCOME THE BLOCKADE WITH ITS STRATEGY? 109
    Qatar's Strength Points 109
    H.H. the Amir's Speech at the 48th Shura Council Session 110
    A Closure to the Blockade 112

REFERENCES 115
APPENDIX 1 121
APPENDIX 2 124
APPENDIX 3 132
APPENDIX 4 134

CHAPTER FOUR: QATAR PUBLIC COMMUNICATIONS SECTOR: MINISTRY OF CULTURE AND SPORTS, SHAPING QATAR'S FUTURE CULTURE 135

   Qatar National Vision 2030 137
      First Pillar: Human development 139
      Second Pillar: Social development 139
      Third Pillar: Economic development 139
      National Development Strategies 140
      National Development Strategy 2011-2016 141
      Sports Goals of the National Development Strategy 142
      Cultural Goals of the National Development Strategy 143
      National Development Strategy 2018-2022 146
      Challenges 147
      Cultural and Sports Goals of the National Development Strategy 2018 - 2022 149
   Intellectual and Religious Approach to Culture 152
      The Holy Quran Universal Solutions 153
      Quran and the perspective of Nature 154
      Quran and the perspective of Work 155
      Quran and the Perspective of Others 155
      Quran and the perspective of Human Dignity 155
      Quran and the perspective of Knowledge 157
      Pillars of the Wijdan Cultural Center 158
      Perspective of Human 158
      Perspective of Others 159
      Perspective of Nature 161
      Perspective of knowledge 161

Perspective of Work *162*
Perspective of Time *163*
Ministry of Culture and Sports Strategy and Plan 164
   Integrating society and values *164*
   Results that reflect the strategy *166*
   Culture and Sports as Means of Communication: *168*
   Doha International Book Fair *168*
   Movement of Theater *169*
   National Sports Day *170*
   Qatar Sports for All Federation *171*
   Awareness Campaigns *172*
Conclusion 172

REFERENCES 175

CHAPTER FIVE: QATAR'S COMMUNICATION STRATEGY: NEW APPROACHES TO ENHANCING QATAR'S BRANDING 177

   Nation Branding 180
   Qatar Branding 184
   Cultural Diversity Shaping Qatar's Branding 189
      Years of Culture *193*
      Cultural Diversity Activities *194*
      Translation *195*
      Expat Communities Radio Stations *196*
   FIFA World Cup Qatar 2022™ and Qatar's Branding 197
      Media Exposure *197*
      New Image Opportunity *198*
      Public Diplomacy *199*
      Engagement and Loyalty *200*
   Education and Research: Global Approach for a Better Future 200
   Tourism: Promoting Unforgettable Experiences in Qatar 204
   Qatar's External Communication Strategy Outline 207
      Background and Strategic Overview *209*
      Goals and Objectives *211*
      Target Groups of Audiences *212*

  Tailoring Key Messages *213*
  Communication Channels and Activities *213*
  Implementation Timeline *214*
  Budget and Human Resources *214*
  Evaluation *215*
 Conclusion 215

REFERENCES 218

CHAPTER SIX: SUCCESSFUL COMMUNICATIONS
STRATEGIES: A WIN-WIN SITUATION FOR ALL 223
 Government Communication Strategies 225
 Planning a good Government Communication Strategy 227
  One Government One Voice: *228*
  Audience Centric Communication: *228*
  Digital and Open by Default: *228*
  Focus on Dialogue and Engagement: *229*
  Driven by Storylines: *229*
  Delivery: *229*
  Results Based: *229*
 Qatar's 8 Points Strategy 230
 Direct Impact of a Government strategy on companies 232
  Government Communication Impact on Public Sector *233*
 Qatar's Communication Strategy For Businesses 236
 Successful Communication Strategies for Private
 Businesses that were also adapted In Qatar's Crisis
 Communication Strategy 239
 What are the components of a successful
 Communication Strategy and how did the state of
 Qatar implement them 241
  Define what appropriate communication is *241*
  Eliminate weak language *242*
  Focus on clarity in communication *242*
  Be intentional with digital communication *242*
  Other effective communication strategies include
  the following *242*

Examples of Successful Marketing and Communications Campaigns 244
   Qatar's Internal Communication Success................................. *244*
   Qatar's External Communication Success................................ *245*
   Conclusion 247

REFERENCES 250

FULL BOOK REFERENCES 252

This book investigates the various communication strategies that Qatar has undertaken to enhance its brand image and engage in practices of nation-branding. The role of reputation, identity, and image play an important role in shaping Qatari domestic politics, along with its foreign policies. This book outlines the various strategies that Qatar has taken to enhance its impact on global political and economic development.

Communication strategies are essential for nation-branding, and specifically in the branding of the Qatari identity. Through communication strategies, Qatar introduced a national narrative, and solidified this narrative in the face of adversities such as the blockade. This book addresses Qatar's communication strategies, throughout the crises affecting Qatar's national identity, including the blockade, to highlight the various threats to Qatar's national image, how it managed, invented, reinvented, and solidified its image, and the benefits emerging from Qatar's communication strategies on a domestic and global level.

This book is divided into six main chapters:
- Chapter One: Communications Strategies Adapting to Technological Developments
- Chapter Two: AI (Artificial Intelligence) Revolutionizing Communication Tools and Practices
- Chapter Three: How has Qatar's communication strategy helped to overcome the blockade?
- Chapter Four: Qatar Public Communications Sector: Ministry of Culture and Sports Shaping Qatar's Future Culture
- Chapter Five: Qatar Communication Strategy: New Approach for the Qatari Brand
- Chapter Six: How do private businesses benefit from the government communications strategy?

In Chapter 1, the authors explore the role of technology in globalization, innovation, and communication. The role of this chapter is to introduce context, specifically how technology has evolved and continues to evolve, along with the implications of this evolution. This chapter outlines the globalized village, the role of social networks, and technology as a political medium. By exploring these sub-topics, this chapter specifically delves into these technological shifts in relation to the Arab Spring in general, and its digital transformation in Qatar in specific. This chapter is significant as it presents the evolution of technology and the emergence of communication strategies. More importantly, it carves out the academic space and literature in light of the Qatari context. Thereafter, this chapter outlines how changes on a global level, specifically in relation to information technology, have necessitated shifts in communication strategies in the Arab World, which continue to resonate in Qatar.

Chapter 2 outlines the role of artificial intelligence in revolutionizing communication tools and practices. In this chapter, the authors explore the various AI technologies emerging in the region, along with practices that inform the development of AI. The role of AI as an emerging technology is important in understanding how Qatar shapes its brand image. AI has introduced significant normative questions related to practices, culture, and society. The Qatari brand thrives on its heritage, national practices, its culture, and its society. The role of AI in Qatar is under-explored, with limited research engaging questions on talent, access, employment opportunities, and more importantly, normative questions on whether AI poses risks in Qatar.

Artificial Intelligence has the potential to disrupt nearly every facet of our lives. It promises to make our daily tasks easier, more accessible, more efficient, and more fun. It will also change the way we live, work, and communicate. As technology continues to evolve, the way we communicate is being challenged from every angle. Do we trust machine-mediated communication? Are we comfortable with the idea of artificial intelligence having a stronger say in our lives? How do we combat the challenges of artificial intelligence and keep communication strategy relevant and effective? Communication strategy is under pressure from AI. The emergence of artificial intelligence has created new challenges for communication strategy. But, it also offers new opportunities. How can we leverage AI while minimizing risks? What are the biggest risks of artificial intelligence and how can you mitigate them? Let's take a look at the challenges and opportunities of artificial intelligence and how they affect communication strategy.

What are the key communication strategies that the Qatari authorities have adopted to secure the country's image and consolidate its international reputation? Today, the question is more important than ever. The world is looking at Qatar, waiting for any news that shows the positive side of this small, oil-rich country. It's no wonder that the country has been the subject of so much scrutiny; with its success, it attracts even more attention than it would if it were a more ordinary place. Who wouldn't want to live in such a tempting place? We'll answer the question of whether the Qatari authorities have done enough to secure the country's image.

These two paragraphs were written by an Artificial Intelligence engine as a demonstration of the latest AI technologies.

Indeed, the image of a country has a huge effect on how other countries deal with it on the international level, in addition to the identity it gives to its own people and to the flow of residents it attracts.

In Chapter 3, the authors explore a specific moment in Qatari history that necessitated the building, solidifying, and communicating of the Qatari national identity. In this chapter, the authors explore the various narratives that emerged in opposition to Qatar, attempting to weaken its brand image. Following these narratives, the chapter delves into the counter-narratives emerging from Qatar. These narratives shed light on the communication strategies Qatar utilized to overcome the threats emerging from the blockade. Thus, this chapter provides a holistic assessment of these narratives and communication strategies, to further explain their effectiveness.

Chapter 4 explores a core tenant of Qatar's brand: culture and sports. This chapter focuses on Qatar's governmental and public communication sector, through using the Ministry of Culture and Sports as a case study. Here, the authors explore how the Ministry creates and weaves sports into the Qatari culture and the Qatari brand. Through focusing on the Ministry's efforts, this chapter outlines the various communication strategies, from effective and successful ones, to those which have room for improvement. This chapter explores the Qatari brand in an in-depth manner, by outlining the role of the Qatar National Vision 2030, the National Development Strategies, and the public sector as a whole in shaping the Qatari brand. Additionally, this chapter identifies the intellectual, religious, and cultural approaches used in communication strategies, further determining how culture becomes a successful and effective communication tool in shaping the Qatari brand.

Chapter 5 investigates new approaches to the Qatari brand. Based on the findings in the previous chapters, communication strategies present the most effective means of turning crises into opportunities. This chapter explores nation-branding, cultural diversity, education, research, and tourism as effective means of shaping Qatar's brand. Here, the authors present the role of soft power, Qatari responses to international allegations that hurt its image and reputation, and how it uses these opportunities to make its mark as a heritage and tourism destination. This chapter also explores the FIFA World Cup Qatar 2022™ and how the state is adapting for this event.

In Chapter 6, the authors extend the analysis and findings to private businesses — a sector that Qatar heavily relies on for its economic growth. By focusing on the private sector, the authors show how the Qatari brand is sustained through the communication strategies employed by private businesses. The authors also present various approaches to help enhance current strategies, in light of their findings.

This book introduces the Qatari brand from the perspective of technology, foreign and domestic politics, and national strategies. The authors present the significance of technological development, implementing new communication strategies, and enhancing domestic solidarity in strengthening the Qatari brand. By addressing crises that Qatar faced, such as the blockade or challenges to the FIFA World Cup Qatar 2022™, the authors explore how internal and external threats aimed at shaking Qatar's brand, or making it fragile, have led to various attempts at solidifying and protecting the Qatari national brand, and also encouraging Qatari nationals and residents to uphold this brand.

Furthermore, the authors point out the ability of the country to protect its national identity and to keep its residents motivated and unwilling to leave in order to avoid aggravating the crisis, and secure its international economic and political relations.

Qatar's ability to overcome the blockade is a result of its successful execution of various strategies, aimed at building an image of prosperity and successfully implementing it. Under Qatar National Vision 2030, Qatar was able to integrate its vision for prosperity in its communication strategies across the public and private sectors. The 2017 blockade presented a real opportunity for the brand to be tested, leading to Qatar benefiting from a long-awaited international sports event as a means of "rebranding" the country. The goals that Qatar sets as a means of building its international brand continue to resonate in local governmental efforts, making Qatar's international and national brand equally important. The Ministry of Culture and Sports has implemented communication strategies upholding Qatar's vision, aiming to create awareness, change perceptions, and integrate health and consciousness into the state's cultural practices.

This book is catered to corporates, students, and academics interested in Qatar and the themes of crisis management, resolution, evaluation, and communication. This book aims to not only inform readers about the current status of communication strategies in Qatar, but also to shed light on what strategies were effective and successful, and how current and future businesses can adopt these strategies to enhance their image. Additionally, this book will present an opportunity for companies to tackle crises affecting their image, by shedding light on proposed effective communications strategies.

CHAPTER ONE

Communication Strategies Adapting to Technological Development

TECHNOLOGY'S IMPACT ON COMMUNICATION

Modern day technology has created unprecedented opportunities, tools and resources in today's digital age, putting the world of information just one fingertip away. Tools such as mobile phones and smart devices have fundamentally changed the way we communicate and access information across different channels and platforms.

This was all made possible with the internet, as it was the essential turning point from the Industrial to the Information Age. This global network based on complex platforms of wireless communication provided the possibility of interactive and fast communication at any chosen time and place.

However, the Internet is not really a new technology. The predecessor, the Arpanet, was first deployed in 1969, but it was in the 1990's when it was privatized and released from the control of the U.S. Department of Commerce that it diffused around the world at extra-ordinary speed. In 1996 the first survey of internet users counted about 40 million users, with China accounting for the largest number of users. Furthermore, for some time the spread of the internet was limited by the difficulty to lay out land-based telecommunications infrastructure in developing countries. This has changed with the explosion of wireless communication in the early twenty-first century (Castells, 2013).

The evolution of these mediums of communication have catapulted the world into a whole new way of living. In fact, information technologies have created fundamental change throughout society, driving it forward from the industrial age to the networked era. In our world, global information networks are vital infrastructure — but in what ways has this changed human relations? (Zaryn, 2013).

HOW HAS TECHNOLOGY CHANGED THE WORLD?

It is safe to say that technological advancements have redefined our society in many aspects.

The internet has changed business, education, government, health care, and even the ways in which we interact with our loved ones — it has become one of the key drivers of social evolution.

With modern technology paving the way for devices such as smart phones and faster, more developed computers, our lives have now been made easier and more connected than ever.

Indeed, the network of networks is an inexhaustible source of information. In addition, the internet has enabled users to move away from their former passive role as mere recipients of information conveyed by conventional media to an active role, choosing what information to receive, how, and when. The information recipient even decides whether they want to stay informed (Zaryn, 2013).

Here are a few main areas where technology has completely shifted, changing life for the better.

Media & Communications

While letters and telegrams might have been the fundamental medium of communication in the past, a simple SMS, text or even voice message and video message can now reach the person within a fraction of a second anywhere in the world. The world of smartphone devices has transformed the planet into a global connected village where information travels faster than light. While there was a time when TV and radio were the only medium of mass media and mass communication, today social media, news applications, internet websites, instant mobile notifications and others are the ways to get across information. In fact, mobile devices and smartphones allow you to do all the things provided by other media tools such as watch, or stream tv shows, videos, movies, music, allowing you to consume news whenever you want, and how you want.

As mentioned by Rungfapaisarn in his paper on the impact of Digital Technology, (Rungfapaisarn, 2019): Digital media has created at least four major disruptions in the media landscape. First, digital media is rapidly replacing print, as evidenced by the gradual disappearance of print media. With the cost of digital media dropping and digital devices like mobile phones improving access to news and information, digital media has rendered print media obsolete.

Second, digital technology has spawned the development of digital media entrepreneurs, who have created a proliferation of media content. Existing media agencies will need to decide how to compete with this influx of agile competitors, or better yet, how to leverage their capabilities as outsourcing partners.

Third, the digital industry has been a boon for video content and technology. Consumers nowadays have an attention span that lasts a few seconds compared to a few minutes in the past. This has forced many media agencies to re-think the way they share their clients' products and services with consumers.

Fourth, with so much digital media bombarding audiences it is not surprising that people have grown wary of what they see and believe. Clever artificial intelligence had created media content dubbed "deep fake", which fooled people initially but has now started raising suspicion. To win over consumers, media businesses will need to convince them that what they are portraying is genuine and not just a lot of bells and whistles. The quality, creativity and relevance of media content and the products and services they represent will also be vital" (Rungfapaisarn, 2019).

The 'art' of communication is unrecognizable in comparison to what our parents would have had to go to in order to speak with relatives, friends and business contacts. We do not go back more than one generation to the world in which our parents were raised. Today's technology has created so many new opportunities at a very fast pace, especially in the world of media, completely transforming this sector and opening up new streams of media and fields that never existed before.

Fintech

Financial Technology, widely known as Fintech, is the merging of the newest technological tools in service of the finance sector and another way in which technology has had a big impact on society. Banks and governments are digitalizing their services to serve a bigger audience more effectively. Paying bills has become a simple task thanks to technology, allowing users to automatically schedule payments when they are due rather than having to remember to mail a check. . Thanks to connectivity over smartphone and a banking app, bill payments online have become a reality.

The tools provided by fintech are changing the way many consumers track, manage and facilitate their finances. According to CNBC: "Fintech investment soared up 18% in 2017 alone. For the estimated near 2 billion people worldwide without bank accounts, fintech provides a nimble option to participate in financial services without the need for the brick-and-mortar. And, to a large extent, that is precisely what fintech has been developed to do - give consumers direct access to their financial lives through easy-to-use technology".

Fintech has even paved the way for new "virtual" currencies that abide by their own sets of rules and regulations. This type of currency is stored and transacted only through designated software, mobile or computer applications, or through dedicated digital wallets, and the transactions occur over the internet through secure, dedicated networks.

Unlike regular money, virtual currency relies on a system of trust and may not be issued by a central bank or other banking regulatory authority. They derive their value based on the underlying mechanism, like mining in cases of cryptocurrencies, or the backing by the underlying asset (Franckenfield, 2019).

Healthcare

Technological advancements have also contributed to enhancing quality of life of patients and to the healthcare industry in general. Healthcare professionals and patients alike now have access to the most cutting-edge diagnostic tools, treatments, materials and minimal invasive procedures. This is in addition to easier access to healthcare professionals thanks to health apps and remote consultations. (Mills, 2019)

"Big data" in healthcare allows the entire field to benefit from comprehensive research studies. These endeavors can access larger and more diverse population groups than ever before. They can also draw from existing studies for comprehensive meta-analyses. This innovation allows medical professionals to stay on top of health care trends, techniques and technologies, in order to automatically identify risk factors and recommend the right preventative treatment by comparing patient data with data from thousands of other patients.

Previously, medical information from visits to the General Practitioner (GP), medical specialist, allied health professionals and the dentists were held in separate locations with different health practitioners and hospitals. Electronic medical records allow all patient histories, test results, diagnoses and relevant information to be stored centrally in an online location. The data allows for more focused and accurate care as well as the ability to see health trends for each individual. Medical billing systems allow hospitals, clinics and medical practices to run much more smoothly (Rauv, 2017).

Shopping

Online shopping has become one of the most popular ways of shopping. With online stores containing thousands and thousands of options and the possibility of shipments overseas, shopping online has rapidly become an international phenomenon. Online shopping allows everything the customer needs be delivered directly to the doorstep.

With technological advances, online shopping and buying through smart devices went into the mainstream naturally. An array of options made consumers compare the prices in stores around the world from the comfort of their couch. Therefore, retailers shouldn't be surprised that nowadays consumers expect shopping to be as easy as pressing a button.

When the technology is used in the right way, it creates numerous opportunities for a customized and improved experience. Overall, rich data on customer behavior allows retailers to offer products or services that match the needs of their clients.

Online customers engage with brands in different ways than several years ago, meaning that technological shifts have rewritten the shopping experience. Retailers can take advantage of the evolving landscape, but only when they deliver customer-oriented services that answer rising demands and expectations. At the same time, they need to be able to assure customers that their sensitive data is safe during checkout.

Payment options should also be adapted to customer habits. The changes in technology made payment companies offer more choices for online consumers to give them more comfortable payment options. As a result, they can go smoothly through a one-click checkout that gives them convenience and personalized experience. In this business every second counts.

Global Village: The Rise of Social Networks

The rise of social media and networking has made it faster and easier to access information around the world. The first social media site to reach a million monthly active users was MySpace – it achieved this milestone around 2004. This is arguably the beginning of social media as we know it.

"Social Network Sites are web-based services that allow individuals to (1) construct a public or semi-public profile within a bounded system, (2) articulate a list of other users with whom they share a connection, and (3) view and traverse their list of connections and those made by others within the system" (Boyd and Ellison 2007, 2).

Whether through a simple tweet, post on Instagram or a status update on Facebook, users can instantly be made aware of different issues around the world.

"Social media has given everyday people the ability to have a voice that can reach millions of people. Before social media was such a big element in our lives, you could have an opinion, or a view on something and only really your close-knit group of friends or family would know about it. But given how easy social media makes it to reach other people, more people are using social media as an outlet to vent, and share their thoughts" (AM Source, 2017).

With 2.3 billion users, Facebook is the most popular social media platform today. Twitter YouTube, Instagram and WeChat follow, with more than a billion users. Tumblr and TikTok come next, with over half a billion users.

In general, young people are more likely to use social media than older people depending on the features that some particular social media channels are offering. This is mainly the reason why some platforms are much more popular among younger people such as Twitter, Instagram, Snapchat and more recently Tik Tok.

As social media matured and its user numbers grew, researchers increasingly placed emphasis on the networked properties of platforms as a constitutive element of social media. It became apparent that social media afforded the emergence of global networks connecting the user not only to other users, but also to information.

Social media platforms have provided new opportunities to consumers to engage in social interaction on the internet. Consumers use social media, such as online communities, to generate content and to network with other users.

As the numbers suggest, the majority of people across the world are connected in some shape or form. Indeed, over 4.66 billion people are connected to the internet, making this virtual community more populated than any country in the world. The resulting impacts on everyday life are prodigious: an average user spends about 13 hours a week online, exchanging e-mails, browsing websites, blogging, tweeting, spending time in social networks or virtual worlds, downloading and uploading movies and documents, sharing photos, taking e-learning programs or shopping. This heavily changed social behavior reflects the emergence of a society of digital age – the Information Society (Radunovic, 2010).

Communications Innovations in Politics

Internet has not only further facilitated communications but has also enabled almost ubiquitous access to information, allowing people across the world to collaborate, create communities, do business, learn, amuse themselves, and even have virtual lives. More importantly, it has empowered the citizenry to take active part in local and international policy-shaping processes and thus significantly affect the international relations and conduct of diplomacy as well.

Such forms of democracy and highly impacted events are naturally the democratic elections that take place in all democratic countries, allowing the rise of new forms of governments and politics. Election campaigns are very critical periods as they shape policies, distribute powers and provide debates about national problems and directions, international agendas and activities.

Indeed, elections can accomplish these goals in relation to the government and political party system existing in a given country which is why election campaigns are the most essential element in creating a candidate and uniting voters behind their ideas and plans. These are practical outcomes and symbolic meaning of electoral campaigns, which are important to the health of democracies. Indeed, the manner in which democracies start by leading their election campaigns can somehow reflect the results of the voting and the overall ruling later on.

In recent years, the practices of these campaigns have started to change drastically with the introduction of new technology mediums such as social media. Around the world, we find that many recent changes in campaigning, despite the historical and political different backgrounds of the countries, all share the same aspects. From political commercials, media appearances, compelling campaign materials, strong visuals to most importantly heavy social media presence, these factors are all common features that can be found in almost all elections around the world.

Technology servicing Modern Democracy

Media is an important backbone of democracy, allowing society to identify issues and choose the best options for resolving them.

While it took only a few years for the internet to grow beyond 50 million users, global social network Facebook as a new service reached that number in less than two years (Ortiz & Ospina, 2019). e-Government services that allow citizens to obtain personal documents, access public information or even vote virtually are listed high on national development strategy plans. Digital signatures are gradually replacing conventional ones, allowing for complete digitalization of paperwork like contracts, certified financial reports or court documents (Radunovic, 2010).

The development of the mass media during the last several decades is characterized by the following main tendencies:

- Convergence: Different media like newspapers, radio, television, telephone and internet are increasingly being fused together, technologically as well as economically.
- Concentration: Media companies are being merged and controlled by fewer owners. This concentration is horizontal (several media under the same owner) as well as vertical (several links in the "food chain" under the same company group). Different media publish news from the same sources.
- Globalization: multinational companies broadcasting across borders own the media. For example, The Ringier, a Swiss-owned company has a massive print business with operations in 10 countries, and a portfolio of about 100 titles.
- Commercialization: Advertisements are sneaked into entertainment as well as news stories. The distinctions between advertisements, news and entertainment are increasingly blurred. Audience groups with less spending money are not considered.
- Commercial influence: Advertisers and owners have influence on editorial decisions (Pavel 2010).

Articles in newspapers, or discussions on radio and television shows about political, economic or social events, for example, have been selected and interpreted by the mass media, and have consequences for how the audience understands and responds to these events. Audience attitudes and their opinions about political figures, for instance, are often if not solely influenced by the impressions that they receive from the mass media. It is their way of getting to know these candidates up close, helping the general public to shape their electoral decisions. Indeed, through the media, the audience can read, watch or hear the views of a variety of experts: politicians, economic analysts, political analysts, cultural critics, academics, among others.

According to a communications study by Sheila Steinberg (2007), there are two main advantages of the mass media performing this function:

"Firstly, audience is exposed to a larger number of different points of view about an issue than would be possible in interpersonal communication alone. Also, the mass media make available a wide range of expertise that individuals might not otherwise have access to. Interpretation can take many forms. Because of that, the downside of the correlation function, that is often regarded as editorializing function of mass media, is that there is no guarantee that interpretations by media commentators and other 'experts' are accurate and valid. There is also the danger that an individual may come to rely too heavily on the views carried by the media and become a passive and uncritical recipient of mass messages.

American Election 2008: A Shift in Political Social Media Campaigns

One of the most relevant examples of a full digitalization of electoral campaigns is the United States Presidential elections of 2008 Barack Obama, the Democrat and junior U.S. Senator from Illinois, and Joe Biden, the senior U.S. Senator from Delaware, defeated the Republican ticket of John McCain, the senior Senator from Arizona, and Sarah Palin, the Governor of Alaska. Obama thereby became the first ever African American to be elected to the presidency as well as being only the third sitting United States Senator elected President, joining Warren G Harding and John F Kennedy.

Three-quarters (74%) of internet users went online during the 2008 election to take part in, or get news and information about the 2008 campaign. This represents 55% of the entire adult population, and marks the first time the Pew Internet & American Life Project has found that more than half the voting-age population used the internet to connect to the political process during an election cycle (Smith, 2009).

The political media system in the United States has undergone massive transformations over the past three decades. The scope of these new media developments is vast, encompassing both legacy sources as well as entirely novel communication platforms made possible by emerging technologies.

The public gained greater political agency through technological advances that allowed them to react to political events and issues, communicate directly to candidates and political leaders, contribute original news, images, videos, and political content, and engage in political activities, such as working on behalf of candidates, raising funds, and organizing protests. At the same time, journalists acquired pioneering mechanisms for reporting stories and reaching audiences. Politicians amassed news ways of conveying messages to the public, other elites, and the press, influencing constituents' opinions, recruiting volunteers and donors, and mobilizing voters (Davis and Owen, 1998; Owen, 2017).

In fact, we can confidently say that the political role of social media in American politics was established during the 2008 presidential election. Democratic presidential candidate Barack Obama's social-media strategy revolutionized campaigning by altering the structure of political organizing. Obama's campaign took on the characteristics of a social movement with strong digital grassroots mobilization (Bimber, 2014).

The campaign exploited the networking, collaborating, and community-building potential of social media. It used social media to make personalized appeals to voters aided by data analytics that guided targeted messaging. Voters created and amplified messages about the candidates without going through formal campaign organizations or political parties. The campaign even aided in creating new social media tools and utilized social media channels in ways never used before. In this unique election, the calculated strategies of Obama's official campaign organization were aided by the spontaneous innovation of voters themselves, especially the young dynamic voters who volunteered and aided the campaign enormously.

Barack Obama's 2008 campaign was indeed one for the history books. This campaign heavily relied on rallying people behind the personality of Obama and the promising future he had within his plans. The slogan "Yes, we can" was the most popular phrase at the time, being used by all sorts of media and social media channels. This diversification helped to diffuse and spread Obama's messages through multiple communication channels, helping to frame recent events and issues through the eyes of the Obama campaign.

Due to the success of the 2008 campaign, President Obama has been called the "first social-media president." It's both a true and a misleading characterization as he continued his path on social media even as he took office, creating the first official handle of the President "POTUS" on twitter. The Obama White House was indeed the first presidency to make use of services like Twitter, Facebook, Snapchat, and Instagram. But on the other hand, these services either didn't exist or weren't used by a broad public before Barack Obama took office in 2009 (Jackson, 2017).

The impact of technology on political communication is not a new phenomenon. Obama, like Jack Kennedy before him, managed to master a new technology before any other politician. Kennedy set the pattern when he learned to use the radio to communicate directly with the public during his fireside chats throughout the Depression and World War II, and Obama did the same with Social Media and Information Technology.

The internet and cell phones indeed added a new dimension to political technology since they are interactive media. In addition to the images presented on the web, the internet allows people to quickly spread ideas, information and organize political protest. Information comes to the public and from the public as well.

Facebook, Twitter, Instagram and Snapchat may help you effectively spread a campaign message that can reach millions of people all at once in real-time. Social media has enabled politicians to create and keep that connection with voters, while also creating the opportunity for the public to engage with political leaders, spread their own message, and advocate on behalf of causes that they are passionate about.

Information Technology in the Arab World

The high level of interest and excitement about the potential impact of social media on collective action is unsurprising. At first glance, this new technology appears able to provide a movement with powerful, speedy, and relatively low-cost tools for recruitment, fund-raising, the distribution of information and images, collective discussions, and mobilization for action (Bennett, 2006).

However, this technology also opens channels of communication and thereby facilitates the alignment of people behind a cause, a person, a regime or other organization. Over the past 25 years, social movements have actively sought out and used new information and communication technologies (ICT), such as the internet and mobile phones, to give voice to their concerns. The growth of access and use of ICT in the Middle East and North Africa provided resources for protesters and governments to influence political and social events. The widespread availability of the internet and mobile phones to facilitate organization and action raises the research question of how ICT affects protest movements (Wilson & Corey, 2012).

In areas where political instability is an omnipresent factor in the midst of difficult economic situations, it is only natural to expect that such mediums that did not exist before would be a main force for the youth to protest and organize large-scale manifestations to express their anger and discontent towards their governments and long established political or religious regimes.

The Middle East and MENA region in general have a few growing economies, however the growth of technology usage in these areas is significantly increasing, especially when it comes to mobile phones. Access to such technological smart tools is heightening the opportunities of information exchange and communication amongst the people and are seen as a technological and generational challenge to the hierarchical social order of many MENA societies.

ICT and the Arab Spring

The growth of social networks, such as the 2009 introduction of Facebook in Arabic, confronts governments with challenges in trying to restrict networking activities and their use for organizing opposition.

This proved to be a major challenge for some of these governments that were still relying on their media channels being the sole source of information for their populations. The recent experience of democracy movements in a number of MENA countries (such as Tunisia, Libya, Egypt and Syria) shows how information and communication technologies during times of social protest and unrest can be significant forces for organization and mobilization. The Arab Spring also serves as an example of the internet evolving to a phase of contested access after less scrutiny in the past (Wilson & Corey, 2012).

Iran was one of the first countries in 2009 to experience first-hand the power of social media against a well-established religious regime in the country. The country has a young population who are very aware and heavy users of these new information technologies.

In the 2009 presidential election, opposition candidate Mir Hossein Mousavi reached out to the young, reform-minded electorate by campaigning extensively via YouTube and Facebook. When the official election results announced his defeat and handed victory to the anti-reformist Mahmoud Ahmadinejad, massive demonstrations erupted, which led the regime to close down press offices. Protesters turned extensively to the internet as a vehicle for the dissemination of information within Iran, both for their own political organization and in order to reach out to the international community. The government responded by shutting down access.

The democratization capacity of the internet was at most an opportunity to promote change, but a brutal regime intent on staying in power at all costs can evidently block it and survive. Nor could the protest movement succeed because the international community, superficially sympathetic, was not inclined to give it genuine support. At that point, the Obama administration had a different kind of deal with the mullahs in mind and therefore had no interest in seeing the democracy movement succeed. The lesson learned in this case would be that liberation technology may be able to build a protest movement, but it can also elicit even more powerful resistance (Berman, 2017).

Indeed, social media played an essential role in January 2011 in Egypt, as the rise of internet social networking sites like Facebook added a new dimension to civil unrest. Massive and possibly the biggest protests the country had seen in this modern age erupted in Cairo's Tahrir Square.

The Egyptian students and young professionals used Facebook to exchange anonymous critiques of the government and hone their strategy. Meetings and protests were organized on Facebook pages and by cell phone. The young people alerted each other to police actions by posting the news via text messaging. Once the demonstrations were launched, attacking police were met by a multitude of arms holding up cell phones, arising from the crowd to record their actions on video. The results were posted on YouTube within a matter of hours (Nelson Fall, 2008).

Communication technology facilitated the mobilization of demonstrators as well as information sharing, so much so that journalists came to speak of the "Facebook Revolution." In contrast to the movement in Iran two years earlier, this one succeeded because of many local and international circumstances forcing Hosni Mubarak from power.

As Anne Nelson writes: "Information technology can be seen as both a cause and effect for protests in the Middle East / North Africa.

As a cause, protests in Tunisia started, in part, to show dissatisfaction that government limited access to YouTube and other internet sources. Residents, especially young people, resented state efforts to control the flow of information. In Tunisia, an early cause was access to YouTube that resulted in public protests and the decision by the government to allow access in January 2011. Similar protests in Syria led to that country allowing access to YouTube in February 2011. In both cases the issue of censorship and blocking of information was a source of protest, but in each country restoring access did little to end the much broader range of issues fueling dissent. As effect, the information dissemination and organizing capacity of ICT were widely used in shaping opinion and events through the Arab Spring.

The Arab Spring context of the protests in many countries was dissatisfaction with high rates of unemployment, especially for the educated young, government corruption, and media censorship. In Tunisia, where the movement started, Internet censorship was a growing issue as noted above. The initiating event for widespread demonstrations was the suicide death in December 2010 of Mohamed Bouazizi in the city of Sidi Bouzid to protest local government corruption. His death prompted protests, assisted in organization by social media. Even with low Internet subscription rates at the time, one quarter of the population in Tunisia was estimated to be online. While limited in access to the Internet, what Tunisia did have was almost 85% penetration of mobile phones, which provided an effective organizational network."

Digital transformation in Qatar

As the world evolves thanks to the transformation of digital technology and the progress this brings with it on all levels, many Middle Eastern countries are also adopting these changes across all governmental levels. The last two decades have witnessed phenomenal growth in digitalization, illustrating its central position in the modern economy.

At the end of 1995, the market capitalization of the top 15 public Internet companies was US$16.7 billion. By May 2016, the valuation of the equivalent top 15 companies had increased more than 125 times and mushroomed to $2.1 trillion. Digital companies have usurped the energy sector's previous dominance in the global economy. Five of the top 10 companies worldwide, in terms of market capitalization, are digital companies (Apple, Alphabet, Microsoft, Amazon, and Facebook). Just 10 years ago, only one digital company (Microsoft) appeared in that same list, which was dominated by oil and gas companies. Moreover, even businesses in traditional industries are going digital.

Following that same path, governments in the GCC region have indeed acknowledged the economic and social benefits that going digital can bring, and have developed ambitious plans and strategies to match it. The GCC countries are among the pioneers in the MENA region applying technological advances to government and public sectors.

Overall, investment in IT in the Middle East and North Africa (MENA) is growing rapidly. With spending on areas of enterprise IT often associated with digital transformation rising significantly, with sales of software as a service expected to jump by 25 percent during the course of 2019. Spending is expected to jump by 19 percent to reach nearly US$3 billion for CRM, and to increase by 12 percent to hit $1.2 billion for BI, analytics, and advanced analytics,including AI (Wright, 2020).

Gulf Cooperation Council (GCC) countries are engaged in ambitious national transformation plans such as the Qatar National Vision 2030, the Saudi Vision 2030, the New Kuwait 2035 Vision, and the UAE's 2021 vision. The full scale of these plans can be realized only by increasing efficiency across sectors, mainly through digitization. A digitized economy requires a skilled digital workforce able to keep pace with the rapidly changing ICT industry. Digital jobs have other benefits, including flexibility and project-based work models that can increase labor force participation, particularly among women.

The Middle East is better positioned for digital transformation than many other regions because it is not over-encumbered with complex legacy IT systems that have been heavily customized over time, according to Alan Pelz-Sharpe, founder of research and analysis consultancy Deep Analysis and author of the bestseller "Practical Artificial Intelligence - An Enterprise Playbook":

"It is easier to leapfrog innovation when you have a fairly basic starting point tech-wise. Clearly Dubai is leading the charge in the Middle East; its Smart Dubai initiative, though very ambitious, has set the tone for others to follow." Smart Dubai, the government entity entrusted with driving Dubai's digital transformation projects, already has for example a mature blockchain strategy, launched in early 2016, which has made the city a global leader in blockchain in government, with some signature projects such as DubaiPay, an online payment portal.

Qatar's Digital Vision

Despite the blockade it has went through, Qatar is leading the way when it comes to digital transformation. "To complete our reform and modernization journey, we set in 2008 the country's future roadmap under QNV 2030, which aims to transform Qatar by 2030 into an advanced country capable of sustaining its own development and ensuring continued decent life for its people ... The Qatar National Vision provides a framework for the development of comprehensive national strategies and implementation plans, while underlining the balance between the achievements of economic growth and the country's human and natural resources." - As stated by H.H. Sheikh Tamim bin Hamad Al-Thani in his speech at the opening of the 42nd session of the Shura Council on 05 November 2013.

A revolution is slowly transforming Qatar's small, vibrant economy of less than three million people. ICT is propelling the country to greater progress and prosperity. And although Qatar has been a late entrant here, having made its first serious moves only in 2005, its leadership is convinced that ICT can bring far-reaching changes. That has been the cornerstone of Qatar's unfolding technology revolution (Al Jaber & Dutta, 2008).

In fact, according to Qatar's official government strategy the vision is divided into three main strategic objectives according to the official Qatar e-Government 2020 strategy:

Strategic Objective 1: Better Serve Individuals and Business – emphasizes the customer focus, serving the people who live and work in Qatar, and the businesses that fuel the nation's economic growth.

Strategic Objective 2: Create Efficiency in Government Administration – maximizes opportunities to make better use of public funds.

Strategic Objective 3: Increase Government Openness – generates economic and political value by collaborating with customers on co-design.

Ministries across Qatar's government have joined to accelerate e-Government initiatives.

In late 2013, the Prime Minister, H.E. Sheikh Abdullah bin Nasser bin Khalifa Al Thani, identified e-Government as a priority and formed a Steering Committee, spearheaded by the Ministry of Information and Communications Technology and composed of eight of the largest ministries.

The Committee was charged with developing and guiding the implementation of a nationwide e-Government strategy. A detailed National Development Strategy document has been established elaborating all the different details and steps taken to achieve QNV 2030.

The strategy has been developed and divided into different areas. As the population of Qatar keeps growing, mainly because of the big number of expatriates, needs have also increased.

During the first period of the National Development Strategy defined between 2011 and 2016, the government focused its efforts on growing the non-hydrocarbon sector. This came as a response to the GCC countries who have been, at various levels and points in time, confronted with a sense of urgency to diversify their still largely hydrocarbon-dependent economies.

The following five years were characterized by the dominance of local government investments in the non-hydrocarbon sector. During the second part of the strategy, Qatar is focusing on diversifying and strengthening its economic sector. Indeed, the 2018-2022 period will be marked by the rationalization of government spending, which will, in general, lead to equilibrium in Qatar's fiscal balance sheet and facilitate wider private sector activities.

The development of government infrastructure includes 8 key components:

1. Improving the government network and deploying the broadband network across government agencies;
2. Establishing a data center to host government data packages;
3. Establishing a crisis response center to support government data;
4. Establishing a cloud technology infrastructure;
5. Expanding the government call center;
6. Establishing the necessary infrastructure needed to activate the use of e-signature;
7. Providing integrated digitization service;
8. Establishing an internet service platform supporting the work of Ministries.

In this context, 29 government agencies are linked to the common technological platform which provides all government services. Related policies have also been developed. Four entities have already benefited from the current host center.

The Government Call Center has deployed and provided technical support to 20 government services. A platform for sharing government data has been established according to standard specifications and practices. It offers nine basic data packages provided by six ministries / agencies: Ministry of Economy and Trade, Ministry of Justice, Ministry of Public Health, courts, Kahramaa and Ministry of Interior (Qatar Second National Development Strategy Document).

These platforms will surely be the base of the digital transformation Qatar is implementing as data is the center of all these reforms. With the right Intelligent Centers installed and the well-established internet infrastructure, Qatar is in fact on the right path to applying these changes.

Steps towards a digitalized future

With the plan and infrastructure being implemented, Qatar has already started obtaining tangible results from solutions and products in the market.

According to a survey by Deloitte in 2017, Qatar is following its own journey. The country has upgraded its plans as part of the new TASMU smart government framework, and is now entering a pilot stage to test proof of concepts behind Next Generation Care initiatives.

As a way to digitalize all government related tasks, Qatar has implemented the Hukoomi Application where users are able to complete more than 650 government related transactions from the comfort of their mobile phones.

In addition, Qatar's updated National E-Health and Data Program (QNeDP), formulated in 2015, outlines a blueprint and set of phased implementation plans behind the integration of various national health management systems (e.g. e-referral, pharmacy, virtual medicine), health data systems, clinical repositories (e.g. clinical data, medication inventory) and external consumer systems (e.g. patient medical records and accounts, population health systems). Furthermore, Qatar's Connected Wellness initiative also includes a Digital Health Coach Service, which uses smartphones and wearables, monitoring food consumption and activity levels to provide real-time user specific health advice. Data collected from the service is even integrated with patient records and monitored by health professionals to provide continuous guidance.

Such programs are well integrated and supposed to be part of the everyday life of citizens.

Qatar's Safe Journey initiative is also a way to introduce a range of new services to enhance car safety and risk management. For instance, it's Connected Vehicle (V2V) project enables vehicles to sense and share perceived threats with other vehicles, based on telematics data.

The Smart Vehicle Monitoring service aims to monitor driving, equipment and maintenance patterns in cars, the data of which can be leveraged to generate demand forecasts for parts, maintenance services as well as informing car insurance schemes.

An enhancement in public transportation is also planned with Qatar's new Connected Transport Network service under its seamless mobility initiative. The service guides user journey planning and booking by recommending the optimal transit package based on real time transport network data and user preferences (e.g. price, distance, time, preferred transport).

Qatar also aims to upgrade its digital tourist guides. The new Digital Travel Guide, for example, aims to deliver location and preference-based points of interest, events, public transportation schedules and offers. The service features Near Field Communication (NFC) and biometric enabled identification, an automated day planner service and online tourist feedback. In conjunction with this, Qatar is also launching Contextual Indoor Navigation, providing indoor information delivery and 'turn-by-turn' navigation for key points of interest such as the airport, malls, and landmarks. Qatar's Augmented City service based on geospatial information and mobile video recognition technologies will also provide assistive contextual real-time information (e.g. descriptive text, interactive videos, targeted offers and event information) on top of smartphone device screens.

REFERENCES

BBVA (2013) The Impact of the Internet on Society. Retrieved from: https://www.bbvaopenmind.com/en/articles/the-impact-of-the-internet-on-society- a-global-perspective/

BBVA Dentzel Z, (2013) How the Internet Changed Everyday Life.

BBVA (2019) The Past Decade and Future of Political Media: The Ascendance of Social Media, retrieved from: https://www.bbvaopenmind.com/en/articles/the-past-decade-and-future-of-political-media-the-ascendance-of-social-media/

Bennett, L. (2006) "Communicating Global Activism: Strength and Vulnerabilities of Networked Politics." In Cyberprotest: New Media, Citizens and Social Movements, ed. van de Donk, W., Loader, B. D., Nixon, P. G., Rucht, D. London: Routledge.

Biance W. (2020) Middle East Digital Transformation retrieved from: https://www.cio.com/article/3513416/middle-easts-digital-transformation-laggard-status-may-be-a-benefit.html

Boyd, Danah M., and Nicole B. Ellison (2007) Social Network Sites: Definition, History, and Scholarship. Journal of Computer-Mediated Communication 13.

Camelia.P (2010) The Role of Mass Media in Modern Democracy, retrieved from: http://management.ucdc.ro/revista/full%20text%202010/Full%20text-15.pdf

CNBC (2018) What is Fintech retrieved from: https://www.cnbc.com/video/2018/06/07/what-is-fintech.html

Deloitte (2017), National Transformation in the Middle East Report, retrieved from: https://www2.deloitte.com/content/dam/Deloitte/

xe/Documents/technology-media-telecommunications/ dtme_tmt_national-transformation-in-the-middleeast/ National%20Transformation%20in%20the%20Middle%20 East%20-%20A%20Digital%20Journey.pdf

Destiny J, (2017) How did the Obama Administration Use Social Media in 2012, retrieved from: https://www.destinyjackson.org/blogs/articles-essays/how-did-the-obama-administration-use-social-media-to-win-the-2012-elections

Gulf Times (2020), Qatar Encourages Digital Transformation in Commercial Transactions, retrieved from: https://www.gulf-times.com/story/663161/Qatar-encourages-digital-transformation-in-commerc

Jake F. (2019) Virtual Currency retrieved from: https://www.investopedia.com/terms/v/virtual-currency.asp

KWANCHAI RUNGFAPAISARN (2019) The impact of digital technology having on media organization Retrieved from: https://www.nationthailand.com/business/30375461

Mark I. Wilson and Kenneth E. Corey (2012), The Role of ICT in Arab Spring Movements retrieved from: https://journals.openedition.org/netcom/1064?lang=en

Mills, T. (2019, September 4). *Council post: How health care apps can improve patient health and support physicians.* Forbes. Retrieved April 29, 2022, from https://www.forbes.com/sites/forbestechcouncil/2019/09/04/how-health-care-apps-can-improve-patient-health-and-support-physicians/?sh=237e0398772b

Ortiz-Ospina, E. (2019, September 18). *The rise of Social Media.* Our World in Data. Retrieved April 29, 2022, from https://ourworldindata.org/rise-of-social-media

Pew Research Center (2009), The Internet's Role in Campaign 2008, retrieved from: https://www.pewresearch.org/internet/2009/04/15/the-internets-role- in-campaign-2008/

Qatar National Development Strategy (2018) Retrieved from: https://www.psa.gov.qa/en/knowledge/Documents/NDS2Final.pdf

Russel B (2017), Social Media New Technologies and Middle East, retrieved from: https://www.hoover.org/research/social-media-new-technologies-and-middle-east

Sandra WK (2018) Ecommerce Shopping Experience, retrieved from: https://securionpay.com/blog/ecommerce-shopping-experience/

Sheila S. (2007), Book: An Introduction to Communication Studies.

Siv R. (2017) The Impact of Technology in Healthcare, retrieved from:https://www.elcom.com.au/resources/blog/the-impact-of-technology-in-healthcare-trends-benefits-examples

Steve. C (2009) The Impact of Technology on Political Communication, retrieved from: https://observer.com/2009/06/the-impact-of-technology-on-political-communication/

Vesna K. (2018) How Social Media Has Transformed Politics, retrieved from: https://strategicsocialmedialab.com/how-social-media-has-transformed-politics/

Vladimir. R (2010) The Role of Information and Communication Technologies in Diplomacy and Diplomatic Services. Retrieved from: https://www.diplomacy.edu/sites/default/files/30112010141720%20Radunovic%20%28Library%29.pdf

CHAPTER TWO
Artificial Intelligence Revolutionizing Communications Tools and Practices

The extent of development that has occurred in the world since computers and the internet became available to the wider public is stunning, including all areas of life and technologies of the fifth generation. This 5G technology and the speed it provides in communication and information transfer has given users the opportunity to complete their tasks with even greater accuracy and speed.

Studying the developments of the world of communications requires anticipating the future through an approach that understands the impact of this technological development that will be reached in the coming years.

WHAT IS ARTIFICIAL INTELLIGENCE?

The first attempt to understand the world of "artificial intelligence" dates back to 1956, specifically in the Dartmouth Artificial Intelligence conference, which formed the first pillar for the emergence of the field of "Artificial Intelligence". In 1956, John McCarthy invited prominent researchers in various fields such as language simulation, learning machines and complexity theories to Dartmouth in New Hampshire to discuss a new topic identified as "Artificial Intelligence".

The invitation letter to the conference made it clear that: "The study is to proceed based on the conjecture that every aspect of learning or any other feature of intelligence can in principle be so precisely described that a machine can be made to simulate it. An attempt will be made to find how to make machines use language, form abstractions and concepts, solve kinds of problems now reserved for humans, and improve themselves".

In fact, this conference was the biggest assembly of scientists to discuss such a matter at that time. It was described as a conference that: "gave birth to the field of Artificial Intelligence as a vibrant area of inter-disciplinary research, and provided an intellectual backdrop to all subsequent computer and development efforts".

Ever since the Dartmouth Conference, scientists have been doing extensive research to define the framework for this new field, in the attempt to set a definition that would have the consensus of the largest number of scientists.

Linguistic Definitions

There is no doubt that linguistic definitions differ from scientific ones, which also differ among themselves. The ability to really define Artificial Intelligence has differed in many ways amongst the most trusted linguistic sources.

The Encyclopedia Britannica for example defines "Artificial Intelligence" as:

"the ability of a digital computer or computer-controlled robot to perform tasks commonly associated with intelligent beings. The term is frequently applied to the project of developing systems endowed with the intellectual processes characteristic of humans, such as the ability to reason, discover meaning, generalize, or learn from past experience".

Meanwhile, the English Oxford Living Dictionary states that: "Artificial Intelligence is the theory and development of computer systems able to perform tasks normally requiring human intelligence, such as visual perception, speech recognition, decision-making, and translation between languages".

Merriam-Webster in the Webster Dictionary defines Artificial Intelligence as:

"1: a branch of computer science dealing with the simulation of intelligent behavior in computers.

2: the capability of a machine to imitate intelligent human behavior".

These different linguistic definitions set a general framework for the interpretation of the term "Artificial Intelligence". It is done by specifying the reference to the field that can be known as "artificial intelligence" without setting a scientific definition of the field. As a result, it makes it necessary for more studies, research and consensus among scientists in this field in order to collectively agree on a definitive and specific connotation of the word.

Scientific Definitions

For decades, scientists have worked hard to find a scientific definition of "Artificial Intelligence" without reaching a unified definition that most of them agree on. In this regard, it is necessary to differentiate between "Machine Learning" and "Artificial Intelligence", something that many find difficult to do.

"Artificial Intelligence is the broader concept of machines being able to carry out tasks in a way that we would consider "smart". In addition, Machine Learning is a current application of AI based around the idea that we should really just be able to give machines access to data and let them learn for themselves" (Marr, 2017).

Another comparison by Avinash Kaushik (2017), explains that "AI is an intelligent machine and Machine Learning is the ability to learn without being explicitly programmed. Currently, ML is the most exciting application of AI."

Moreover, we are able to encounter a definition emphasizing the human role, in both fields: "Artificial Intelligence is a machine pretending to be a human. Machine Learning is a machine pretending to be a statistical programmer. Managing either one requires a data scientist." (Sterne, 2017).

A much deeper definition comes from Tom Mitchell (2006), who stated that: "This question covers a broad range of learning tasks, such as how to design autonomous mobile robots that learn to navigate from their own experience, how to data mine historical medical records to learn which future patients will respond best to which treatments, and how to build search engines that automatically customize to their user's interests. To be more precise, we say that a machine learns with respect to a particular task T, performance metric P, and type of experience E, if the system reliably improves its performance P at task T, following experience E. Depending on how we specify T, P, and E, the learning task might also be called by names such as data mining, autonomous discovery, database updating, programming by example, etc."

In the search to define "Artificial Intelligence", the focus is not really on the word "artificial", because it simply means man-made.

A group of scientists has agreed on Pei Wang's (2019) definition, which may be the most agreed on and accurate definition in this field. It indicates that "Intelligence is the capacity of an information-processing system to adapt to its environment while operating with insufficient knowledge and resources."

In this way: "Intelligence is defined as a strategy of problem-solving that is fundamentally different from computation. However, this does not inhibit this working definition from being used to guide the design of an AI system that is implemented in a computer."

The issue of defining "artificial intelligence" needs further studies and research, but there is a convergence in the general definitions of this concept and this field. It is crucial to resolve this issue at a certain moment to allow for the development of the necessary legislations and regulations for this field.

"We find that while AI researchers tend to define AI in terms of ideal thinking / behavior, policy documents tend to define AI in terms of human thinking / behavior. An important consideration in this comparison is that definitions adhering closely to the technical functionality of AI systems are more inclusive of technologies in use today, whereas definitions that emphasize human-like capabilities are most applicable to hypothetical future technologies. Therefore, regulatory efforts that emphasize AI as human-like may risk overemphasizing concern about future technologies at the expense of pressing issues with existing deployed technologies" (Kraft, 2020).

The Organization for Economic Co-operation and Development (OECD) states that: "An AI system is a machine-based system that can, for a given set of human-defined objectives, make predictions, recommendations, or decisions influencing real or virtual environments. AI systems are designed to operate with varying levels of autonomy." (OECD, 2019).

American legislatures (H.O.R 2020), in their introduced bill in March 2020 to establish the National Artificial Intelligence Initiative, state that, "the term "Artificial Intelligence" means a machine-based system that can, for a given set of human-defined objectives, make predictions, recommendations or decisions influencing real or virtual environments.

Artificial intelligence systems use machine and human-based inputs to:
(A) perceive real and virtual environments;
(B) abstract such perceptions into models through analysis in an automated manner; and
(C) use model inference to formulate options for information or action."

The definition developed by Wang is based on determining the field to which this concept applies. It is based on the ability to adapt to the lack of resources in identifying problems or issues, and to find appropriate options and solutions and implement them with complete independence, in a continuous and cumulative manner.

This means that the self-learning process increases the ability to adapt in an environment where resources are constantly evolving, to develop the ability in tackling specific issues in specific circumstances and implement appropriate solutions to them.

However, we can certainly conclude that the use of artificial intelligence is adapted to purpose it serves, meaning the goal it serves or the function it performs. Artificial intelligence systems are independently based on collecting the largest amount of information and analyzing it based on many variable data. This is in order to reach the most accurate expectations of solutions related to specific issues and to implement them while continuing the process of automatic learning to develop future performance.

The technical definition serves the development of the sector and sets the scientific framework for it. However, the general definition, based on its descriptive identification, allows the development of the regulatory frameworks required for this field in order to ensure its exploitation for the benefit of humanity.

Who is controlling what?

There is no doubt that the rapid development of artificial intelligence technologies presents many challenges on different levels, particularly the level of specialization required to keep pace with the development in terms of setting general frameworks and controls for the field.

The Extents of AI

To date, private companies may be leading this development, but they need these technologies to develop and expand their businesses knowing that a large part of this development is to serve governments.

AI technologies serve military and security industries which are based on monitoring, analysis and control at the level of smart programs that serve weapons by developing and operating them.

Another level is security programs that are based on intelligence, control, and analysis techniques, and anticipate the future based on a rapid analysis of available data about any person or issue.

On the other hand, the expansionary technological programs of companies in various fields highlight the ability to analyze customer data, in order to anticipate their future options. This allows comparison to necessary products or services.

In the current stage of AI development, private companies are leading the research and development, especially companies like Amazon, Google, IBM, Microsoft and many others.

This development raises many concerns with artificial intelligence technologies, specifically when it comes to the extent of these programs' independence. The relationship between the development of this software and the extent of its independent self-learning and developing itself is a direct relationship. A well-developed system means a higher degree of independence. This is what poses the greatest problem in this field which is based on the following questions.

What is the amount of independence that will be given to machines under the control of the human being? How can this delicate balance be found between the independence of machines and the submission to their founder's will?

Many have expressed fears about this rapid development. Elon Musk, one of the pioneers of innovative industries that rely on artificial intelligence technologies, displayed a hesitant approach: "I think we should be very careful about artificial intelligence. If I were to guess like what our biggest existential threat is, it's probably that. So, we need to be very careful with the artificial intelligence. Increasingly scientists think there should be some regulatory oversight maybe at the national and international level, just to make sure that we don't do something very foolish. With artificial intelligence we are summoning the demon. In all those stories where there's the guy with the pentagram and the holy water, it's like yeah, he's sure he can control the demon. Didn't work out" (Washington Post, 2014).

In fact, Elon Musk co-founded OpenAI in 2015, an artificial intelligence laboratory, with the stated goal of discovering and enacting the path to safe artificial general intelligence.

These fears of new technologies for artificial intelligence are legitimate concerns. It is not the first time that humanity has encountered a technological development that threatens the existing social system and the rules governing the sectors affected by new technologies and their relations with other sectors.

Setting a framework for AI

The world has witnessed many similar developments throughout history. The focus was always to make the best use of technology, while finding solutions to any potential negative aspects. Therefore, the need is clear to produce new frameworks benefiting from their positive effects and allowing them to be incorporated into new societal system.

According to Tom Wheeler (2020): "A key lesson of history is that effective regulation focuses on prioritizing the effects of the new technology, rather than the ephemeral technology itself. The transformational nature of a new technology is not per se the primary technology itself, but rather the secondary effects enabled by that development. We didn't regulate the railroad tracks and switches; we regulated the effects of their usage, such as rates and worker safety. We didn't regulate the telegraph (and later telephone) wires and switches, but whether access to them was just and reasonable. History's road map is clear: if there is to be meaningful regulation of AI, it should focus on the tangible effects of the technology."

In this context, governments seem to be behind in following this development in terms of legislation to regulate the field of artificial intelligence, or agreements and understandings among countries.

However, this does not mean that there are no organizing initiatives. Many countries have witnessed specific measures in this area, to put in place regulatory controls.

In fact, in April 2018 the European Commission published the communication "Artificial Intelligence for Europe", in which it outlined the EU's approach to make the most of the opportunities offered by Artificial Intelligence and to address the new challenges that it brings with it.

This communication emphasized the GDPR (General Data Protection Regulation) for the EU which took effect on 25 May 2018. The GDPR "lays down rules relating to the protection of natural persons with regard to the processing of personal data and rules relating to the free movement of personal data."

The communication detailed how the GDPR "ensures a high standard of personal data protection, including the principles of data protection by design and by default. It guarantees the free flow of personal data within the Union. It contains provisions on decision-making based solely on automated processing, including profiling. In such cases, data subjects have the right to be provided with meaningful information about the logic involved in the decision (GDPR, art. 13 (2) f), 14 (2) g) and 15 (1) h)). The General Data Protection Regulation also gives individuals the right not to be subject solely to automated decision-making, except in certain situations. (GDPR, art.22)".

The United States is also catching up on the regulation work of artificial intelligence. In fact, Congress is reviewing a bill establishing the National Artificial Intelligence Initiative. The original text of the bill acknowledges "that AI has the potential to change every sector of the United States economy and society". (H.O.R 2020)

The bill highlights that "the Federal Government lacks clear understanding of the capabilities of artificial intelligence and its potential to affect various social and economic sectors, including ethical concerns, national security implications, and workforce impacts."

The purposes of the Initiative shall be to:
1. "ensure continued United States leadership in artificial intelligence research and development.
2. lead the world in the development and use of trustworthy artificial intelligence systems in public and private sectors.
3. maximize the benefits of artificial intelligence systems for all American people; and
4. prepare the present and future United States workforce for the integration of artificial intelligence systems across all sectors of the economy and society."

However, efforts to regulate the field of artificial intelligence are so recent that at times they do not keep up with the rapid evolution AI. This is the case with regards to the international cooperation on AI, where relatively few actions were taken.

One of the main actions taken by governments collectively was in May 2019. A total of 42 countries among which members and non-members of The Organization for Economic Co-operation and Development (OECD) signed a global framework, highlighting the necessity to start regulating the AI technological evolution. The summary of this framework states:

- AI should benefit people and the planet by allowing inclusive growth, sustainable development and well-being.
- AI systems should be designed in a way that respects the rule of law, human rights, democratic values, and diversity. They should include appropriate safe-guards, such as enabling human intervention where necessary to ensure a fair and just society.
- There should be transparency and responsible disclosure around AI systems to ensure that people understand when they are engaging with the systems and can challenge their outcomes.
- AI systems must function in a robust, secure and safe way throughout their lifetimes. Potential risks should be continually assessed and managed.

- Organizations and individuals developing, deploying or operating AI systems should be held accountable for their proper functioning in line with the above principles.

The OECD recommends that governments:
- Facilitate public and private investment in research and development to spur innovation in trustworthy AI.
- Foster accessible AI ecosystems with digital infrastructure and technologies, and mechanisms to share data and knowledge.
- Create a policy environment that will open the way to deployment of trustworthy AI systems.
- Equip people with the skills for AI and support workers to ensure a fair transition.
- Co-operate across borders and sectors to share information, develop standards and work towards responsible stewardship of AI.

At the same time, governments are facing the challenge of regulating AI. They should find the means to introduce AI into the government itself, thereby potentially improving services for citizens and developing the work of public service professionals. AI might mean a major facelift for government and present a real challenge on government roles and functions.

Governments should keep the interests and well-being of citizens as a top priority when regulating artificial intelligence. The development of this field is not supposed to be at the expense of freedom, privacy, and the interests of citizens.

Governments should consider specific strategies for applying AI to their work, "make AI a part of a goal-based, citizen-centric program; get citizen input; build upon existing resources; be data-prepared and tread carefully with privacy; mitigate ethical risks and avoid AI decision making; and, augment employees, do not replace them." (Mehr, Ash, and Fellow, 2017).

Artificial Intelligence can do a lot of good in the hands of well-equipped government agencies. Therefore, it is crucial for governments and government agencies to be aware of such artificial intelligence programs, or indeed ahead of the curve, to help enhance programs for their citizens.

Governments should also be responsible in preserving the human values embedded in societies while the world of artificial intelligence develops. In particular, this value system is essentially linked to the essence of humanity and its future, and it may be difficult to translate it accurately into data that machines understand and work to respect.

New and ethical concerns on Artificial Intelligence, and human values

Having an ethical approach for artificial intelligence presents a real challenge. It is true that automated machines built with self-learning algorithms might be able to understand ethics and values to a certain extent. Machines understand clearly recognized data, and transforming values and ethics to clear science is not an easy job.

Responsible AI

Finding an ethical approach to artificial intelligence is not an easy task. AI is influencing our daily life in many aspects and it will dominate most of the aspects in the future. We can find AI almost everywhere, and its use will increase over time, to enter all areas of our lives. Therefore, there is an urgent need for a new moral approach to artificial intelligence.

Artificial intelligence based on machines with self-learning algorithms will be able to understand the value systems only to a certain extent. Machines understand explicit and specific data, and converting values into explicit science is a difficult undertaking:

"Developing AI responsibly requires the means to elicit and represent human values and translate these values into technical requirements. It also requires us to develop the means to deal with moral dilemmas and values preferences and evaluate systems in terms of their contribution to human wellbeing" (Dignum, 2018).

Han Yu (2018) conducted extensive research regarding ethical approaches for AI. Based on many papers presented by a group of researchers on this topic, he suggested to look at the ethics of AI in four main areas:

(1) Ethical dilemmas,
(2) Individual ethical decision frameworks,
(3) Collective ethical decision frameworks,
(4) Ethics in human-AI interactions.

These four fields define the main problematic issues with regards to making AI ethical:

1. Ethical Dilemmas are about three major schools of understanding ethics: Consequentialism (the ends justify the means), Deontology (not to deliberate harm), and Virtue (to act on specific values).
2. Individual Ethical Decision Framework is about creating possible ways towards developing a general ethical decision-making framework for AI. That means how to train an AI agent to make ethical autonomous decision through extensive data regarding different scenarios, past example cases and game theories.
3. Collective Ethical Framework: Not only each specific AI is programmed morally and individually, but this also requires a cohesion among one another to assure proper ethical standards.
4. Human-AI interaction: It is about the challenge of measuring benefits and risks when AI is interacting with humans. The issue that arises is commonly known as the Trolley Problem: if there were five people tied to a rail track and one person tied to another and a trolley was directed to kill them and you had the switch to flip the line, would you do it? Issues such as these need to be resolved by society in general and AI researchers. These issues will become imperative later as AI develops and becomes more integrated in our lives.

Achieving Ethical AI

Virginia Dingum (2018) argues that any intelligent system should be responsible. This approach is somehow a developed version of the human intelligence, where responsibility is not fundamental to intelligence. It will not be easy to have a responsible machine in the ethical sense.

Dingum sets out three main pillars for responsible AI. Firstly, society should be ready to take responsibility regarding the impact of AI, an undertaking which should be collective work by researchers, developers, governments, legislatures, and citizens through hard work in research and education to develop the necessary regulations.

Secondly, responsible AI needs a well-developed algorithm to allow AI agents to reason and act according to ethics and human values.

Thirdly, responsible AI requires people's participation from different cultural backgrounds to shape a framework and to create a form of governance that assures responsibility in the evolution of AI systems.

One crucial element that almost all researchers agree on is the importance of dialogue amongst ethicists and researchers in artificial intelligence (Anderson, Anderson, 2017).

This effort is much needed to find a common language for both parties, since it would be really challenging for ethicists to translate ethics into readable code language in order to allow developers to transform ethics into smart algorithms for machine functioning in ethical fashion. This might require a new philosophical approach for values and ethics to get to the core of it, or add new readings for many concepts, and make it more AI compatible.

As Daniel Dennett (2006) stated in a talk at the International Computers and Philosophy Conference: "AI makes philosophy honest."

Many approaches and suggestions were presented regarding how to create an ethical AI approach.

UNI Global Union suggests that a "full transparency in an AI system should be facilitated by the presence of a device that can record information about said system in the form of an 'ethical black box' that not only contains relevant data to ensure transparency and accountability of a system, but also includes clear data and information on the ethical considerations built into said system."

One of the most substantial studies (IEEE, 2019) published on ethical AI recommends a road map to achieve ethical, Autonomous and Intelligent Systems (A/IS):

- The first step is identifying the norms of the community relevant to the tasks and roles that the A/IS system is designed for.
- The system should be capable to respond to any changes in the norms of the society in which the A/IS system is deployed. The system should ensure transparency to the users, stakeholders and the community about those changes and amendments in the norms.
- The A/IS system should identify ways in which people can easily resolve any norm conflicts in full transparency. The resolution of norm conflicts should be documented by the system and available to users, the relevant community of deployment, and third-party evaluators.
- An evaluation should be put in place to ensure the proper incorporation of the cultural norms within the A/IS system. It must document the similarities and differences in norms applied to the system itself and to other human users. Also, it needs to include a mechanism to assess any biases in the system's accessibility and performance that can be considered as a disadvantage for a certain social group or a demographic group. The system should also allow for use of strong verification and validation techniques for assessing the system's safety and norm compliance by different regulators and accident investigators (IEEE 2019).

As mentioned earlier, the work to regulate the AI field is still at early stages, but many independent initiatives have been launched internationally to explore the question of ethical artificial intelligence. The Secretariat of the European Parliament published in March 2020 a study that summarizes the main ethical initiatives and the main issues discussed in regard of ethical AI (ERPS, 2020).

In fact, it is still a challenge to ensure an ethical AI approach. A lot of research is still needed to "investigate the representation and determination of ethical principles, the incorporation of these ethical principles into a system's decision procedure, ethical decision making with incomplete and uncertain knowledge, the explanation for decisions made using ethical principles, and the evaluation of systems that act based upon ethical principles" (Anderson, Anderson 2007).

Artificial intelligence is affecting our lives in many ways and developing at a high speed. What is crucial to our study is to understand how AI is influencing the field of communications.

Artificial Intelligence techniques in communications

The entry of machines and smart programs created major changes and added new dynamics to many industries. This will also be shown to a greater degree when 5G is entrenched in our daily life and in everything that affects us.

The Various Models of AI

Wireless communications are a cornerstone of how human beings interact in the 21st century. From bluetooth, to WiFi, to 5G, they have revolutionized our world. Furthermore, AI has a strong hand in how that revolution has occurred.

Both the Neural Network and the Markov Model are ways that Artificial Intelligence is being practiced in fields such as wireless communications, with other advancements such as Fuzzy Logic.

Artificial Neural Networks are models based on the brain within the central nervous system. "They are usually presented as artificial nodes or 'neurons' in different layers connected via synapses. The learning properties of artificial neural networks have been applied to resolve extensive and diverse tasks that would have been difficult to solve by ordinary rule-based programming" (Serrano, 2018).

In general, Neural Networks are a "collection of simple computational units interlinked by a system of connections. The number of units can be very large and the connections intricate. Neural Networks are used for many applications of pattern classification and pattern recognition" (Science Direct, 2015).

Another definition of Neural Networks by Rondeau & Bostian (2009) defines it as "signal processing elements that perform simple operations on data. However, the collection of artificial neurons and clever learning algorithms allow networks to build and adapt to represent and process data in interesting ways. In signal classification, they take multiple noisy input items and provide accurate answers to the type of modulation represented".

Some examples include image and speech recognition, textual character recognition, and domains of human expertise such as prediction of financial market indicator and medical diagnosis.

Moreover, researchers did extensive work to study the use of neural networks in marketing, specifically in predicting choice making among consumers.

In fact, "when neural network performance is compared to the predictive results that would be obtained using traditional marketing models, without exception the neural network model exhibits equivalent or better out-of-sample predictive accuracy than any of the comparative statistical methods examined. This portends great usefulness for the use of artificial neural network modeling for prediction of consumer choice and suggests potential applications of the neural network methodology to numerous other marketing applications" (West, Brockeh, Golden, 1997).

In addition to Neural Networks, Artificial Intelligence uses another model based on calculating probabilities of sequences: The Hidden Markov Models (HMM).

In fact, the HMM are based on augmenting the Markov chain: "A Markov chain is a model that tells us something about the probabilities of sequences of random variables and states, each of which can take on values from some set. These sets can be words, tags, or symbols representing anything, like the weather. A Markov chain makes a very strong assumption that if we want to predict the future in the sequence, all that matters is the current state. The states before the current state have no impact on the future except via the current state. It's as if when to predict tomorrow's weather you could examine today's weather, yet you weren't allowed to look at yesterday's weather" (Jurasky, Martin, 2019).

Indeed, a Hidden Markov Model is a tool for representing probability distributions over sequences of observations. It is used in almost all current speech recognition systems, in numerous applications in computational molecular biology, in data compression, and in other areas of artificial intelligence and pattern recognition (Ghahramani, 2001).

The importance of Hidden Markov Model is the ability to study hidden events in a sequence of observable events. "A Markov chain is useful when we need to compute a probability for a sequence of observable events. In many cases, however, the events we are interested in are hidden. We do not observe them directly. For example, we don't normally observe part of speech tags in a text. Rather, we see words and must infer the tags from the word sequence. We call the tags hidden because they are not observed. A hidden Markov model (HMM) allows us to talk about both observed events (like words that we see in the input) and hidden events (like part-of-speech tags) that we think of as causal factors in our probabilistic model (Rondeau & Bostian, 2009).

Another technique of artificial intelligence used in communications is Fuzzy Logic. The best way to explain Fuzzy Logic is to see a bottle: while the bottle may not just be entirely full or empty, most binary forms of logic will not comprehend that. In terms of binary truth values, a bottle is viewed as full or empty. But if one accounts for the quantity of liquid in the bottle, one may say that the bottle is "almost full." Under this way of speaking, "almost full" becomes a fuzzy predicate and the degree of truth of "the bottle is almost full" reflects the amount of liquid in the bottle.

Another way of looking at this technique is the following: we cannot exactly establish whether it will rain tomorrow or not, due to our incomplete knowledge about our world. However, we can estimate to which degree this is probable, possible or necessary.

As for the main differences between probability and possibility theory, the probability of an event is the sum of the probabilities of all worlds that satisfy this event, whereas the possibility of an event is the maximum of the possibilities of all worlds that satisfy the event. Intuitively, the probability of an event aggregates the probabilities of all worlds that satisfy this event, while the possibility of an event is simply the possibility of the "most optimistic" world that satisfies the event. Hence, although both probability and possibility theory allow for quantifying degrees of uncertainty, they are conceptually quite different from each other. That is, probability and possibility theory represent different facets of uncertainty" (Straccia, 2014).

These technologies are fascinating and life changing for humans. Evolution will certainly continue at a rapid pace. Many studies and research aim to develop a new network that combines two or more of the techniques mentioned above to create a Hybrid Intelligent Network: "A hybrid intelligent system is one that combines at least two intelligent technologies. For example, combining a neural network with a fuzzy system results in a hybrid neuro-fuzzy system.

The combination of probabilistic reasoning, fuzzy logic, neural networks and evolutionary computation forms the core of soft computing, an emerging approach to build hybrid intelligent systems capable of reasoning and learning in an uncertain and imprecise environment." (Lecture notes B219).

Hybrid Intelligent Networks are systems that operate in a similar fashion to the brain. They are ones that have a complex Network Structure, and Hybrid Dynamical Evolution: "The brain is in essence, not only a computer but also a hybrid intelligent network with much more complicated structures and behaviors/functions. Therefore, unveiling the neuronal modeling and activity could be one of the key steps toward understanding how the brain works and then emulating the brain functions. It is tacitly assumed that the brain is a complex brain network with complicated structures and much more complicated dynamical behaviors" (Guan, Hu, Shen, 2019).

Such measures can increase the efficiency in multiple fields such as medicine, communications and security measures.

Another important technology for Artificial Intelligence to be more effective in certain circumstances is the Edge Computing. It is a new perspective regarding data centers and their relation to operations and relations to the network.

"Edge computing is a new form of decentralized computing. Edge computing is done at or near the source of generated data, often with difficulties to reach locations such as wind turbines and oil rigs, as opposed to sending data to the cloud to be processed and analyzed. Bringing operations closer to the edge of a network reduces the distance and time the data has to travel between a client and server. It also accelerates the data-to-insights process" (Ouissal, 2020).

Edge computing provides Artificial intelligence with a new form of connectivity and data sharing network. This will result in faster data processing and response to situations, especially for emergency ones. "By solving the proximity problem, you solve the latency problem. The on-device processing approach ensures that only non-critical data is sent over the network and that critical data can be acted upon immediately. That is important for latency-sensitive applications, such as autonomous vehicles, where having to wait milliseconds may be untenable" (Hamilton, 2018).

This technology is becoming more crucial for many services, like autonomous vehicles, retail advertising, smart speakers, healthcare devices, security solutions, retail advertising, and video conferencing. "The decentralized approach of edge computing also decreases bandwidth. Data processing starts at the point of collection and only the data that needs to be stored is sent to the cloud. That makes edge computing more efficient and scalable and reduces network load" (Hamilton, 2017).

These developed technologies will have a significant influence on all aspects of life. They will influence the way we communicate and interact with information related to businesses and brands. It will give the chance for morecustomized communications strategies and provide new effective tools to execute them. Nonetheless, the question would be: to which extent?

Best Artificial Intelligence Practice from a communications perspective

The Artificial Neural Networks are divided into three main categories: pattern classification, prediction and financial analysis, or control and optimization (Rumelhart, Widrow, Lehr, 1994). Other researchers (Li, 1994) made a wider selection of categories that fall under ANN: approximation, optimization, classification, prediction, generalization, relation, abstraction and adaptiveness.

In fact, many industries are using this technique through different technologies and solutions:

- Airline security control
- Investment management and risk control
- Prediction of thrift failures
- Foreign exchange systems
- Prediction of stock price
- Handwriting recognition

- Petroleum exploration
- Weather forecasting
- Speech recognition

Artificial Neural Networks play an important role in developing techniques used for digital media analysis, classification, and representation.

Deep learning architectures have been successfully used for image retrieval, natural language processing, large scale media analysis problems and feature learning (Tefas, Losifidis, Pitas, 2013).

The Artificial Neural Networks is applied to our daily use, especially when it comes to social media. All major social media applications use neural networks to manage the huge amount of data uploaded instantly on these platforms and to understand users' preferences, selections and orientations.

Facebook announced in 2016, a new Artificial Intelligence initiative that uses various deep neural networks such as DeepText that can understand the textual content. Similar techniques are used to browse the internet for specific content of interest.

Pinterest makes relevant recommendations through a neural network called PinSage, where part of the development is using the TensorFlow and PyTorch deep-learning frameworks on Amazon Web Services (AWS). The deep-learning model places each image according to a theme, within one giant "graph" of other images.

The created data every day in different fields related to our daily life routines is immense, with currently no possibility to track and analyze it quantitively and qualitatively.

Communications firms are increasingly relying on Artificial Intelligence techniques. Reading thousands of articles for one client and analyzing them would take days of work, while using a Natural Language Processing tool gets the job done in minutes. But to understand more about what Natural Language Processing is, we need to explore some of the straightforward definitions, including that of SAS, one of the main leaders in analytics:

"Natural language processing (NLP) is a branch of artificial intelligence that helps computers understand, interpret and manipulate human language. NLP draws from many disciplines, including computer science and computational linguistics, in its pursuit to fill the gap between human communications and computer understanding" (SAS, 2020).

Meanwhile, Microsoft's definition presents a more practical version from an end user perspective: "Natural language processing (NLP) is used for tasks such as sentiment analysis, topic detection, language detection, key phrase extraction and document categorization. NLP can be used to classify documents such as labeling documents as sensitive or spam. The output of NLP can be used for subsequent processing or search. Another use for NLP is to summarize text by identifying the entities present in the document. These entities can also be used to tag documents with keywords, which enables search and retrieval based on content".

Another technology that increases effectiveness for communications teams is speech recognition and conversion, like Google Cloud Speech API, which allows users to accurately convert speech into text using an API powered by Google's Artificial Intelligence technologies.

Google cloud Speech API applies deep learning neural network algorithms for automatic speech recognition (ASR), and allows us to meet users where they are globally, with voice recognition that supports more than 125 languages. It also combines the best of Google's technologies in Text-to-Speech and Natural Language to unlock useful cases like voice bots and sentiment analysis for speech.

In addition, communications firms use artificial intelligence to monitor and analyze social media and media platform to track where a client is mentioned and monitor how people perceive the brand.

Artificial intelligence is needed to observe all the sources by creating a large amount of data and analyzing it. This is done in order to check for any relevant response needed. Some examples of this technology include:

- Hootsuite: Search streams in the Hootsuite dashboard allows monitoring conversations relevant to specific business sectors, industries and products. It helps monitor what people are saying based on keywords, hashtags, locations and even specific users.
- Google Alerts are offered by Google which monitors the web as a content change detection and notification service. It automatically surfs the web, based on key words and sends notification when matching content is found.

The web search in general is a major field powered by artificial intelligence due to the large data processed, and the process needed to find instant results. "Neural networks and artificial intelligence have also been applied to web searching in result ranking and relevance as a method to learn and adapt to variable user interests" (Serrano, 2018).

The web searching engines are one of the most useful tools for marketers and communications professional. Many jobs and projects start with a search in the form of research.

Artificial Intelligence is deeply changing our way of communication, as well as how we create the necessary messaging, push it to audiences, analyze the impact, and evaluate the strategies implemented.

A crucial element of any communication strategy are press releases. Would Artificial Intelligence present a new tool to write down press releases, replacing communications specialists in this skilled task? In fact, the right question would be: when will AI write for PR?

An impressive amount of work is in progress to develop an unsupervised transformer language model. "Statistical language modeling plays an important role in many areas of natural language processing including speech recognition, machine translation and information retrieval. The prototypical use of language models is to assign probabilities to sequences of words" (Mitchell, Lapata, 2009).

In this regard, OpenAI, a leading artificial intelligence company based in San Francisco, has generated significant progress in this field. GPT-3 (Generative Pretrained Transformer 3) is an unsupervised transformer language model, and a developed version of GPT-2.

OpenAI announced a significant amount of progress in GPT-3, especially in the accuracy of text produced: "We find that GPT-3 can generate samples of news articles which human evaluators have difficulty distinguishing from articles written by humans" (Brown, Mann, Ryder, Subbiah, 2020).

On the other hand, there are limitations on many levels: "GPT-3 shares some limitations common to deepest learning systems – its decisions are not easily interpretable. It is not necessarily well-calibrated in its predictions on novel inputs as observed by much higher variance in performance than humans on standard benchmarks. It retains the biases of the data it has been trained on" (Brown, Mann, Ryder, Subbiah, 2020).

AI can write a press release today, but it will need some data entries which are created by humans. Soon, it could become a fully automated writing process.

To conclude how AI is changing the communications field, it is important to summarize that artificial intelligence will help corporate communications through the following areas:

- Monitoring media and social media for relevant mentions to business and brand.
- Analyzing people's sentiments through comments and posts.
- Writing press releases and media reports.
- Identifying and extracting names, places, businesses, events, data and more.
- Translating texts and audios to different languages for a wider distribution.
- Marketing studies for the audience to reach a better impact.
- Creating messages in relevance to vision and mission, and specific occasions.

- Delivering news to a wide range of platforms, in very innovative ways using virtual and augmented reality applications.
- Creating crisis alerts at early stages and suggesting to contain it, which enables faster responses to crises in very precise and accurate manners.
- Converting speech to text.
- Monitoring fake news and videos relevant to the business or the brand, which can help expose lies and identify deception.
- Suggesting story angles for journalists and bloggers based on thorough and accurate market research covering interests and trends.
- Evaluating communications strategies for competitors and suggest better approaches.
- Engaging the right influencers who would be able to engage specific audience for a better influence.

Benefiting from artificial intelligence systems has become a necessity for various fields. Indeed, it has become important for the pioneers of these fields to develop proposals and plans for the new AI systems that serve them greatly in their work.

This is what global companies such as Amazon, Google and others have succeeded with at this stage, by studying and anticipating the market for better results in marketing their products.

This automatically applies to the field of communications, since artificial intelligence systems were integrated. But there is a need to develop a set of new systems and software that serves the field of communications. We have seen the greatest possibility in writing press releases and other writings, although this technique is not completely ready until now.

How could the State of Qatar implement AI effectively

The efforts of governments individually and collectively date back months and years to regulate and organize the work of AI, while the efforts of researchers in this field go back to the year 1956.

The legislation expected in the coming years must be inspired by the existential values of the human being. Regulations should be based on a clear value system, taking into account the development of artificial intelligence towards a great benefit to humanity, by preserving the basic values based on human dignity, and in particular the freedom and justice that constitute the essence of human existence.

A great governmental effort is required to keep pace with the development of artificial intelligence, considering the concerns it poses at the level of privacy, security, control and independence. This also needs to go hand in hand with most of the futuristic visions being applied lately by many countries in the GCC, including Qatar's National Vision 2030.

In fact, Qatar is one of the few countries that are taking these matters to another level by establishing a National Artificial Intelligence Strategy for the country. The document states that:

"Our vision is to have AI so pervasive in all aspects of life, business and governance in Qatar that everyone looks up to Qatar as a role model for AI+X nation" (QCRI,2019).

In this regard, it is necessary that the State of Qatar takes certain measures towards artificial intelligence, particularly at five levels:

- First, developing legislative measures and regulations in regards to the applications of artificial intelligence in the State of Qatar. There is an urgent need that sets the general framework to keep pace with this development, and to maintain society's values and culture.
- Second, sharing experiences is a must. There is a need to make use of the experiences of the development of artificial intelligence existing in the world. Developing a new approach for research and development, in artificial intelligence that serves the strategic goals of the State of Qatar.
- Third, taking advantage of foreign investment opportunities in the areas of artificial intelligence, and building an investment

portfolio in major AI pioneer companies. Furthermore, investing in companies and institutions that focus their research and work on developing this field, while protecting humans and a universal set of values, and limiting the implications of pure commercial development of artificial intelligence.

- Fourth, preparing the appropriate work environment to keep pace with the development of artificial intelligence, in terms of creating an efficient workforce that can adapt to the rapid development of this field. In fact, only 13% of Qatar nationals hold jobs in the ICT and the ICT related sectors. GCC countries will face a gap of 3.1 million jobs for nationals by 2025 in these sectors.
- Fifth, taking advantage of the existing artificial intelligence systems, in various fields. This includes governmental institutions and private sectors for more effective integration of AI systems in their daily work.

It seems clear that the field of communications will change significantly with the presence of smart systems that perform a range of tasks that currently require a large number of employees. This includes developing existing systems used only for monitoring towards new systems that follow up, analyze, propose plans, produce the necessary materials for execution and implement after approval by the authorized party.

The bet on the field of communication is a bet on the future. The development it witnesses in this field gives it great importance in the work of governments to communicate its message to internal and external audiences.

Communication strategies have become an irreplaceable necessity for the work of governments and their official agencies to explain public policies and strategic directions.

The technological development in the world of communication added many independent players in the process of transferring information and bridged the distance between people and centers of events. Therefore, governments need new strategies, plans, and technologies to clarify their vision, direction, and policies.

War today, is a war of ideas, words, rumors and piracies, all happening in the digital world.

REFERENCES

Anderson, M., & Anderson, S. L. (2007). *Machine Ethics: Creating an Ethical Intelligent Agent.* AI Magazine. https://doi.org/10.1609/aimag.v28i4.2065 .

Artificial Neural Network. Artificial Neural Network - an overview | ScienceDirect Topics. (2015). https://www.sciencedirect.com/topics/earth-and-planetary-sciences/artificial-neural-network

Brown, Tom B.& Mann, Benjamin & Ryder, Nick & Subbiah, Melanie (2020), Language Models are Few-shot learners. https://www.thetalkingmachines.com/sites/default/files/2020-12/neurips-2020-language-models-are-few-shot-learners-paper.pdf

Cheng, B., & Titterington, D. M. (1994). Neural Networks: A Review from a Statistical Perspective.

Copeland, B. J. (2020, August 11). *Artificial intelligence.* https://www.britannica.com/technology/artificial-intelligence .

Desoukie, B. O. A. (2019, August 13). *How Artificial Intelligence Changes Media In The Middle East.* Communicate Online | Regional Edition | Advertising, marketing, public relations and media in the Arab world and beyond. https://www.communicateonline.me/digital/how-artificial-intelligence-changes-media-in-the-middle-east/ .

EPRS, E. P. R. S. (2020). The ethics of artificial intelligence: Issues and initiatives, Study, Panel for the Future of Science and Technology EPRS, European Parliamentary Research Service Scientific Foresight Unit (STOA) – March 2020.

Global Union, U. N. I. (2018). Top 10 Principles for Ethical Artificial Intelligence.

Google. *Speech-to-Text: Automatic Speech Recognition | Google Cloud.* Google. https://cloud.google.com/speech-to-text/?utm_campaign=emea-emea-all-en-dr-bkws-all-all-trial-e-gcp-1009139 .

Ghahramani, Zoubin, "An introduction to Hidden Markov Models and Bayesian Networks",International Journal of Pattern Recognition and Artificial Intelligence, Hidden Markov Models, Applications in Computer Vision, Edited By: Horst Bunke (University of Bern, Switzerland) and Terry Caelli (University of Alberta, Canada), volume 45, June 2001. https://doi.org/10.1142/4648

Guan, Z.-H., Hu, B., & Shen, X. (2019). Hybrid Intelligent Networks. *Introduction to Hybrid Intelligent Networks*, 1–26. https://doi.org/10.1007/978-3-030-02161-0_1

Hamilton, Eric, (2018) — Last Updated: 27 Dec'18 2018-12-27T08:37:12 00:00, & Name*. (2018, December 27). *What is Edge Computing: The Network Edge Explained.* Cloudwards. https://www.cloudwards.net/what-is-edge-computing/.

H.O.R (2020), House Of Representatives, H.R. 6216 To establish the National Artificial Intelligence Initiative, and for other purposes. House of Representatives, United States.

Hybrid Intelligent Systems. (2019). Lecture.

IEEE SA - Artificial Intelligence Systems (AIS). IEEE SA - The IEEE Standards Association - Home. https://standards.ieee.org/initiatives/artificial-intelligence-systems/index1.html?utm_expid=.qavZBKmuRnmUw2AK_BZo7g.1.

Jurafsky, D., & H. Martin, J. (2019). *Speech and Language Processing.* https://web.stanford.edu/~jurafsky/slp3/A.pdf.

Kaushik, A. (2017, November 6). *Artificial Intelligence: Implications On Marketing, Analytics, And You.* https://www.kaushik.net/avinash/

artificial-intelligence-machine-learning-implications-marketing-analytics/.

Krafft, P. M., Young, M., Katell, M., Huang, K., & Bugingo, G. (2020). Defining AI in Policy versus Practice. *Proceedings of the AAAI/ACM Conference on AI, Ethics, and Society.* https://doi.org/10.1145/3375627.3375835

Lecture notes, B219, 03B219Lect_Week11 (murdoch.edu.au)

Li, Eldon Y. (1994). "Artificial neural networks and their business applications", Institute of Information Management, National Chung Cheng University, http://eli.johogo.com/pdf/neural.pdf

McFarland, M. (2019, April 17). *Elon Musk: 'With artificial intelligence we are summoning the demon.'*. The Washington Post. https://www.washingtonpost.com/news/innovations/wp/2014/10/24/elon-musk-with-artificial-intelligence-we-are-summoning-the-demon/.

Mehr, H., Ash, H. and Fellow, D., (2017). *"Artificial intelligence for Citizen Services and Government"*, Ash Cent. Democr. Gov. Innov. Harvard Kennedy School, August 2017.

Mitchel, T. (2006). The discipline of Machine Learning. Pittsburg; School of Computer Science, Carnegie Mellon University.

Mitchel, J., & Lapata, M. (2009). Language Models Based on Semantic Composition.

Monett, D., Lewis, C. W. P., Thórisson, K. R., Bach, J., Baldassarre, G., Granato, G., … Winfield, A. (2020). Special Issue "On Defining Artificial Intelligence"—Commentaries and Author's Response. *Journal of Artificial General Intelligence, 11*(2), 1–100. https://doi.org/10.2478/jagi-2020-0003

Organisation, O. E. C. D. (2019). *Recommendation of the Council on Artificial Intelligence*. OECD Legal Instruments. https://legalinstruments.oecd.org/en/instruments/oecd-legal-0449.

Ouissal, Said, (2020)" what is Edge computing?", https://www.quora.com/What-is-edge-computing/answer/Said-Ouissal-1

Papazian, S., Risl, M., Bohsali, S., & Matar, A. (2017). *Empowering the GCC digital workforce Building adaptable skills in the digital era.* https://www.strategyand.pwc.com. https://www.strategyand.pwc.com/m1/en/reports/empowering-the-gcc-digital-workforce-full-report.pdf.

QCAI, National Artificial Intelligence Strategy Qatar (2019). https://www.motc.gov.qa/sites/default/files/national_ai_strategy_-_english_0.pdf

Rumelhart, D. E., Widrow, B., & Lehr, M. A. (1994). The basic ideas in neural networks. *Communications of the ACM, 37*(3), 87–92. https://doi.org/10.1145/175247.175256

Rondeau, T. W., & Bostian, C. W. (2009). *Artificial intelligence in wireless communications.* Artech House.

SAS. (2020). *What is Natural Language Processing?* https://www.sas.com/en_us/insights/analytics/what-is-natural-language-processing-nlp.html.

Seabrook, J. (2019). *"Can a Machine Learn to Write for The New Yorker?",* The New Yorker. https://www.newyorker.com/magazine/2019/10/14/can-a-machine-learn-to-write-for-the-new-yorker.

Serrano, W. (2018, September 6). *The Random Neural Network and Web Search: Survey Paper.* SpringerLink. https://link.springer.com/chapter/10.1007/978-3-030-01054-6_51.

Straccia, Umberto (2014), Foundations of Fuzzy logic and Semantic Web Languages. Boca Raton: Chapman and Hall. 2014.

Tefas, Anastasios, Iosifidis, Alexandros, and Pitas, Ioannis (2013), *"Neural Networks for Digital Media Analysis and Description",* Engineering Applications of Neural Networks, Springer, 2013

Virginia, D. (2018). Responsible Artificial Intelligence: Designing AI for Human Values".

Wang, P. (2019). On Defining Artificial Intelligence. *Journal of Artificial General Intelligence, 10*(2), 1–37. https://doi.org/10.2478/jagi-2019-0002

Webster, M. *Artificial Intelligence.* https://www.merriam-webster.com/dictionary/artificial intelligence.

Patricia M. West, Patrick L. Brockett and Linda L. Golden (1997), *"A Comparative Analysis of Neural Networks and Statistical Methods for Predicting Consumer Choice"*, Marketing Science, 1997, Vol. 16, No. 4 (1997).

Wheeler, T. (2020, May 6). *History's message about regulating AI.* Brookings.https://www.brookings.edu/research/historys-message-about-regulating-ai/.

Yu, H., Shen, Z., Miao, C., Leung, C., Lesser, V. R., & Yang, Q. (2018). Building Ethics into Artificial Intelligence. *Proceedings of the Twenty-Seventh International Joint Conference on Artificial Intelligence.* https://doi.org/10.24963/ijcai.2018/779

CHAPTER THREE
Qatar Blockade History and Crisis Management

QATAR: A QUICK LOOK

The State of Qatar is a small peninsula and a promising success story. It borders the Persian Gulf with a land border with Saudi Arabia. Over 11,571 square kilometers territory is the home of approximately 2.7 million inhabitants according to the latest statistics compiled in 2020, with over 94 different nationalities a part of the population. According to Leo Benedictus (2013), immigrant workers mostly from South Asia outnumber the native population of Qatar by eight to one, the biggest ratio of migrants to citizens in the world.

"We share many things in common; but most importantly Qatar and Singapore have proved that size does not determine a country's success" said H.E. Mohammed Bin Abdulrahman Al Thani, Qatar's Minister of Foreign Affairs, after a meeting with his Singaporean counterpart in Doha in April 2018.

This young country is the land of massive untouched oil and gas reservoirs, and the possessor of huge investments and assets around the globe, which guarantees it a thriving economy and a GDP that is among the highest in the world. Qatari citizens are indeed among the richest people in the world, with a high purchasing power ability (Benedictus, 2013). Qatar is the largest producer of liquefied natural gas (LNG) in the world and has massive reserves. Being heavily import-dependent has never presented a financial challenge (Stewart, 2017).

Qatar is also part of the Gulf Cooperation Council, which was founded in 1981 and includes Bahrain, Kuwait, Oman, Qatar, Saudi Arabia, and the UAE. Since 1981, the GCC has grown as a socio-economic powerhouse in the region, promoting stronger relationships amongst the members to ensure stability in the Gulf (Naheem, 2017).

Doha shares with Tehran the world's largest gas field, which gives an economic incentive to its growing ties with Iran. This relationship has caused some issues with major neighboring GCC states, especially KSA, UAE and Bahrain due to the political conflicts and tension with Iran that has been building for many years. Having been the poorest among the six Gulf States - before joining the Middle East oil club some 50 years ago - Qatar adopted a number of distinguished and diversified economic strategies instead of relying solely on gas revenues. In this process, *The Qatar Investment Authority* was established by the Qatari administration in 2005 with the objective of facilitating the state's implementation of its economic diversification vision by seeking the most important investment opportunities in the world. Since then Qatar acquired increasing investments worth billions of dollars in different sectors worldwide. In the real estate sector, beside large ownerships in New York, San Francisco, Los Angeles, Singapore and France, the Qatari government possesses property in London which is equivalent to more than the Queen of England herself. In fact, Qatar owns 34% of the top 15 London Skyscrapers.

Qatar's technological investments include those in Silicon Valley, while in the travel and tourism industry, in addition to state-owned Qatar Airways, Doha has acquired shares in British Airways, Heathrow Airport and Saint Petersburg Airport. In Germany, Qatari shareholders in Deutsche Bank, Siemens, Volkswagen and other corporations are dominant, and while the buying of Paris Saint Germain football team is the main stone of its sports investment plan, purchasing the Italian luxury brand Valentino is the most significant asset in fashion, not to mention its assets and investments in India, Japan, Brazil, and wherever the opportunity looms (CNBC report, 2017).

Away from its economic potential, Qatar has a well-equipped military force, especially with a powerful air defense. Yet the strength point at the military level lies in Qatar's two foreign military bases: Al Udeid Base, which is the largest US military base in the Middle East; and Tariq Bin-Ziyad military base, Turkey's most strategic armed presence in the region (Mouchantaf, 2017).

The presence of the American and Turkish military bases on Qatari lands boosts the positioning of Doha as an oasis of tranquility and progress and amplifies its stance in the region.

Socially, Qatari citizens enjoy affluent living at all levels; financially, medically, educationally, and culturally, since Doha is not only a city with a flourishing economy, but also a destination of rich cultural identity, and a gathering arena for some of the best international universities, healthcare service providers and sports agencies in the world, in addition, of course, to reputable public educational and medical care institutions.

As for previous market supplies before the blockade, 80% of food items that Doha consumes are supplied via its borders with KSA for instance, as no more than 1% of its alimentary requirements are produced locally. Simultaneously, building supplies and other materials worth billions are transported yearly into Qatar territory through its one and only land portal with KSA.

On the other hand, prior to the opening of Hamad International Port in September 2017, Doha lacked a modern port that enabled the smooth letting in of vehicles, machinery, and other big imports and supplies, as well as the exportation of its gas and oil containers out to Japan, Pakistan, and other clients around the world. Accordingly, it relied on the ports of neighboring Dubai and Abu Dhabi in order to facilitate its trade and fill this gap, leading to a significant impact when the aerial, sea and land blockade decision was taken by Saudi Arabia, United Arab Emirates, Bahrain, and Egypt against Qatar on 5 June 2017.

THE CRISIS: 5 JUNE 2017

An article that Qatar News Agency allegedly published on 23 May 2017 was later proven to be hacked. The article had falsely claimed that His Highness the Amir Sheikh Tamim Bin Hamad Al Thani allegedly cautioned against confronting Tehran and expressed support for Hamas and Hezbollah. The blockading countries coalition pointed its finger at Qatar, accusing it of cooperation with rival Iran, financing and hosting terrorism, as well as meddling in Gulf states' internal affairs, announcing thus the following sanctioning measures against Doha on 5 June 2017:

- Cutting off diplomatic and trade ties with Qatar.
- Closing air, sea and land routes with Qatar.
- Calling on GCC citizens to leave Qatar, and asking Qatari nationals to fly back to their country (Gulf Times, Stewart, 2017).

Countries including Saudi Arabia, the UAE, Bahrain, and Egypt- and later the Maldives, in addition to Mauritania, fully cut diplomatic and economic ties with Qatar in the early morning on 5 June 2017.

Saudi Arabia also announced that Qatari troops would no longer be part of the GCC unified army in Yemen, while the UAE sent strong warnings to its citizens and residents to refrain from publicly sympathizing with Qatar (Al Rawi, 2019).

Bahrain's Ministry of Foreign Affairs issued a statement as well, saying it would withdraw its diplomatic mission from the Qatari capital Doha within 48 hours, and that all Qatari diplomats should leave Bahrain within the same period. Saudi Arabia followed making the announcement via its state-run Saudi Press Agency. Both the UAE and Egypt made the announcement on their state-run news agencies within minutes of each other.

At around 10 am, Qatar responded by saying there was "no legitimate justification" for four Arab nations to cut diplomatic ties. Qatar also said the decision was a "violation of its sovereignty", vowing to its citizens that it will not affect them (Al Jazeera, 2017).

The Demands

Simultaneously, the blockading partners enlisted 13 demands that Qatar should obey in order to lift the blockade:

- Scale down diplomatic ties with Iran and close the Iranian diplomatic missions in Qatar, expel members of Iran's Revolutionary Guard and cut off military and intelligence cooperation with Iran. Trade and commerce with Iran must comply with US and international sanctions in a manner that does not jeopardize the security of the Gulf Cooperation Council.
- Immediately shut down the Turkish military base, which was under construction, and halt military cooperation with Turkey inside of Qatar.
- Sever ties to all "terrorist, sectarian and ideological organizations," specifically the Muslim Brotherhood, the Islamic State, Al Qaeda, Fateh Al Sham (formerly known as the Nusra Front) and Lebanon's Hezbollah. Formally declare these entities as terror groups as per the list announced by Saudi Arabia, Bahrain, UAE and Egypt, and concur with all future updates of this list.
- Stop all means of funding for individuals, groups or organizations that have been designated as terrorists by Saudi Arabia, UAE, Egypt, Bahrain, US and other countries.
- Hand over "terrorist figures", fugitives and wanted individuals from Saudi Arabia, the UAE, Egypt and Bahrain to their countries of origin. Freeze their assets, and provide any desired information about their residency, movements and finances.
- Shut down Al Jazeera and its affiliate stations.

- End interference in sovereign countries' internal affairs. Stop granting citizenship to wanted nationals from Saudi Arabia, UAE, Egypt and Bahrain. Revoke Qatari citizenship for nationals where such citizenship violates those countries' laws.
- Pay reparations and compensation for loss of life and other financial losses caused by Qatar's policies in recent years. The sum will be determined in coordination with Qatar.
- Align Qatar's military, political, social and economic policies with the other Gulf and Arab countries, as well as on economic matters, as per the 2014 agreement reached with Saudi Arabia.
- Cease contact with the political opposition in Saudi Arabia, the UAE, Egypt and Bahrain. Hand over files detailing Qatar's prior contact with and support for opposition groups, and submit details of their personal information and the support Qatar has provided them.
- Shut down all news outlets funded directly and indirectly by Qatar, including Arabi21, Rassd, Al Araby Al Jadeed, Mekameleen and Middle East Eye, etc.
- Agree to all the demands within 10 days of list being submitted to Qatar, or the list will become invalid.
- Consent to monthly compliance audits in the first year after agreeing to the demands, followed by quarterly audits in the second year, and annual audits in the following 10 years. (Al Jazeera, 2017).

The 13-point ultimatum as seen by many analysts was in fact a way to limit the sovereignty of Qatar and to significantly cut short its role as a strategic player in the region.

The demands were multi-layered, each serving a specific goal that ensures the maintenance of Saudi Arabia's policies. The most flagrant demands were the ones asking for the immediate cutting of ties with Iran, serving the ultimate goal of further isolating Iran from the rest of the region.

The points also targeted other groups which were classified as terrorists by Saudi Arabia and the US such as Al Qaeda, Hamas and Hezbollah. Saudi Arabia has serious ideological differences with Hezbollah, and, like Hamas, receives its financial support and training from Iran, which is enough to be in the Saudi blacklist. At the same time, the significant improvement of the Saudi relations with Israel is another reason that bitter enemies of Israel - Hezbollah and Hamas, are in a disadvantaged position via Saudi Arabia.

Another very important factor within these points is the importance of the Qatari media outlet Al Jazeera. Blockading countries claimed Qatar's funded media were creating soft power by instigating unrest and complications throughout the region. Al Jazeera has acquired a large Arab audience because it has aired opposing views and news and airs programs which have criticized most Arab governments. For this reason, it has been banned from time to time by nearly all of Qatar's immediate neighbors.

Qatar's Turkish military base was also a point which was raised as a concern by the blockading countries, as they claimed that Turkey is a powerful ally for Iran's policies in the region and having such a military base in a GCC country allegedly causes a threat to the Saudi Arabian authorities.

With these 13 points, Qatar was basically asked for "alignment" with the blockading countries, in other words asking Qatar to receive orders from them.

Reasons given for the blockade

Qatar's Government categorically denied the fake news article which sparked the blockade, stating that the QNA website had been hacked. After proving that the first accusations were in fact false and resulted from a Blockade country hack, many analyzed that the blockade was long in the process and planned in advance.

Firstly, Saudi Arabia and its allies accused Qatar of adopting a non-neutral behavior - being part of the conflicts in Iraq, Syria,

Yemen, Afghanistan and wherever the opportunity of backing armed militias and anti-Gulf factions was available, instead of agreeing to conciliatory strategies and conforming with regional affiliations.

Secondly, the fact that Qatar owns Al Jazeera Media Network broadcasting independent news regardless of the priorities of the blockading countries caused a major issue of dispute between Qatar and blockade countries (BBC, 2017).

Indeed, some claimed that Al Jazeera had become a divisive issue since it was launched in 1996. Hundreds of complaints by Arab countries had been filed, including several cases that caused diplomatic tension in the region which were attributed to the way Al Jazeera handles and covers sensitive topics and taboos. The channel's coverage was also alleged to be partly responsible for the issue of the 2014 withdrawal of some GCC ambassadors from Qatar, as it was accused of biased coverage on certain topics and countries during and after the Arab Spring events due to ideological or political differences (Al Rawi, 2017).

Thirdly, blockading countries alleged that Qatar supported extremism and terrorism, interfered in the internal affairs of its neighbors, co-operated with Iran, harbored dissidents and opposition figures from other countries, and engaged in critical and unfriendly media coverage of its neighbors (Al Ansari, Baaboud et Al, 2018).

QATAR'S RESPONSE: ABSORB, SAFEGUARD, PREVENT

Qatar has long practiced an ambitious foreign policy with different priorities than its neighbors, but two key issues have irritated them in recent years. One is Qatar's support for Islamist groups, and Qatar recognizes that it has been assisting people in certain organizations such as the Muslim Brotherhood, but denies the support of Al Qaeda or Daesh-related military groups. The other key issue is that of

Qatar's close ties with Iran, with which the Qatari state shares the largest gas field in the world, keeping in mind the fact that Iran is the Shiite Muslim power that is the main regional rival of Saudi Arabia, which is Sunni Muslim (Atanasiu, 2017).

With the blockade imposed, a first of its kind in the Middle East, Qatar was faced with a significant test to resist and at the same time guarantee security amongst its citizens and ensure their future.

Official Statements

Qatari spokespeople did not engage in escalated media talk, on the contrary, a robust and solid denial was issued initially (24 May 2017) to discredit the fake news.

According to the Government Communications Office, the QNA website "has been hacked by an unknown entity" and "a false statement attributed to His Highness the Amir Sheikh Tamim Bin Hamad Al Thani has been published".

"The statement published has no basis whatsoever, and the competent authorities in the State of Qatar will hold all those [involved] accountable" (BBC, 2017).

It was later on revealed on 17 July 2017, through an investigation with the US federal intelligence agency, which concluded that Abu Dhabi was responsible for the cyberattack (Mostafa, 2017).

A report by the Washington post (2017) stated the below:

"The United Arab Emirates (UAE) orchestrated the hacking of a Qatari government news site in late May in order to plant a false story with incendiary quotes attributed to His Highness the Amir Sheikh Tamim Bin Hamad Al Thani".

Quoting unnamed US intelligence officials, the paper said senior members of the Emirati government discussed the plan on 23 May. But the officials said it was unclear if the UAE hacked the websites or paid for them to be carried out, the newspaper said.

The report said it was unclear whether Saudi Arabia, Bahrain and Egypt had also taken part in penetrating Qatari government websites.

The hacking took place on 24 May, shortly after a lengthy meeting between US President Donald Trump and Gulf leaders in Saudi Arabia.

These hacking and surveillance acts are examples of vertical (top-down) online political jamming activities, which are meant to compromise, undermine, weaken, and pressure oppositional groups and members (Al Rawi, 2019).

Qatar did not deny the negative impact that the blockade caused, yet an official statement by the press office of the Ministry of Foreign Affairs published on its website further highlighted that the siege: "will not affect the normal course of life of citizens and residents of Qatar." Such declarations were evidenced successively by the media coverage of the rapid supply of alternatives that Oman, Lebanon, Iran, Kuwait, Turkey and other allies ensured (Gulf Times, Stewart, 2017).

Qatar's Foreign Minister assured to Al Jazeera on 7 June 2017 that "Qatar will never surrender to the pressure being applied by its Arab neighbors and won't change its independent foreign policy to resolve disputes that have put the region on edge".

"We are not ready to surrender, and will never be ready to surrender, the independence of our foreign policy," H.E. Sheikh Mohammed Bin Abdulrahman Al Thani said during the interview (Al Jazeera, 2017).

Following the issuance of a '13 points' list of demands, Qatar categorically rejected it on 12 June, and stated that these demands were more of an "insult" to the sovereignty of the State.

None of the requirements was met since many of them relied on false pre-conceptions about Qatar's behavior from the start. Indeed, the Foreign Minister of Qatar declared on 4 July 2017 that "the list is unrealistic and impossible to achieve" (Atanasiu, 2017). According to Marwan Bishara, Senior Political Analyst at Al Jazeera (2017): "The tone of these demands and the underlining approach does not only show total ignorance of international relations and a lack of understanding about what state sovereignty means, but it also goes to the heart of a lack of coherence and preparation by the four countries over putting a document like this together. This could be, for some who are supportive of Saudi Arabia and the United Arab Emirates, the start of a negotiating position - the starting bid, and now Qatar could counter-bid. But to be honest, I don't think that's even a starting bid. The US state department had made it clear that this [list with demands] needs to be reasonable, actionable and based on facts. There has to be evidence provided - and of course there is no evidence provided.

What we know is that this has nothing to do with "terrorism". If you accuse it of doing so, then you have to provide evidence. Qatar has made it clear that it does not support Fateh Al Sham, ISIL, Al Qaeda and so forth. The Muslim Brotherhood is not considered a "terrorist" organization by the UK, by the United States and by most countries around the world. This list shows that these four countries are not interested in a solution to the crisis. What they are asking for is a complete and total humiliating surrender by Qatar of its sovereignty. That is not going to happen. This is counter revolution 2.0. This is the second phase of the attack on the Arab Spring and what's left of it, which is very little."

Government's Information Strategy

The Qatari administration was able to identify and react to the crisis rapidly. They fathomed the Saudi-backed strategy of rapid, multi-fronted attack that aimed primarily at shocking Doha, thereby dispersing its efforts and defense capabilities, so that it might get overwhelmed and give in quickly. However quite on the contrary, the administration of Doha restored a calm, absorbent communication strategy - the H.H. the Amir kept silent for a while (until July 2017), as the Minister of Foreign Affairs and a few senior diplomats were appointed to serve as the spokespersons of the State of Qatar.

The government even actively encouraged its citizens to develop and grow local businesses for homegrown products, increasing the country's level of self-sufficiency, something that was never required previously. In fact, many local businesses have now flourished thanks to the blockade, pushing the Qatari people to rely on their businesses and their joint local efforts to meet the demands of the local market.

Keeping the internal communication going on a daily basis reflected that the crisis management committee regarded their people as the main priority in the crisis, and helped to calm their concerns and strengthen their trust in their leadership as they saw in the media continuously how the adopted policies paid off instantly.

On the same level of diplomacy, signing the US-Qatari counter terrorism treaty one month after the crisis on 11 July 2017 came as an important moment to counter the Saudi-nurtured narrative around its alleged support for terrorism.

Such communication policy of calmness and evidence-based content helped the avoidance of unneeded tensions and distasteful media disputes that the opponent would have profited from. It also reflected a well-crafted media handling based on picking the right spokesperson to tell the truth, clearly, and rapidly, with a smart decision-maker backstage.

International Lobbying

Diplomatically, H.E. Mohammed Bin Adbulrahman Bin Jassim Al Thani, who has occupied the position of the Director of the Economic Affairs Bureau of Qatar before being appointed as the country's Minister of Foreign Affairs, knew the added value that his government's assets and investments in the international markets could inject into Doha's talks with its partners in the world about the crisis at hand.

With the aim of lobbying for Qatar's position among intellectuals and political strategists, the Foreign Minister held discussions at several international institutions of particular cultural reputation. It is no secret that the sympathy and support that Qatar received from international partners are the by-products of its smart economic planning that the investment authority was in charge of over the recent years that helped at setting up a positive international PR for Qatar. Qatari officials additionally increased their public diplomacy efforts in Washington, D.C. and other key capitals in Europe and Asia to counter the intense lobbying of the 'Quartet' states (Ulrichsen, 2017).

The Qatari Foreign Minister's efforts were well noticed as he first travelled to Moscow, London and France to try and rally international support for Qatar.

Indeed, German Chancellor Angela Merkel spoke out during a visit to Mexico City in support of Qatar on 6 June, affirming that: "We have to see that the political solution of conflicts ... such as the situation in Syria, such as the situation in Libya or the situation in Iraq, won't happen if certain players are no longer even included in the conversation, and that includes Qatar, it includes Turkey, it includes Iran".

Moscow joined the support on 10 June during a visit of H.E. the Qatari Foreign Minister to his Russian Counterpart Sergey Lavrov, who called for talks to end the crisis and for contradictions to be resolved through dialogue, adding that Arab states should unite to effectively fight "terrorism".

France, Italy and the UK expressed their sympathy as well during the next few days with Britain's Foreign Secretary Boris Johnson saying he would urge Saudi Arabia, the United Arab Emirates and Bahrain along with Egypt "to ease the blockade on Qatar". Meanwhile, the French President Emmanuel Macron kept working to ease the tensions between Qatar and its neighbors, with Italy also promising to continue economic cooperation with Qatar (Al Jazeera, 2017).

The Turkish President was also among the first to take action in terms of helping to reduce the tensions. On 6 June 2017, Turkish President Recep Tayyip Erdogan spoke by phone with the leaders of Qatar, Russia, Kuwait and Saudi Arabia on lowering tensions, presidential sources said. "The importance of regional peace and stability was underlined in the talks, as well as the importance of focusing on the path of diplomacy and dialogue to lower the current tension," according to the sources.

Kuwait's Amir even asked Qatar's Amir to postpone a planned speech, to give all parties time to solve the crisis.

Doha embraced the visit and the mediation initiative by Sheikh Sabah Al Ahmad Al Jaber Al Sabah, the Amir of Kuwait (7 June 2017): "Sheikh Sabah briefed Sheikh Tamim on his efforts to resolve the crisis between Qatar and each of the Kingdom of Saudi Arabia, the United Arab Emirates, Al Jazeera reported".

This initiative disrupted the Saudi-led blockade even more in front of the international community and pushed it towards slight moderation and accepting negotiations indirectly in order to reach consensus instead of imposing its demands.

Qatar's Economic & Social Strategy

The people of Qatar did not immediately react to the blockade as they assumed it was another political crisis that will be resolved within hours. Indeed, the initial response from the resident population of Qatar was relatively calm, with the only sign of panic being stockpiling of certain foodstuffs. The confident expectation of the majority of Qatari people was that the issue would be over in a matter of days or, at worst, a couple of weeks. But, instead of improving, the blockade became increasingly tense.

Indeed, the blockade had an immediate economic effect on Qatar's market and its people:
- Qatar's stock market dropped dramatically (it lost 10% of its value in 10 days).
- Hundreds of air flights in and out of Hamad International Airport were restricted due to the Gulf States' airspace closure.
- Shipping and transportation (in/out) was halted – trade and commercial exchange stopped.
- Markets ran out of some essential products.

- Companies and investors whose stadiums and infrastructure projects construction were underway were left in worrisome state as shipping was not only hampered, but also got costly and time consuming.

Socially, Qatari citizens also suffered the split of families that the crisis caused by obligating non-Qatari nationals to leave back to their homelands due to the imposed policy by the blockading nations of sending Qataris residing in the blockading countries back home (BBC, Qatar Crisis, 2017).

However, immediate measures were put in place at all levels to cope with the airspace, land, and sea closure ramifications. Significant amounts of funds were injected into the market in order to contain the drop in the stock market.

Qatar's government deposited over $10 billion in local banks to offset a pull-out of deposits by foreign institutions due to the country's diplomatic crisis, Qatari central bank data showed (Reuters, 2017).

Thousands of flights were re-routed, and Hamad International Airport regained its usual busy schedule in few days thanks to the Iranian air-space opening for air traffic. Food and other essential market products were imported from Iran (10 June) and Turkey (17 June), and prices were subsidized by the government before reaching supermarket shelves. Shipping routes with Dubai and Abu Dhabi were replaced by re-routing towards the ports of the Sultanate of Oman and Kuwait. This was the case until September 2018, when Hamad international Port was inaugurated and revived the country's booming import and export movement, in addition to calming the fears of investors whose infrastructure and huge construction projects faced potential material and equipment shortage (Mindscape, 2018).

The Central Bank regularly responded to concerns about the Qatari Riyal trading by reassuring people that their money was safe. The stock exchange plummeted (about 9%) in the first few days while fluctuating afterwards, but Qatar emphasized that the International Monetary Fund recognizes the local money as an official currency, a status secured by the country's huge cash reserves (Allgui, 2017).

Diplomacy Outcome

On the military side, Doha activated its updated bilateral defense treaty with Turkey signed in April 2016 straight away (Bozkurt, 2019).

Indeed, on 10 June when Turkish President Erdogan vowed to stand by Qatar and after the approval of the Turkish parliament, on 8 June there was the approval of deployment of additional Turkish troops to Qatar. The bill, first drafted in May, passed with 240 votes in favor, largely with support from the ruling AK party and nationalist opposition MHP (Al Jazeera, 2017).

This fortified Qatar's stance in the face of Saudi Arabia and its allies and gave locals and residents a feeling of greater security.

Diplomatically and thanks to the Foreign Minister's visits in which he openly made use of Qatar's economic weight and investments to draw political leaders into supporting a mediated solution to the dispute, Qatar was able to reduce the tone of the 13 demands.

In fact, on 6 July the Foreign Ministers of the quartet, meeting in Cairo, opted to prolong the boycott without applying the expected further escalation, in a decision which was interpreted as a result of international pressure for de-escalation (Ellsworth, 2018).

On 18 July, diplomats from the four nations (Bahrain, UAE, Egypt & Saudi Arabia) said they were no longer insisting Qatar comply with the demands and instead wanted it to commit to six broad "principles". The principles were combating terrorism and extremism, denying financing and safe havens to terrorist groups, stopping incitement to hatred and violence, and refraining from interfering in the internal affairs of other countries, the New York Times reported (July 2017). Finally, by definition, a crisis embeds both danger and opportunity, and one could not tackle the crisis of Qatar without noticing how the country recognized and treated the danger rapidly and seized the opportunity to enhance its image, improve self-sufficiency and work on achieving improved security in many areas.

For instance, instead of showing any negative impact that the blockade caused, Qatar responded to hurricane Harvey in the USA in September 2017 by donating 30 million dollars to help victims. This portrayed indirectly Qatar's economy was unaffected by the crisis. Expanding local agriculture was an additional entrepreneurial opportunity that Doha seized (several thousand cattle importations were made to satisfy market needs of fresh milk and dairy), in addition to speeding up the execution of fundamental infrastructure and vital assets that were needed for self-sufficiency (Hamad Port), and getting more resilient by learning how to find alternatives to stand up again rapidly (Al Jazeera, 2017).

In fact, many experts agreed that although the countries of the GCC share a common legacy, ethnicity, religion and language, the deceptive homogeneity of the Gulf Arabs has not prevented conflict from occurring between the relatively young states of the region, of whom many achieved full independence only in the second half of the twentieth century. As state nations rather than nation states, nationalism has long been a top-down effort by some monarchies in an attempt to replace an inclusive form of *'Khaliji'* identity with a more exclusive one (Crieg, 2019).

However, with its intelligent communication strategy, Qatar was able to achieve national unity amongst Qataris. Regardless of the historical existence of different components of Qatari identity, the 5 June 2017 blockade proved that Qatar was socially unified when it came to national security (Al Hammadi, 2018).

H.H. THE AMIR'S SPEECH: A TURNING POINT

The peak moment of the Qatari communications strategy was on 21 July 2017 – some 50 days after the Saudi-backed blockade, when H.H. the Amir of Qatar, Sheikh Tamim Bin Hamad Al Thani, addressed the blockade for the first time in person, through a televised speech that lasted 16 minutes.

H.H. the Amir's Legacy

During the speech, H.H. the Amir appeared strong and confident and expressed readiness for dialogue, although he reiterated that he: "would not accept any dictation and won't compromise his country's sovereignty". The televised speech showed H.H. the Amir seated behind his desk, with a photo of his father, the Father Amir of Qatar, to his right, and a photo of him with his son to his left. The setting of this speech clearly meant to send a double message to the audience. The first message of confidence was meant to the people of Qatar assuring them that the legacy of their ruling family will continue. The second message of certainty and defiance was meant for the blockading countries, a reminder that H.H. the Amir's legacy will not be submissive, and that Qatar's rulers will keep its sovereignty a reality. A powerful visual message which showed that H.H. the Amir's continuity is unshaken despite all challenges produced by the blockade (QNA, 2017).

Audience

H.H. the Amir's speech was aimed at communicating to the internal and external audiences Doha's entire communication strategy by adopting a tone of self-assurance and calmness in the face of waves of fake news and allegations that the media in blockade countries regularly published.

The Amir started by expressing gratitude to his people and their reactions following the blockade: "All those who live in this country have become spokespersons for Qatar. Here I would like to recognize, with great pride, the high moral standard exercised by our people despite the campaign of incitement, as well as the siege." He communicated his sense of pride and admiration for the residents of Qatar in their resilience and behavior towards the blockade nations. Defiantly, the Qatari leader affirmed that everything was business as usual in his country despite the blockade. H.H. the Amir declared that the ongoing crisis had made Qatar more autonomous and resilient, focusing on the positive outcomes of the crisis.

The Amir then continued to address the siege that Qatar was suffering from, and said: "It has become evident to those near and far that this campaign and the steps that followed it had been planned well in advance, and that its plotters and implementers carried out an attack on the sovereignty of the state of Qatar by planting statements that had not been spoken, in order to mislead public opinion and the world and achieve predetermined goals." This was a clear message to the international community as well as the blockade countries that Qatar had been a victim of a pre-determined plan.

H.H. the Amir carried on by stating that many countries sympathized with Qatar and condemned the unjust blockade, showing the futility of blockade countries and especially Saudi Arabia to rally public opinion on their side. H.H the Amir continued: "Moreover, in a similar political stance, Western political, civil and media institutions reject diktats and impositions. This is evident from the international reaction to the conditions that some have tried to impose on us, especially controlling our external relations, infringing on the independence of our policy, shutting down media outlets and controlling the freedom of expression in our country."

H.H. the Amir was also intent on thanking all of Qatar's international allies by naming them to emphasize their roles in the international community, and this included a mention of Kuwait in particular:

"We highly value the mediation efforts undertaken by my brother, His Highness Sheikh Sabah Al Ahmad Al Jaber Al Sabah, Amir of the sisterly State of Kuwait, which Qatar has supported from the outset. This is an opportunity to express my thanks once again for what he did and continues to do. We hope that his sincere efforts will be culminated in success. We also appreciate the American support for this mediation, as well as the constructive positions of Germany, France, Britain, Europe in general and Russia."

The Amir also thanked Turkey for "putting into force quickly a cooperation agreement signed between us and meeting our basic needs".

View on Terrorism

The Amir went on to discuss how Qatar did not agree with many policies that fellow GCC countries were conducting, yet they never intervened or imposed any sanctions or regulations on them. H.H. the Amir also addressed the topic of terrorism and how some countries are imposing their view of terrorist organizations on others. The Amir clearly directed his address at the blockading countries, disclosing their unfair and unjust policies.

"Any solution to the crisis must be based on two principles: first, the solution should be within the framework of respect for the sovereignty of each State. Secondly, it should not be in a form of orders by one party against another, but rather as mutual undertakings and joint commitments binding to all".

Maintaining that Doha is combatting terrorism and extremism "relentlessly and without compromise," and doing so with the international community's blessing, H.H. the Amir blasted the quartet for waging an "unprecedented smear campaign" against Qatar.

The Amir also made sure to address the Palestinian issue in order to re-focus the view of the Arab and international community on it as a way to revert to the big picture of uniting the Arab front: "I cannot end this speech without expressing solidarity with the brotherly Palestinian people, especially our people in Al Quds (Jerusalem), and denouncing the closure of the Al Aqsa Mosque, the first of the two Qiblas and the third of the two Holy Shrines, hoping that what is happening in Al Quds be an incentive for unity and solidarity instead of division."

Qatar's Future

The Amir also made sure to address his nation with positive messages of hope for the future, as he quoted from the Holy Quran by saying: "Despite the bitterness caused by these steps, the most prevalent proverbial wisdom in the Qatari society these days is: 'Every cloud has a silver lining', which corresponds with the Quranic verse: *'But perhaps you hate a thing and it is good for you.'*"(Verse 216, Al-Baquarah, the Holy Quran).

Following this statement, H.H. the Amir encouraged the Qatari people to explore their full potential: "We are called upon to open our economy to investments and initiatives so that we produce our own food and medicine, diversify our sources of income, achieve our economic independence through bilateral relations of cooperation with other countries, in our geographical environment and worldwide, and on the basis of mutual interests and mutual respect. We also call upon ourselves to develop our educational, research and media institutions, as well as our sources of soft power at the international level and with the interaction of the best national, Arab and foreign expertise. All of this of course will be in cooperation with the residents in our country who work, contribute and live with us, and who stood with us throughout this crisis."

A clear message was sent by H.H. the Amir to the people of Qatar that he believed in their potential and that they would be the ones to help Qatar stand independently: "As we pass through this test with honor and dignity, I am addressing you to emphasize that Qatar needs every one of you to build its economy and protect its security. We require diligence, creativity, independent thinking, constructive initiatives and interest in academic achievement in all disciplines, self-reliance and fighting indolence and dependency."

The Amir thereby addressed his nation and empowered his people to take responsibility and bring glory to their nation.

Speech Reactions

The Amir's speech marked a positive turning point in the blockade. H.H. the Amir successfully shifted the focus from the 13 demands list to the struggle of dealing with extremism and terrorism and to the humanitarian issues caused by the blockade. Locally, the Amir succeeded as well at uniting his people around him and pushing Qatari citizens and residents to work together for a better future and to achieve more for their nation.

The Amir's speech was a comprehensive one sending several messages to his fellow citizens, to the blockade countries and to the international community as well. He was polite, positive and asked for unity and open to dialogue, while also being assertive that Qatar will not lose its sovereignty. The Qatari leader maintained the friendliness and harmonious approach as the basis for reconciliation with the four blockading countries, which came in stark contrast to the language they were using to attack Qatar.

In addition, another positive element was Qatari diplomacy taking immediate actions and constantly communicating its plans and actions to its people and to the world.

Quite predictably, Arab newspapers in the UAE and Saudi Arabia were quick to criticize the Amir's speech. The Saudi newspaper Okaz highlighted the "victimization" discourse adopted by Qatar.

COMMUNICATION OUTLETS

Qatar handled public diplomacy during the blockade by being open and transparent; its diplomats spoke to both government representatives and key elites, and made media appearances that emphasized the state's "victim in control" position through different media and social networks outlets (Allagui, 2017).

Qatar's communications approach focused on three elements:

1. Show concern;
2. Prove that Qatari leaders are in control;
3. Display commitment to stakeholders.

MEDIA

After the cyber-attack, the blockading nations reverted to using media. A media war flared during the crisis between the two sides and the media outlets at the center of the conflict have been politicized and weaponized to sway opinion and garner support, both within the GCC and outside as well, and to shape narratives (Al Shabnan, 2018).

Local & GCC Coverage

In the first days of the crisis, audiences found themselves spectators of an information war playing out before their eyes. Newspaper stories, TV shows, and news programs on TV satellite channels were filled with discussions in which one side insulted the other. Moreover, readers and viewers in the region witnessed low standards of media practice and a lack of media ethics (Allagui & Akdenizli, 2019).

Al Jazeera channel, initially a main and direct reason behind the blockade was turned into the voice of Qatar. According to the allegations of the blocking countries, one of the main reasons behind the blockade was to shut down Al Jazeera channel. The station's global and regional credibility gained during peacetime made it a highly potent public diplomacy tool, which allowed the state to shape public opinion. Qatar reinvented and specifically adapted the state-sponsored broadcasting model to the contemporary media environment, thus allowing its operator to regain control over the narratives transmitted to the world with high impact.

The rift between the Saudi-led blockading nations and Qatar intensified the media war in reporting negatively on each other's respective economies. The Saudi and UAE media, Al Arabiya and Sky News Arabia, focused their reporting on the economic consequences faced by the Qatari economy. Furthermore, they framed these economic consequences mainly as a result of severing of economic ties and the sanctions placed on Qatar. On the Qatari side, Al Jazeera focused their reporting around two aspects:
1. Refuting reports that indicate damage inflicted on the Qatari economy as a result of sanctions by the blockading nations, and instead praising fiscal measures adopted that contained the economic damage.
2. Reporting on economic hardships faced by Gulf countries, mainly Saudi Arabia, and their effect on social cohesion (Al Shabnan, 2018).

Qatar also invested in lobbying and advertising campaigns abroad, mainly to gain support and prove that the blockade violated international law, as well as to eliminate or at least address the supposed image of supporting terrorism inflicted by the blockading countries. For example, according to The New Arab, Saudi Arabia funded TV advertising spots that were placed on NBC4 on July 23, 2017, targeting politicians in Washington; the message was that Qatar finances terrorism and destabilizes allies in the region ("Anti-Qatar Terrorism Ads", 2017).

Sky News Arabia aired a UAE-sponsored documentary referring to Qatar's alleged support of Al Qaeda. Qatar, on the other hand, invested in newspaper ads, promoting its position as a strategic U.S. partner in fighting terrorism, creating jobs and hope abroad, while other ads highlighted shared education values between the U.S. and Qatar (Reinl, 2017).

Art Expressions

Music has also been used to demonstrate national pride. The locally recorded "One Nation" (an anthem "in solidarity with

Qatar") was released in June 2017 and involved both local and international musicians. Its lyrics highlighted Qatar's strength and ended with the following lines: "We stand tall, above it all. Rain will fall, to plant the seeds that feed us all. We stand united, behind our leader with all our might. With you we rise, our nation's pride" (Freer, 2017). Saudi label Rotana released a "diss track" "Goulou Li Qatar" ("Say to Qatar") a song that the coalition against Qatar launched as part of its lobbying in line with dedicating the key messages of its media headlines, news bulletins, talk shows and all its media vehicles with the same objective.

Ahmed Al Maadheed, a local Qatari young artist, was also catapulted to fame thanks to his "Tamim Al Majd" (Glorious Tamim) portrait. It initially started when in December, Al Maadheed was getting ready for Qatar National Day which takes place on the 18th of December. His creativity inspired him to post a video on Instagram of himself painting the portrait of what we now know as "Tamim Al Majd".

When he painted it on his car, it was merely for celebrating Qatar National Day, but when the blockade started on June 5th, he painted the same portrait on a canvas and posted it on Instagram to show his support during the shocking initial days of the blockade.

The portrait became so famous it spread out beyond canvases and bumper stickers; people were very creative with showing this beautiful artwork. T-shirts, phone covers, and cafés even use the portrait on coffee foam (Odeh, 2018).

This piece of art became a way to defy the blockade and show the support of the people to their Amir.

International Sympathy

Building on the gained international sympathy, additional news articles emerged about the tragedy of camels and sheep trapped between borders. Famished and dying camels owned by nomadic Qatari farmers were forced to trek back to Qatar unattended and without water or food due to the expulsion of the farmers from Saudi Arabia. Photos and videos of these scenes distributed by media networks such as Al Jazeera provoked disdain towards Saudi Arabia. Video footage was distributed showing starving and injured animals on Saudi borders, juxtaposed with an emergency shelter organized by the Qatari Ministry of Environment at the nearby Qatari border.

Qatar thus became a victim deserving of sympathy as its human and animal population suffered abuse and violation of rights. This message conveying care and concern has been carried through consistently; it is emphasized through Qatar's position towards its expatriates from the blockade countries since they were given the choice to stay. Such a message portraying Qatar as the good and caring neighbor only adds to the desired image it aims to convey: the country's "grandeur" (Allagui, 2017).

Doha also aired stories of its nationals who were visiting or even residing in KSA and other blockade states and the suffering they went through upon the evacuation decision. Students of Emirati fathers and Qatari mothers who were residing in Qatar were suddenly asked to leave the country in a matter of days, local entrepreneurs ran short on business because of lack of external supplies, and relatives were separated and would miss out on important events such as weddings, Eid and other family gatherings (Al Jazeera Beyond the Blockade, 2018).

Yemen War Coverage

Negative news coverage of the war in Yemen increased significantly after the start of the Gulf crisis with respect to the role of the Saudi-led coalition in Yemen's current war (Gasim, 2018).

Al Jazeera's coverage on the so-called "Decisive Storm", or the Arab coalition's operations to restore the UN recognized government in Yemen, shifted drastically following the Gulf crisis that resulted in the expulsion of Qatar from the coalition. Before the crisis, Al Jazeera's reporting framed the conflict and the Arab coalition's operations in a positive manner and emphasized the danger and violations of the Iranian-backed Houthi rebels and Ali Abdullah Saleh, the ousted Yemeni president who is aligned with the Houthis. Following the crisis and Qatar's expulsion from the coalition, Al Jazeera's reporting focused on the civilian and humanitarian toll that the Arab coalition has caused while framing the operations by the coalition as a failure in achieving their goals while at the same time causing devastating human loss of life. What is also significant in their post-crisis reporting on Yemen is that the coalition is Saudi-led. Moreover, Al Jazeera changed terminology by ceasing to use "Arab Coalition" and instead uses "Saudi-led Coalition" (Al Shabnan, 2018).

Social media

Social media is the most common platform for people to share their immediate opinions on any subject matter, and the Gulf crisis was no exception to this trend. Qatari citizens and Arabs in general quickly took to social media to express views and concerns about the crisis. Internet penetration in Qatar is a significant 93 per cent, according to a 2016 study by Northwestern University in Qatar. The study reported Internet penetration also at 93 per cent in Saudi Arabia and at 100 per cent in the UAE (AFP, 2017).

Twitter is the world's largest micro-blogging social media site and the third biggest social networking site. Because of its widespread use, Twitter has the potential to be a strong force in political acknowledgement, allowing the immediate expression of opinions with a wide spread ratio to other users. Consequently, residents in the State of Qatar used Twitter to express their difficulty in coping with the blockade.

In fact, Twitter, Facebook and Snapchat were awash with the topic after the announcement of the blockade and #cuttingtieswithqatar was briefly the number one trend worldwide on Twitter immediately after the blockade began.

The Gulf crisis had its temporal logic rooted in the hacking pretext. However, the controversy surrounding this event was precipitated by considerable online bot activity against Qatar. Generally speaking, the hashtags that tended to reveal the existence of bots were those that ostensibly appeared to be Saudi-based, according to the user input locations on Twitter. Indeed, an examination of the bots' biographies reveals that they were all in opposition to the Al Thani ruling family and the Qatari government (Jones, 2019).

Twitter: A Coping Mechanism for the people

The diplomatic rift between Qatar and the blockading nations was clearly manifested on social media; many pro-Qatari Twitter users changed their profile pictures to show the image of the Amir of Qatar with the statement "We're all Hamad," while anti-Qatari users employed various hashtags to condemn Qatar, such as "#Qatarsupportsterrorism" or calling the H.H. the Amir's father "the Gulf's Qadaffi" (Al Rawi, 2019).

However, a BBC Arabic investigation (2018) later revealed that the majority of tweets using these hashtags immediately after the blockade were pushed by fake accounts known as "bots". Bots are automated accounts, which attempt to manipulate public opinion by artificially boosting the popularity of social media posts.

In Qatar, social media helped to increase the public's support for H.H. the Amir as the dust of the sudden blockade settled. The face of the Amir spread everywhere on Social Media thanks to the stylized portrait of the Amir, "Tamim the Glorious" (Tamim Al Majd), which even spread to huge banners on skyscraper windows, cars, shop windows and walls of homes.

Indeed, locally social media enabled people to engage in campaigning for their country by being part of viral virtual rallies like "#Tamim_Al_Majd" which drove a nationwide conversation and stirred patriotic feelings in the midst of the blockade among citizens and residents.

As a reaction to the blockade, the whole Qatari nation united as one voice to support the Qatari Amir. The Qatari people began to introduce themselves on social media as descending from one tribe: Qatar. They replaced their family or tribal name with their new tribal name— Al Qatari—such as Ali Al Qatari, Ibrahim Al Qatari, Ahmed Al Qatari, Wadha Al Qatari, Noof Al Qatari, and so on (Hammadi, 2018).

Popular influencers such as Mohamad Al Dhahi, who runs the "Doha Live" Snapshat account, transformed overnight into a source of news about the blockade. Even Qatari social media influencers shared a bond after the crisis that helped them express the people's true opinions and strengthen the patriotic feelings of Qataris (Beyond the Blockade, 2018).

A UAE hashtag claiming the Emirates would snatch the FIFA World Cup 2022™ from Qatar - #UAEwillhosttheWorldCup – also reached a level of popularity, notoriety and amusement far beyond the region. The response from Qataris on Twitter was quick to follow: #youaredreaming.

Another hashtag that was trending in the UAE, #Qatarfundsterrorism, mirrored accusations by the Emirates and its allies that Doha funds extremist groups in the region. Meanwhile in Qatar, "Oh God, keep Qatar safe" was trending in Arabic, as well as #iloveqatar among the country's sizeable English-speaking expat community (AFP, 2017).

And Twitter users had great fun at the expense of Jamil Al Ziabi, the editor of a Saudi newspaper, who said he was concerned about Qataris having to get used to food shipped from Iran and Turkey, after Saudi Arabia cut exports. He said: "I am really worried because I don't believe Qatari stomachs can get used to such products so quickly," Ziabi said. This sparked another trending hashtag in Arabic - #Qataristomach (Pressform, 2017).

Social Media also became one of the only ways of communication between Qatar and other Gulf countries especially when it came to relatives separated from their Qatari family sharing news, pictures or other personal events of their lives, since the blockade prohibited blockade nations citizens from visiting Qatar.

Twitter's direct influence on the crisis

As this was the first diplomatic crisis that was sparked by an online hacking incident, the effect of the blockade was clearly displayed on social media platforms, especially Twitter.

Al Jazeera analyzed more than 2.3 million tweets from almost 2,400 accounts, published between June 2017 and October 2018.

The analysis found that bots played a significant role in the online conversation about the blockade.

"In the two months before the Gulf Crisis started, a network of Twitter accounts was set up specifically to have anti-Qatar messages in their bios," Marc Owen Jones, Assistant Professor of Middle East Studies at Hamad Bin Khalifa University in Doha and Fellow of the Exeter Institute of Arab and Islamic Studies, told Al Jazeera (2019).

"If you see a huge amount of accounts created on the same day tweeting on the same topic and they don't really interact with people, you can be almost certain they're bots," he said.

"A lot of the obviously fake accounts we saw in the Qatar case were ones ... [where] the combination of the creation date and anti-Qatar messages in their bios suggest that [a] network was specifically set up against Qatar," he told Al Jazeera.

"The goals of these networks is not just to manipulate trends but it's to get real people to adopt these hashtags. This is something we saw a lot in the GCC Crisis, where some hashtags were started by bots."

Al Jazeera's analysis found that as time progressed and the blockade was forgotten by the majority of the world, bots were still being created to increase the reach of political tweets.

Twitter an official channel

The Government Communication Office of the State of Qatar launched its own official Twitter account to disseminate accurate reports about Qatar and to counter any fake news and disinformation being circulated against the country.

Indeed, Twitter took on an important role in informing the Qatari people during the blockade.

From the Qatari government's side, the internet, through the official websites of Qatari official institutions, aided news reach. The social media presence played an important role in the crisis, mainly through Twitter, where all the press conferences and advancements were posted on official accounts. These posts served to inform the public of the latest happenings instantly.

On the other hand, many international officials also found that the best way to express their opinion about the blockade was through their twitter accounts.

U.S. President Donald Trump was one of the first to express his support for the blockade on Twitter:

"During my recent trip to the Middle East I stated that there can no longer be funding of Radical Ideology. Leaders pointed to Qatar - look!" He wrote on 6 June 2017.

He added: "So good to see the Saudi Arabia visit with the King and 50 countries already paying off. They said they would take a hard line on funding extremism, and all reference was pointing to Qatar. Perhaps this will be the beginning of the end to the horror of terrorism!" Other UAE officials responded as well: "We need a guaranteed roadmap to rebuild confidence after our covenants were broken," UAE State Minister for Foreign Affairs Anwar Gargash said on Twitter.

Gargash also accused Doha of turning to "money and media and partisanship and extremism" in a series of tweets. The UAE went as far as to ban demonstration of sympathy toward Qatar on social media, making such actions punishable by a jail term of up to 15 years and a fine of at least AED 500,000. Soon after, Bahrain declared that any expression of sympathy toward Qatar or opposition toward the measures taken by the Government of Bahrain would result in a fine and up to five years' imprisonment. Initially and throughout the many attempts of the blockade countries to cast out Qatar even on social media, the Qatari people showed resilience and loyalty even through their social media accounts and hashtags.

Most of the blockade countries attempts were quickly exposed or immediately shut down by Qatari residents. Qatar's control over the story helped the country's leaders secure their people's trust and support. The hashtags #TamimAlMajd (meaning: Glorious Tamim) as well as #WeAreAllTamim are just a few examples of the trending support online. The country's swift response to the blockade proved a great sense of control in managing the crisis; it may even lead one to believe that some response plans and negotiations were already in the works (Allagui, 2017).

An overall sense of responsibility to defend their nation through the only medium that they had helped Qataris feel more united than ever and responsible to help their country stand back on its own feet without the aid of any of the blockading countries. Thanks to many social media campaigns supporting Qatar's position, they were able to encourage each other to develop local businesses, local agriculture and farming and many other industries to serve the local market and Qatar's residents.

HOW DID QATAR OVERCOME THE BLOCKADE WITH ITS STRATEGY?

Qatar's Strength Points

The four blockading countries expected to reap the benefits of their escalation policy quickly and expected a rift between the country leadership and its social community.

However, the Qatari administration proved that it succeeded at identifying the crisis promptly and created a well-crafted communication strategy that was able to face the attacks made on Qatar, strengthening its position with its people and helping them to defend their position as well. The strategy was indeed reflected by responding properly and instantly to the crisis, internally and externally, throughout the lengthy period of escalation.

Choosing well-informed and reliable spokespeople such as the Qatari Foreign Minister, H.E. Mohammed Bin Abdulrahman Al Thani, was crucial. Through his large volume of meetings, he was able to create a counter diplomatic move aimed at informing international and regional powers of the humanitarian consequences of the crisis on the one hand and refuting the claims and accusations of the siege states on Doha on the other.

In fact, the Qatari diplomacy was able to achieve tangible results, reflected by a broad European backing for Qatar's position, through the rejection of the siege and sanctions approach as the only means to resolve political disputes between countries.

Doha mastered the art of distinguishing between types of targeted audiences and the significance of communicating with a tailor-made content approach for every audience. In this way, Qatar was able to create social media campaigns and content series to engage people, stories of a human nature to gain international backing, as well as holding discussions about the crisis in reputable international institutions and diplomatic chambers such as the UK House of Lords and Chatham House, to lobby for Qatar among intellectual and political elites.

The Foreign Minister knew exactly how to communicate with the Qatari people by using their most popular channel during the crisis: Twitter. Every move was announced and documented on Twitter through his official channel, amassing a big number of retweets, reactions and spread on social media. Indeed, he is recognized as one of the most active Foreign Ministers in the region on Twitter.

It was clear that the communications strategist in Doha knew the significance of using various channels of media and social media properly. Each medium functioned to target a specific audience: social media to reach masses and the youth, international TV channels to communicate with Western leaders and help to shape public opinion.

The swift and effective implementation of the communications strategy made it clear that contingency plan had likely been set beforehand. Qatar adopted prevention tactics through the flow of evidence-based, ethical, and continuously updated information towards both local and international audiences, which kept rumors dormant and hampered any opportunities for the blockading nations to hit back.

Harmonious performances throughout the crisis reflected effective coordination and non-stop fine-tuning backstage (Mostafa, 2017).

H.H. the Amir's Speech at the 48th Shura Council Session

As a final result of the policies and strategies implement and just a few years since the blockade began, Qatar had triumphed over the blockade's economic impact. By November 2018, Qatar was no longer spending any of its financial reserves to offset the embargo's negative effects and, as a result, its economic prospects are promising.

To mark the beginning of a new legislative term, His Highness the Amir Sheikh Tamim Bin Hamad Al Thani inaugurated the 48th ordinary session of the Shura Council in September 2019. He outlined the country's economic achievements and said the Gulf state will keep developing its food security and renewable energy sectors while working to further diversify its economy.

H. H. the Amir's speech was divided into describing the tangible economic growth that Qatar has witnessed, as well as expressing admiration for the resilience of Qatari citizens and residents.

H.H. the Amir was quoted as saying: "We've overcome the obstacles of the blockade and we're also closer to achieving Qatar's national vision for the year 2030", (Al Jazeera, 2019).

During his speech, the Amir was confident and proud of the achievements of his country. He laid down the economic accomplishments of Qatar during the past three years, stating that the country has grown economically and thereby surpassed expectations.

The Amir stated: "Reports indicate a significant progress in the field of economic diversification, encouraging the private sector, increasing the production capacity of power generation plants and establishing an advanced agricultural and livestock-fish production system".

The growth witnessed by Qatar's economy in various sectors, including education, health, food and agriculture, following the blockade are part of successful programs adopted by the state to diversify its economy.

H.H. the Amir also made sure to stress the "Human Capital" of Qatar: "Development is not measured by buildings and facilities only, but rather by the ability of human beings to plan, build and maintain them, and by the schools that educate them and the universities from which they graduate, as well as the quality of education, culture and the prevailing values and ethics".

This was a clear message of recognition and thankfulness to his fellow nationals and residents in the state of Qatar. With such messages, the Amir made sure to give back to his people for the loyalty they showed him and ensured they were aware that they are an essential asset of their country.

H.H. the Amir, known not to miss an opportunity to thank the citizens and expatriates living in Qatar, renewed his support and gratitude for their hard work and assured them that their needs are also one of his main concerns : "Our fellow resident brothers who live with us in Qatar are not here as a result of a favor conferred on them, but by virtue of their work, which is indispensable to us, and by means of their appreciated contribution to the building of this country."

A Closure to the Blockade

With this speech, H.H. the Amir clearly put an end to the economic aspect of the blockade, sending a clear message to his rivals and friends alike that Qatar grew stronger and overcame all obstacles thrown its way.

Ironically, Qatar owes its current success to the Saudi-led coalition's economic and diplomatic severance. Had it not been for the blockade, Qatar would not have been so motivated to fortify its global reputation. While lobbying and communications strategies won over many policy officials and academics, Qatar most effectively solidified a positive relationship with the US by enhancing America's military cooperation with the country (Hickert, 2019).

Qatar has managed to bring itself out from under the Saudi-UAE sphere of influence. After announcing its decision to quit OPEC — which gathers 14 member states including Saudi Arabia and the UAE — Qatar sent another message to these countries through the decision of H.H. the Amir not to attend the annual summit of the Gulf Cooperation Council (GCC) in Riyadh in person. Instead, Qatar was represented by the Minister of State for Foreign Affairs, lowering the level of representation.

In addition, Qatar continued to claim a moral high ground and raise its voice about human rights in the Middle East, in contrast to Saudi Arabia and the UAE. Besides their disastrous track record in Yemen, both Saudi Arabia and the UAE continue to be implicated in severe human rights abuses which are regularly exposed by the international media (Kucukasi, 2019).

In January 2021, the blockade on Qatar was officially lifted after announcing that relations between Qatar and the four Arab blockading countries had been fully restored.

With a solemn but visibly pleased air, the Kuwaiti Foreign Minister made the announcement on the evening of 4 January, after a phone call involving Kuwait's Amir H.H. Sheikh Nawaf Al-Ahmad Al-Sabah, Qatar's Amir H.H. Sheikh Tamim bin Hamad Al-Thani and Saudi Arabia's Crown Prince Sheikh Mohammed bin Salman Al Saud.

"[I]t was agreed to open the airspace and land and sea borders between the Kingdom of Saudi Arabia and the state of Qatar, starting from this evening," Kuwaiti Foreign Minister H.E. Ahmad Nasser Al-Sabah said. After a more than three-year-long blockade on Qatar, the decision brought the crisis to an end (The African Report 2021).

Indeed, the announcement was made ahead of the 41st Gulf Cooperation Council (GCC) Summit, which kicked off on 5 January in the north-western Saudi city of Al-Ula, with the Kuwaiti Foreign Minister calling the meeting an opportunity for "reconciliation". Saudi Arabia's King H.H. Sheikh Salman bin Abdulaziz Al-Saud opened the summit by urging "regional unity".

The Saudi Crown Prince embraced the Amir of Qatar upon arrival in Al-Ula. The two leaders reportedly even rode the same car together and had private discussions at another occasion.

Michael Greenwald, former U.S. Treasury attaché to Qatar and Kuwait, said the agreement was just a "first step." "This is a political resolution," he told CNBC's "Capital Connection". He said the opening of airspace is helpful ahead of the Qatar 2022 World Cup, and the nations want to "boost themselves economically" while preparing for a new U.S. administration.

But Greenwald, who is also a director at investment management firm Tiedemann Advisors, said more needs to be done. "There needs to be a much stronger, detailed framework put in place so that this does not happen again," he said.

However even though this crisis may have ended, it is undeniable that Qatar transformed the challenge of the blockade into an opportunity to grow as a country, showing the world how its diplomacy and crisis communications strategy was a success.

REFERENCES

Andreas Krieg (2019), Divided Gulf, The Anatomy Of A Crisis https://newbooksnetwork.com/andreas-krieg-divided-gulf-the-anatomy-of-a-crisis-palgrave-2019/

AFP, 2017, Qatar's Foreign Minister Calls in Press Conference for the Blockade to be lifted Retrieved from: https://www.france24.com/en/20170619-qatar-demands-blockade-lifted-before- gulf-crisis-talks

Ahmad el Rawi 2019, Cyberconflict, Online Political Jamming, and Hacking in the Gulf

Retrieved From Cooperation Council International Journal of Communication, https://ijoc.org/index.php/ijoc/article/view/8989/2600

Al Araby 2019, Two years on, Qatar has beaten the Saudi-led blockade (2019). Retrieved from:

https://www.alaraby.co.uk/english/indepth/2019/6/5/two-years-on-qatar-has-beaten-the-saudi-led-blockade

Al Jazeera (2017) Qatar donates 30m to help Harvey victims in Texas. Al Jazeera.

Retrieved from https://www.aljazeera.com/news/2017/09/qatar-donates-30m-harvey-victims-texas-170908042945728.html

Al Jazeera (2017) Arab States issue 13 Demands to end Qatar-Gulf Crisis. Al Jazeera.

Retrieved from https://www.aljazeera.com/news/2017/06/arab-states-issue-list-demands-qatar-crisis-170623022133024.html

Al Jazeera English (2018, Feb 15) Qatar: Beyond the Blockade.

[Video File] Retrieved from https://www.youtube.com/watch?v=Dc6n31wIuHI

Al Jazeera 2019, Emir Qatar Overcame Obstacles Gulf Blockade. Retrievedfromhttps://www.aljazeera.com/news/2019/11/emir-qatar-overcome-obstacles-gulf-blockade-191105075057081.html

Al Jazeera 2019, Fake Twitter Accounts Influencing Qatar Crisis. Retrieved from: https://www.aljazeera.com/news/2019/07/fake-twitter-accounts-influencing-gulf-crisis-190717052607770.html

Al Jazeera June 2017, Turkish Parliament approve of Turkish Troops Deployment in Qatar. Retrieved from: https://www.aljazeera.com/news/2017/06/turkey-fast-track-troops-deployment-qatar-170607151127104.html

Al Jazeera 2017, Qatar Foreign Minister Interview: Qatar Not Ready to Surrender. Retrieved from: https://www.aljazeera.com/news/2017/06/qatar-fm-ready-surrender-170608142453812.html

Alshabnan, Ali (2018), The Politicization of Arab Gulf Media Outlets in the Gulf Crisis, Global Media Journal. http://www.globalmediajournal.com/open-access/the-politicization-of-arab-gulf-media-outlets-in-the-gulf-crisis-a-content-analysis.php?aid=86958

Banu Akdenizli & Ilhem Allagui1 (2019), The Gulf Information War and the Role of Media and Communication Technologies https://ijoc.org/index.php/ijoc/article/view/8988

BBC (2017) Qatar Crisis: What you Need to Know. BBC. Retrieved from http://www.bbc.com/news/world-middle-east-40173757

BBC (2017) Qatar camels caught up in Gulf crisis. BBC. Retrieved from http://www.bbc.com/news/world-middle-east-40346329

BBC, (2017) Middle East News Qatar says state news agency hacked after report cites Emir criticizing US https://www.bbc.com/news/world-middle-east-40026822

Benedictus, L. (2013) Qatar: 12 things you need to know. The Guardian. Retrieved from https://www.theguardian.com/global/2013/jun/25/qatar-12-things-you-need-to-know

Cinzia Bianco and Gareth Stansfield, 2018, The intra-GCC crises: mapping GCC fragmentation
https://www.chathamhouse.org/publication/ia/intra-gcc-crises-mapping-gcc-fragmentation-after-2011

CNBC International (2017, Jun 29) What does Qatar own around the world? CNBC Explains. [Video File]. Retrieved from https://www.youtube.com/watch?v=8mZl9AePmHs

CPD Blog 2017, Qatar's Crisis Management Comms Plan. Retrieved from:
https://www.uscpublicdiplomacy.org/blog/qatar%E2%80%99s-crisis-management-comms-game-plan

Ebrar Sahika Kucukasci 2019, The Saudi Led Blockade Won't End Anytime Soon, but Qatar has moved on. Retrieved from:
https://www.trtworld.com/opinion/the-saudi-led-blockade-won-t-end-anytime-soon-but-qatar-has-moved-on-26803

Egypt Today 2017, What does Qatari Emir's Speech Mean. Retrieved from:
https://www.egypttoday.com/Article/2/13184/What-does-Qatari-emir%E2%80%99s-speech-mean

Gabriel Collins, J.D., Baker Institute (2018), "Anti-Qatar Embargo Grinds Toward Strategic Failure"
https://www.bakerinstitute.org/media/files/files/7299ac91/bi-brief-012218-ces-qatarembargo.pdf

Gamal Gasim (2018), The Qatari Crisis and Al Jazeera's Coverage of the War in Yemen
https://www.arabmediasociety.com/the-qatari-crisis-and-al-jazeeras-coverage-of-the-war-in-yemen/

IAStube (2017, Jun 24) 2017 Qatar Crisis Explained. [Video File]. Retrieved from https://www.youtube.com/watch?v=zHI5DcZWhSw

Kristian C. Ulrichsen* (2017), Lessons and Legacies of the Blockade of Qatar
https://www.insightturkey.com/commentaries/lessons-and-legacies-of-the-blockade-of-qatar

Lea Hickert (2019), Qatar Crisis Blockade Embargo, Fair Observer Retrieved from https://www.fairobserver.com/region/middle_east_north_africa/qatar-crisis-blockade-embargo-saudi-arabia-uae-gulf-news-khaleej-38004/

Lobelog (2017), Was Emir Tamim's Speech A Turning Point In The Qatar Crisis? Retrieved from
https://lobelog.com/was-emir-tamims-speech-a-turning-point-in-the-qatar-crisis/

Mariam I. Al Hammadi – 2018, Presentation of Qatari Identity at National Museum of Qatar: Between Imagination and Reality
https://www.jcms-journal.com/articles/10.5334/jcms.171/

MARC OWEN JONES 2019, Propaganda, Fake News, and Fake Trends: The Weaponization of Twitter Bots in the Gulf Crisis
file:///C:/Users/maya.ghorayeb/Downloads/8994-37168-1-PB.pdf

Memri Staff- May 25, 2017, Uproar In The Gulf Following Alleged Statements By Qatari Emir Condemning Gulf States, Praising Iran, Hizbullah, Muslim Brotherhood And Hamas
https://www.memri.org/reports/uproar-gulf-following-alleged-statements-qatari-emir-condemning-gulf-states-praising-iran

Mirela Atanasiu, 2017, Book: Qatar Crisis In The Recent Security Context Of The Middle East.

Mohammed Ahmad Naheem, June 2017 The dramatic rift and crisis between Qatar and the Gulf Cooperation Council (GCC).
https://www.researchgate.net/publication/319693755_The_dramatic_rift_and_crisis_between_Qatar_and_the_Gulf_Cooperation_Council_GCC_of_June_2017

Mostafa, H. (2017) ادارة الازمة الخليجية... نموذج قطر الناجح. Alaraby Aljadeed.

Retrieved from https://www.alaraby.co.uk/opinion/2017/9/7/-1إدارة-الأزمة-الخليجية-نموذج-قطر-الناجح

Mouchantaf, C. (2017) A Huge Military Buildup is Underway in Qatar. But who will man the systems. Defense News. Retrieved from https://www.defensenews.com/global/mideast-africa/2017/12/15/a-huge-military-buildup-is-underway-in-qatar-but-who-will-man-the-systems/

Noor Odeh, 2018, The artist behind Tamim Al Majd portrait. Retrieved from: https://www.qatarliving.com/forum/welcome-qatar/posts/artist-behind-tamim-al-majd-portrait

Pressform (June 2017), Qatar Crisis Turns Hostile on Social Media, Retrieved from https://pressfrom.info/us/news/world/-58344-qatar-crisis-turns-hostile-on-social-media.html

Reuter, 2017, Qatar deposited over $10 bln in banks to offset crisis outflows Retrieved from: https://www.reuters.com/article/qatar-banks-deposits-idUSL5N1KI3X6

Stewart, D. (2017) Qatar's resilience – a lesson to all on how to respond positively to a crisis. Gulf Times. Retrieved from http://www.gulf-times.com/story/566847/Qatar-s-resilience-a-lesson-for-all-on-how-to-resp

The GCC Crisis at One Year, 2018, Al Ansari, Baaboud et Al. Retrieved from: http://arabcenterdc.org/wp-content/uploads/2019/05/The-GCC-Crisis-at-One-Year.pdf

The Africa Report.Com. Saudi Arabia ends its Qatar blockade, but dispute is not over. (2021, January 7). https://www.theafricareport.com/57423/saudi-arabia-ends-its-qatar-blockade-but-dispute-is-not-over/

The New York Times 2017, Countries That Broke Ties With Qatar Indicate Some Flexibility on Demands. Retrieved from: https://www.nytimes.com/2017/07/18/world/middleeast/

qatar-crisis-demands-saudi-arabia-tillerson.html?rref=collection%2Fsectioncollection%2Fmiddleeast&_r=0

The Qatar Crisis, its Regional Implications, 2018, and the US National Interest
https://smallwarsjournal.com/jrnl/art/qatar-crisis-its-regional-implications-and-us-national-interest

Washington Post 2017, UAE Hacked Qatari Government sites
https://www.washingtonpost.com/world/national-security/uae-hacked-qatari-government-sites-sparking-regional-upheaval-according-to-us-intelligence-officials/2017/07/16/00c46e54-698f-11e7-8eb5-cbccc2e7bfbf_story.html

Wikstrom, C. (2017) Glorious Tamim: 'you won and you were silent'. Aljazeera. Retrieved from https://www.aljazeera.com/indepth/features/2017/07/glorious-tamim-won-silent-170718093327234.html

APPENDIX 1
Calendar of Events of Blockade from June to September 2017

- On 24 May, Qatar state run news service Qatar News Agency is hacked.
- On 5 June, Saudi Arabia, Bahrain, Egypt, the UAE, Yemen and the Maldives break diplomatic relations with Qatar.

  They accuse it of supporting "terrorists" and of being too close to Iran, Saudi Arabia's regional rival. It is the biggest diplomatic crisis to hit the region in years.

  Riyadh and its allies close land and maritime borders, suspend air links and expel Qatari citizens.

  Saudi Arabia also closes the Riyadh bureau of Qatari broadcaster Al Jazeera.

  Qatar claims its neighbors are pursuing a "policy of domination and control" and insists it will not back down.
- On 6 June, Mauritania joins the boycott and Jordan trims its diplomatic presence in Doha.
- On 7 June, the United Arab Emirates says the measures against Qatar are "not about regime change" but rather about "change of policy."

  The UAE's State Minister for Foreign Affairs calls Qatar "the main champion of extremism and terrorism in the region".
- On 9 June, Saudi Arabia and its allies publish a list of people and organizations they accuse of involvement in "terrorism" with support from Qatar. Doha calls the accusations unfounded.

- On 12 June, Qatar's Foreign Minister denounces sanctions against his country as "unfair" and "illegal".
  Turkish President Recep Tayyip Erdogan calls the sanctions "inhumane and un-Islamic."
- On 16 June, a Qatari official accuses Riyadh and its allies of laying "siege" to his country.
- On 19 June, the UAE Foreign Minister says a blockade of Qatar could last "years."
  Doha demands the "blockade" lifted before talks on resolving the standoff.
- On 20 June, the U.S. State Department says it is "mystified" that Saudi Arabia has yet to produce a clear list of demands. President Donald Trump presses Qatar to "immediately" stop financing terrorism. He discusses the situation with Saudi Arabia's new Crown Prince, Mohammed Bin Salman. However, Secretary of State Rex Tillerson speaks to both sides of the dispute. Tillerson says Saudi Arabia is set to present Qatar with a list of demands, which he hopes "will be reasonable and actionable." That comes days after the Pentagon, which maintains a huge airbase in Qatar, agrees to sell Doha $12 billion worth of F-15 fighter jets.
- On 22 June, Bahrain, Egypt, Saudi Arabia, and the UAE send a list of 13 demands to Qatar, giving Doha 10 days to comply. Among the demands are shutting down Al Jazeera, curbing relations with Iran and closing a Turkish military base in the emirate.
  On 24 June, Qatar rejects the 13-point demand list.
- On 1 July, Qatar says that the demands were "made to be rejected."
  US President Trump reiterates the next day that financing for terrorism must stop.
- On 3 July, the ultimatum is prolonged for 48 hours.
- On 17 July, The Washington Post breaks story revealing that

the UAE was behind hacking of Qatar News Agency.
- On 21 July, His Highness Sheikh Tamim Bin Hamad Al Thani, Amir of the State of Qatar addresses the nation on TV.
- On 17 August, Saudi Arabia reopens the border with Qatar to facilitate the annual Hajj Pilgrimage.
- On 19 September, his Highness Sheikh Tamim Bin Hamad Al Thani, Amir of the State of Qatar, addresses the opening session of the United Nations General Assembly and meets with US President Donald Trump.

APPENDIX 2
Qatar ready for dialogue but won't compromise on sovereignty

H.H. the Amir Sheikh Tamim Bin Hamad Al Thani addresses citizens and residents on the Gulf crisis

22 Jul 2017 - 2:12 – QNA

The full text of the speech of H.H. the Amir is as follows:

In the name of Allah the Most Merciful, The Most Compassionate. Distinguished citizens, and all those who live on the good land of Qatar, brothers and sisters,

In these circumstances that our country is passing through, I wish to address your conscience in the language of reason.

We speak in rational terms in assessing the phase we are going through, to plan the promising future that our people have proved aptly worthy of, and touched by the spirit of solidarity, harmony and defiance that prevailed and frustrated the hopes of those who banked on the opposite side because of their ignorance of the nature of our society and our people.

As you know and since the onset of the blockade, day to day life in Qatar has continued as normal. The Qatari people instinctively and naturally stood up to defend the sovereignty and independence of their homeland.

All those who live in this country have become spokespersons for Qatar. Here I would like to recognise, with great pride, the high moral standard exercised by this people despite the campaign of incitement as well as the siege. They combined the solidity of stance and magnanimity of behaviour that has always characterized the Qatari people. They have amazed the world by maintaining a high level of tenacity in tackling the situation, despite the unprecedented incitement in tone and language, the honor-related prejudices, and the unparalleled blockade in the relations between our countries.

This was tantamount to a true moral test where our society has achieved great success, as we have proved that there are basic principles and norms that we observe even in times of conflict and dispute, because we respect ourselves first and foremost. I call upon all to continue this approach, and not slip into what is inappropriate for us, nor for our principles and our values. The sons and daughters of this country have realised, with common sense and political awareness, the seriousness of this campaign against their homeland, and the goals of the siege imposed on it.

They have seen through the heavy curtain of fabrications and incitement, without blurring or distorting their vision, and were able to understand the implications of the attempt to impose pressure on this country, and the gravity of the subservience to language of incitement, threats and diktats.

It has become evident to those near and far that this campaign and the steps that followed it had been planned well in advance, and that its plotters and implementers carried out an attack on the sovereignty of the state of Qatar by planting statements that had not been spoken, in order to mislead public opinion and the world and achieve predetermined goals.

Those who took these steps did not realize that the people of the world do not accept injustice so simply, and people do not believe the forgeries of those who do not respect their minds. After all, there are limits to the efficacy of orchestrated propaganda that is not believed even by the very people who forged them.

Therefore, Arab and non-Arab countries that have a respected public opinion stood with us, or at least did not stand with the siege despite the extortion they were subjected to.

The States that have taken these steps have banked on the effect that terror-supporting charges would have in the West, while appealing to the sentiments and preconceived notions of some marginal discriminative forces in Western societies.

It soon became apparent to them that Western societies are like us, in that they do not accept levelling the accusation of terrorism purely due to political dissension, or for purposes such as suppressing pluralism at home, or distorting the image of other countries and isolating them at the international level. This behavior itself, although far from being just, ultimately inflicts damage on the war on terror.

Moreover, in a similar political stance, Western political, civil and media institutions reject diktats and impositions.

This is evident from the international reaction to the conditions that some have tried to impose on us, especially controlling our external relations, infringing on the independence of our policy, shutting down media outlets and controlling the freedom of expression in our country.

We know that there have been differences with some GCC countries over Qatar's independent foreign policy. We too do not agree with the foreign policy of some member states of the GCC, especially over the attitude towards the aspirations of the Arab peoples, supporting just causes, and distinguishing between legitimate resistance to occupation and terrorism, in addition to other issues.

However, we do not try to impose our opinion on anyone. We have never thought that these differences would spoil the sense of amity. There are many commonalities for which the GCC as a regional organization has been established.

Some brothers thought they were living alone in this world, and that money can buy everything.

They have committed yet another mistake, as many States and institutions have reminded them that this world is not for them alone, and that many countries do not favor immediate interests over principles and long-term interests, and they have come to know that even underprivileged countries have dignity and will, and that they cannot impose things that history has long left behind.

They have tried to undermine two principles that humanity has made sacrifices for. First, the principle of sovereignty and the independent will of States; secondly, freedom of expression and the right to information. Freedom of expression is meaningless if the citizen does not have the right to access information. Qatar has quashed the monopoly on information through the media revolution it started, and it is no longer possible to go back. This revolution has become an achievement for all the Arab peoples.

We have been very saddened to see how some countries have used defamation and fictions against Qatar to stir political malice against us in the West. This is a disgrace under all norms: first because the allegations are baseless, and secondly because they have wrongfully prejudiced a sister country. Do we not teach our children at a young age that lying and malicious snitching are two of the worst vices? Is slander and tarnishing a reputation not a crime punishable by law in all civilized countries?

The Emir said that Qatar is fighting terrorism, relentlessly and without compromises, and there is international recognition of Qatar's role in this regard. It does this not because we want to appease anyone in the East or the West, but because we consider terrorism, in the sense of it being an act of aggression against innocent civilians for political ends, a heinous crime against humanity; and because Qatar believes that the just Arab causes are impeded by terrorism, which affects Arabs, Islam and Muslims.

We disagree with some on the sources of terrorism. For example, we say that religion is a moral motive, and not a source of terrorism that could lie in radical ideologies whether religious or secular. Even these extreme ideologies become a source of terrorism only in socio-political environments that create frustration and desperation.

While the disease of terrorism must not be underestimated, we cannot ignore other issues in our world. We believe that the whole world, including our region, also suffers from problems such as poverty, tyranny, occupation and others. This suffering needs to be addressed, as it is also a significant root cause of violent extremism and terrorism.

I do not want to underestimate the scale of suffering and pain caused by the siege, and I hope that this malevolent approach in dealing among brothers will come to an end, and that differences may be resolved through dialogue and negotiation, for this approach has tarnished the image of all GCC countries in the eyes of the world.

It is high time to stop making the citizens of our countries pay the price of political differences among governments. Our Arab region has known the method of revenge and collective punishment of citizens of the other country in case of disagreement with its government, and we have so far succeeded in avoiding this here in the Gulf. But the countries that asked the Qataris to leave, separated members of the same family, and asked their citizens to give up their jobs, their families and leave the State of Qatar, have decided to use this method.

This behavior on their part is not only against international law, but it also affects their own citizens, the values and the norms of dealing between people.

As you know, we did not retaliate, and we have let the citizens of the other countries make their own decisions to stay in Qatar or depart, each according to their own circumstances and will.

Any solution to this crisis in the future must include arrangements to ensure that this retaliatory approach in dealing with innocent citizens will not be repeated when there is a political dispute between governments.

Despite the bitterness caused by these steps, the most prevalent proverbial wisdom in the Qatari society these days is: "Every cloud has a silver lining", which corresponds with the Quranic verse: "And perhaps you may hate something which is good for you."

This crisis has driven Qatari society not only to explore its human values as I have indicated, but also to draw on its sources of strength that lie in its unity, will and determination. Further, the efficiency with which the government, with its various ministries and other state institutions, dealt with the crisis to cater for all the needs of the population, has ensured that the people did not feel any difference in their daily lives.

The same qualified persons in technical, administrative, political and media fields who dealt with the situation rationally, calmly and with resolve, are capable of building our economic independence, protecting our national security and strengthening our bilateral relations with States in this world.

We are called upon to open our economy to investments and initiatives so that we produce our own food and medicine, diversify our sources of income, achieve our economic independence through bilateral relations of cooperation with other countries, in our geographical environment and worldwide, and on the basis of mutual interests and mutual respect. We also call upon ourselves to develop our educational, research and media institutions, as well as our sources of soft power at the international level and with the interaction of the best national, Arab and foreign expertise. All of this of course will be in cooperation with the residents in our country who work, contribute and live with us, and who stood with us throughout this crisis.

On numerous occasions I have directed our institutions to pursue the pursuit a policy of economic openness and diversification. At this stage, this is no longer a matter of luxury for us, but a binding and inevitable course of action, leaving no room for complacency. This is the responsibility of all of us, government and business community alike.

This crisis has helped us identify the shortcomings and obstacles in determining Qatar's national, political, economic and independent identity and in deciding to overcome and surpass these obstacles.

As we pass through this test with honor and dignity, I am addressing you to emphasize that Qatar needs every one of you to build its economy and protect its security.

We require diligence, creativity, independent thinking, constructive initiatives and interest in academic achievement in all disciplines, self-reliance and fighting indolence and dependency. This is not just wishful thinking, and these are not mere dreams. Our goals are realistic and practical, based on the continued determination that Qataris have shown during this crisis. This is not just a passing wave of enthusiasm, but rather the basis for further awareness in building the homeland.

Qatar is going through an important phase that has provided opportunities, not only to build upon, but also to bridge the gaps and address shortcomings, if any. We are not afraid of identifying errors and correcting them.

Under my direction, the government will do whatever it takes to achieve this vision, including the required economic openness, the removal of obstacles to investment, and the prevention of monopolies in the context of building the national economy and investing in human development. I have also directed the government to allocate newly-discovered gas revenues that God has blessed us with to investment for our future generations. Qatar has lived well so far without it.

We will also continue to work on the international arena to deepen bilateral cooperation and conclude bilateral agreements between Qatar and other countries.

We highly value the mediation efforts undertaken by my brother, His Highness Sheikh Sabah Al Ahmad Al Jaber Al Sabah, Emir of the sisterly State of Kuwait, which Qatar has supported from the outset. This is an opportunity to express my thanks once again for what he did and continues to do. We hope that his sincere efforts will be culminated in success. We also appreciate the American support for this mediation, as well as the constructive positions of Germany,

France, Britain, Europe in general and Russia. I would like to commend the important role that Turkey has played in the rapid adoption and direct implementation of our Strategic Cooperation Agreement that had been previously signed, and to thank it for its immediate response to meet the needs of the Qatari market.

I also thank all those who opened their airspace and territorial waters when our brothers closed theirs.

We are open to dialogue to find solutions to lingering problems, not only for the interest of our States and peoples, but also to spare the efforts that are being wasted in vain by countries moved by malicious scheming against their brothers in the international arena, so that these efforts may be invested in serving the causes of the Ummah.

Any solution to the crisis must be based on two principles: first, the solution should be within the framework of respect for the sovereignty and will of each State. Secondly, it should not be in a form of orders by one party against another, but rather as mutual undertakings and joint commitments binding to all.

We are ready for dialogue and for reaching settlements on all contentious issues in this context.

I cannot end this speech without expressing solidarity with the brotherly Palestinian people, especially our people in Al Quds (Jerusalem), and denouncing the closure of the Al Aqsa Mosque, the first of the two Qiblas and the third of the two Holy Shrines, hoping that what is happening in Al Quds be an incentive for unity and solidarity instead of division.

In conclusion, I would like to thank you for your solidarity, cohesion, determination, resolve and civilized behavior, and to congratulate you on the spirit of nobility, love and amity prevailing in our land nowadays. These are our assets, our provision and energy to counter the great challenges in the way ahead.

May Allah's Peace, Mercy and Blessings be upon you all.

APPENDIX 3
H.H. the Amir of Qatar's Speech at 48th Advisory Council Session
November 2019

By virtue of God's support, credit for our success in containing most of its negative impacts is attributable to maintaining our calm and decisive approach in handling this crisis, revealing all its related facts to the whole world...as well as strengthening our bilateral relations with friendly and allied countries.

The Qatari people, with their noted magnanimity, stood up together as one man in defense of their homeland's sovereignty and principles, because they realize that renunciation of the independent decision-making is conducive to losing the homeland itself along with its wealth and potentials.

Qatar's Gross Domestic Product (GDP) at current prices grew in 2018 by about 15% and non-hydrocarbon GDP by about 9%. The importance of that has been further boosted by the fact that the government has sought this year to restore balance to the State budget, by cutting public expenditure, without affecting priority projects.

As a result of the efforts to cut expenditure and increase efficiency, the big budget deficit in 2017 was turned into a surplus. Although the spending was reduced, the general State budget has continued to attach importance to and focus on priority sectors, especially education, health and investment in infrastructure.

The private sector has participated in QR. 27 billion worth of major projects over the last five years.

I will focus hereinafter on the most important initiatives, projects and policies we have adopted, and which show that we have overcome the negative impacts of the blockade, and that we are steadily moving towards achieving the goals of Qatar National Vision 2030.

Reports indicate a significant progress in the field of economic diversification, encouraging the private sector, increasing the production capacity of power generation plants and establishing an advanced agricultural and livestock-fish production system

The progress made is notable, but we have much still to do in the areas of economic diversification, food and medicine security, renewable energy, revitalization of the private sector and cutting red-tape that hinders progress and advancement.

Development is not measured by buildings and facilities only, but rather by the ability of human beings to plan, build and maintain them, and by the schools that educate them and the universities from which they graduate, as well as the quality of education, culture and the prevailing values and ethics.

Rights, brothers and sisters, are not privileges or a mere sense of superiority engendered by identity or unwarrantable transcendence towards others, because humility is a proof of self-confidence, and showing respect to others is a reflection of self-respect. The responsibilities of citizenship also require being appreciative of those who have worked hard in building this country, and this includes our resident brothers.

Our fellow resident brothers who live with us in Qatar are not here as a result of a favor conferred on them, but by virtue of their work, which is indispensable to us, and by means of their appreciated contribution to the building of this country.

Source:
https://www.gco.gov.qa/en/speeches/his-highness-speech-at-the-opening-of-the-48th-advisory-council-session/

APPENDIX 4
The Gulf Information War and the Role of Media and Communication Technologies
Ilhem Allagui1 - Banu Akdenizli (2019)

Press Release by Government Communications Office (GCO)
Allah the Whole Mighty said in the Holy Quran: "Dost thou not see how Allah sets forth the similitude of a good word? It is like a good tree, whose root is firm and whose branches reach into heaven" (Ibrahim, Verse 24). Based on the principles of our true Islamic religion, our humanitarian values and our authentic Qatari culture, we call on all those who live on this good land to rise and continue to avoid responding similarly to the abuses that spread in various means of mass communication. We also call upon you to show more responsibility, of which you are well known, and not to insult countries, their leaders or peoples, while guaranteeing the right of every Qatari citizen and resident to express their opinion for showing the truth and reality in a peaceful manner, always keeping in mind the Islamic and Arab values.

CHAPTER FOUR:
Qatar public communications sector: Ministry of Culture and Sports, shaping Qatar's future culture

(This chapter was written ahead of the governmental changes in October 2021. After this change the Ministry title is "Ministry of Culture", and the content of this chapter applies to the work of multiple ministries.)

While Qatar and the Qatari people truly showed signs of resilience and strength during the blockade period, it is truly impressive as well how far the Qatari government has come in applying advanced communications strategies throughout their work.

Indeed, the Qatar National Vision 2030 embodies a huge improvement for the country by implementing the latest state-of-the-art technology to serve the people of Qatar.

The Qatari Ministry of Culture and Sports is a clear example of how developed communication strategies serve the governmental sector. Notably, for the position it holds in the institutional system in Qatar, based on its specialization and role.

The Ministry of Culture and Sports policy is mainly characterized by being the biggest part of the communication strategy of the State of Qatar. The Ministry assumes a crucial communication and interaction role within the community, as it aims to encourage society to adopt new social and cultural patterns, and focus on a set of universal values, hoping to positively affect the life of individuals and to guarantee the achievement of developmental goals. In this regard, the main vision of the Ministry of Culture and Sports is: "Towards a Conscious Society with an Authentic Conscience and a Healthy Body».

The National Development Strategy of 2018-2022 states that the Ministry is "an efficient and creative cultural, sports and youth system backing the society in its action towards improvement whilst preserving its principles and values." Through the interpretation of the communication strategy, we notice that: the word "towards" means working to reach a certain goal in the future, which signifies changing the current reality for a new one (presumed to be better than the current one). The word "society" confirms working with the community to make a change regarding certain perceptions or behaviors, establishing new foundations that serve the common interests of people. After all, the main purpose is to affect the society, mainly the Qatari citizens and eventually all people living in Qatar.

The Ministry will mostly work to achieve awareness on an individual level, thereby working to guarantee a more "aware" society. The goal of the Ministry indicates the necessity to influence society in order to move it from a certain system to a new system state in the three fields: culture, sports and youth. In this way society can be more efficient and creative, all while preserving the values and principles linked to the traditions and heritage of the country.

These objectives indicate that the work of the Ministry falls within a more comprehensive communication strategy, a part of which is implemented by the Ministry through its work. In this context, the Ministry works through different means, communicating with the public to ensure the necessary interaction with the programs, projects and activities offered by the Ministry and the affiliated parties. The Ministry has indeed put in place a strategy that is aligned with the Qatar National Vision 2030 and with the first and second National Development Strategies, with a values system adopted by the Ministry in order to influence society by implementing tools adopted by the Ministry in its work in order to reach its goals.

QATAR NATIONAL VISION 2030

Qatar's leaders were visionary in creating a forward-thinking development plan, leading to the long-term prosperity of the nation. Thus, Qatar National Vision 2030 was adopted in 2008, to outline Qatar's sustainable development roadmap. H.H. the Amir – in his former role as Heir Apparent – emphasized the importance of this vision: "Qatar National Vision 2030 builds a bridge between the present and the future. It envisions a vibrant and prosperous country in which there is economic and social justice for all, and in which nature and man are in harmony. We need to galvanize our collective energies and direct them toward these aspirations. Strong Islamic and family values will provide our moral and ethical compass. The welfare of our children, and of our children yet to be born, demands that we use our resource wealth wisely. Qatar must continue to invest in its people so that all can participate fully in economic, social and political life" (QNV 2030, 2008).

In fact, H.H. the Amir summarized the 2030 vision by stressing the main pillars of this vision and the importance of all people to lead the implementation and for everyone to play a role, in order to guarantee prosperity today for this generation and for the generations to come. In this way Qatar is able to create a diversified economy, while preserving nature. In fact, to summarize Qatar vision 2030, one could select a single word: balance. The challenge is how to maintain a balance in a rapidly developing country, between the needs of this development and the human and social transformations which it brings with it. A balance between today and tomorrow, between modernization and tradition.

Qatar National Vision 2030 presents a development path that is compatible with the views of its leadership and the aspirations of its people: "The National Vision defines broad future trends and reflects the aspirations, objectives and culture of the Qatari people. By shedding light on the future, the Vision illuminates the fundamental choices that are available to Qatari society. Simultaneously, it inspires Qatari people to develop a set of common goals related to their future" (QNV 2030, 2008).

Qatar's National Vision as defined on the official website, is the long-term outcomes for the country, rather than the processes for reaching these outcomes. It provides a framework within which national strategies and implementation plans can be developed.

Indeed, the National Vision defines the characteristics of Qatar's future, challenges, and opportunities. This is achievable through managing and balancing five main challenges:
- Modernization and preservation of traditions
- The needs of this generation and future generations
- Managed growth and uncontrolled expansion
- The size and the quality of the expatriate labor force and the selected path of development
- Economic growth, social development, and environmental management

The basic principles of Qatar's National Vision are to ensure the well-being of citizens on two levels. The first guarantees their physical existence by ensuring security, stability, and fair opportunities. The second level is based on a value system that ensures the development of society, by protecting public freedoms, achieving justice, and preserving values and traditions.

In fact, Qatar National Vision 2030 is focused on four main pillars for sustainable development: human development, social development, economic development and environmental development.

First Pillar: Human development

The development of Qatar's economy depends heavily on the oil and gas sectors, posing many future challenges. Qatar National Vision focuses on human development as one of the main pillars of evolution. These include ongoing plans to ensure educational and research institutions and programs that provide advanced learning opportunities to ensure a new generation of competitive youth in a new world order based primarily on the knowledge economy.

In addition to the educational system, the State of Qatar is working to ensure a healthcare system that cares comprehensively for citizens. Qatar is aware of the challenges posed by the need for specialized and professional labor capital in many fields, and in this context seeks to recruit foreign labor, within the framework of a legal system to ensure the work and human rights of the labor force.

Second Pillar: Social development

The State of Qatar strives to ensure the progress and prosperity of society by working to strengthen the cohesion of society, especially the cohesion of the family, and helping Qataris to develop the necessary knowledge and acquire the needed skills to be able to face the challenges of the times.

Opportunities are also promoted to ensure an effective role for women in society and in the state's future. In this context, it works to promote openness to other cultures, to ensure the values of tolerance and justice, and to encourage dialogue that would be in harmony with Islamic and Arab culture.

Third Pillar: Economic development

The Qatari economy has maintained its stability and growth, relying mainly on the oil and gas sector. Ensuring prosperity requires a balance in how these resources are used, to ensure their sustainability for future generations. On the other hand, these resources must be used to build a diversified economy, based on different sectors that ensure sustainable development regardless of the oil and gas sectors. This is done by stimulating the economy towards new initiatives, projects, and investments, by creating appropriate investment opportunities, and by establishing financial, advisory, and sponsoring institutions.

This path presents two major challenges. The first is to stimulate the private sector to lead economic development at the state level by encouraging entrepreneurs, providing training opportunities and securing the necessary financial support.

The second challenge is related to the size of the economy itself, and this is related to the ability of the public services structure to cope with the rapid development, which calls for parallel development servicing economic growth. The answer to these challenges lies in an open economy, based on flexible rules that serve its movement, an inexpensive social protection system, and a cash reserve capable of coping with crises.

Fourth Pillar: Environmental development

The Qatari Government seeks to protect and preserve the environment. This path of development must therefore be pursued responsibly and respectfully, by balancing development requirements with environmental needs. The pillar of environmental development is important for Qatar, especially with a shortage of natural resources such as water, and due to diminishing hydrocarbon reserves. In addition, this factors in environmental pollution and corrosion, as well as global environmental risks such as global warming. Meeting these challenges at the environmental level requires a high capacity to identify them, and to develop the necessary plans to prevent and to face them.

National Development Strategies

The development of the Qatar National Vision 2030 came together with several National Strategies developed by the State in order to keep track of the progress made.

This initiative started in 2011 and continues until today, with each part of the national strategy focusing on main aspects for progress and development.

National Development Strategy 2011-2016

When the Qatar National Vision 2030 was established in October 2008, it set the general framework for the progress of the State of Qatar by achieving sustainable development, which guarantees the welfare of the Qatari people and moves the country forward.

In order to implement and achieve these objectives, the National Development Strategy of Qatar 2011-2016, adopted in March 2011, was created. This was considered to be the first developmental strategy for the State of Qatar, aiming to create a balance by responding to five main challenges:

- Updating and preserving traditions
- Achieving the balance between the needs of the current generation and the next generations
- Controlling the targeted economic development and avoiding undisciplined expansion
- Conforming the volume and quality of incoming labor to keep track of the targeted development
- Adapting between the economic and the social development and protecting the environment (Qatar National Development Strategy, 2011)

On the economic level, such a strategy stressed the necessity to achieve sustainability alongside economic prosperity. Indeed, major steps were needed for expanding the field of the productive basis and fostering economic stability and efficiency, as well as reaching an economic variety guaranteeing such sustainability. As for the strengthening of human development, the Qatar National Vision set a group of goals based on raising healthy citizens and to guarantee an efficient labor force through building knowledge and skills on the individual level.

As part of social integration, such a strategy drew up a plan to foster family cohesion, and secure social protection and foster comprehensive development in addition to enhancing public security and safety and creating an active and sports-oriented culture within the society. This was to be achieved while maintaining, preserving and fostering Qatari traditions.

As for environmental integration, the National Development Strategy stressed the necessity of protecting main natural resources such as water and air, in addition to managing nature and the environmental heritage in a sustainable manner. It also highlighted the necessity to increase environmental awareness amongst the people of Qatar.

Sports Goals of the National Development Strategy

The National Development Strategy set a main focus on sports as an inspiration for a healthy and active society. This was to be achieved through educating the public on the importance of an active and healthy lifestyle, and increasing opportunities for the people of all ages to participate in physical activities. In addition, it planned to provide adequate and available sports and leisure facilities to increase the number of talented sportspeople, and promote their development through programs as well as sponsoring athletes to improve their chances of success. Within the strategy a set of results were to be achieved:

- Increasing the community's participation in sports and physical activities:
  This would be achieved by stressing the importance of sports as a tool to build a cohesive and healthy society. Physical activity provides health benefits and reflects the performance of a person and their social communication. The strategy focuses on achieving such a result on all age categories, notably children and youth, to encourage them to adopt a sports culture from childhood.

- Equipping the country with accessible sports facilities:
  The relevant ministries would ensure the adequate facilities to achieve the first point, including by providing the sports and leisure facilities that ensure an optimal environment for training and practicing sports.
- Raising sports to the distinction level:
  Reaching sports distinction is a goal, as it reflects the position of the State and its interest in backing and developing sports talents. Notably, this would derive benefit to the State pertaining to sports investment and the resulting opportunities as well as increasing awareness of the importance of sports, in addition to supporting the development of tourism and industries linked to sports.

Cultural Goals of the National Development Strategy

The National Development Strategy was able to achieve positive social development by using culture as a platform to build national identity and encourage dialogue and understanding among cultures. Additionally, the National Development Strategy also aimed to protect cultural heritage and develop it as an integral component of the Qatari national identity.

Cultural heritage does not only play a role in shaping the national identity, but has also significantly boosted the position of the State of Qatar and its image as a unique cultural destination and an epicenter for cultural exchange. Through using culture, the State of Qatar has also contributed to improving education among youth. Young people are the means to which the State attracts and sponsors cultural talents to stimulate the growth of the cultural sector. The growth of the cultural sector also depends on the research and information collected and disseminated on the factors that contribute to the growth of the sector, along with the existing potential the sector has. The Strategy further outlines a set of results that it aims to achieve:

- Increasing demand and support for cultural activities:
Preserving and boosting the cultural identity of any state constitutes a goal to be achieved by governments globally; in the case of the Qatari government, the preservation and boosting of the nation's cultural identity is a top priority for the Qatari state. In this context, the National Development Strategy stresses the importance of fostering and increasing cultural activity within the country. The strategy specifically focuses on fostering local and social awareness of the national culture, whilst encouraging the inter-cultural and intra-cultural understanding. In this context, rich cultural programs were developed to involve society, through festivals, exhibitions, conferences, workshops, round-tables, and translations. In addition to developing cultural institutions, the strategy also encourages research, arts development, with the focus on improving communication strategies. By standardizing the dissemination of information, the strategy along with its relevant institutions promote cultural production, specifically engaging both heritage and our modern conception of tradition and culture.
- Fostering cultural diplomacy and increasing cultural exchange:
In the past years, the State of Qatar played an important role in encouraging religious dialogue through different international and regional initiatives such as the annual forum of the United States of America and the Islamic World, the Dialogue Center for Religions and other projects and initiatives. These initiatives span across regional and international forums. The National Development Strategy highlights the importance of cultural diplomacy to create and promote communication with the varying cultures worldwide. Cultural diplomacy serves to encourage the closeness of peoples and promotes the growth of positive relations between countries. The strategy promotes cultural exchange programs

and the cultural projects in common with many countries through exhibitions, artists' programs and others in hopes of improving cultural diplomacy.

- Improving the administration of traditional resources and fostering their governance:

  The National Development Strategy focuses on the importance of the cultural heritage as a stability factor during major economic changes and how these changes impact or reflect on the social changes that manifest within Qatar. This situates cultural heritage as an important factor that could be affected by economic and social changes. Thereby, the strategy encourages the inclusion of cultural heritage through promoting common cultural bonds, the closeness among citizens, and the social cohesion of this ever-increasing diverse society through mainly identifying existing common historical roots. In this context, the strategy works to improve the management of traditional resources through a modern system to guarantee, preserve and manage the safety of the sites as well as expand the viable touristic opportunities.

- Supporting the participation of the future generation in culture:

  Cultural awareness functions as the cultural bond among generations, and is one of the most vital determinants of the national identity of any nation. Therefore, the National Development Strategy seeks to invest in the youth in general, and to promote cultural awareness specifically, all by engaging in projects guaranteeing the participation of the youth in cultural programs and projects. This form of cultural awareness aims to introduce the youth to the nation's culture and its national identity from childhood, through schools, and embed it within the social consciousness to enhance their capacity to create, analyze and discover new innovative contributions to the Qatari culture.

- Increasing the talents in the cultural sector:
  The strategy stresses on the necessity to increase talents in the cultural field, in which these talents comprise of many arts, such as writing, acting, painting, playing music and directing, through set programs implemented by the parties and the institutions working in the different fields of the cultural sector.
- Improving the media support of the culture:
  Media is considered the main source of communication with the public for any sector. Thus, the media functions as a necessary medium for the culture sector to create the necessary communication to guarantee the development of the sector. Knowing the media structure and its prestige in our era, it remains a part of the culture of any society and one of the criteria that expresses the cultural limit of the society, in addition to being a primary means to develop the society's culture. In this context, the National Development Strategy seeks to develop a proactive relationship with media outlets, and promote its role in transferring the society's image and establish a communication channel with the public in regards to the achievement of the goals of developing the cultural sector.

National Development Strategy 2018-2022:

The second National Development Strategy for the years 2018-2022 came in the same framework as the follow up for the first Development Strategy of 2011-2016 in the context of the four development pillars as set by the Qatar National Vision 2030, in order to achieve sustainable development. This strategy adopted the definition of sustainable development as the one that satisfies the needs of the modern times without affecting the capacity of the future generation to satisfy their needs. It also stresses that the sustainable development envisioned for the State of Qatar characterizes the collective aspirations of the people of the world towards peace, freedom, improvement of the living conditions and living in a safe environment (National Development Strategy 2018-2022).

The National Development Strategy 2018-2022 is a strategy aimed at enhancing the sustainability of the nation's economic prosperity by developing the country's infrastructure and growing the private sector. In addition, it considers achieving economic diversification and promoting human development by presenting a complete and comprehensive healthcare system, enhancing the quality of education and training, employing an efficient labor force and achieving safety and security measures. The strategy also focuses on cultural enrichment and sporting distinction, in addition to sustainable development and the preservation of the environment. It is noticeable that economic prosperity along with cultural enrichment and sports are significant contributors to the nation's development, as the strategy emphasizes.

Such a strategy considered the progress made in the National Development Strategy 2011-2016 in various fields, notably in the fields of culture and sports through building a cultural structure and promoting the cultural movement, whilst focusing on promoting national identity and showing the local cultural components. An additional focus is placed on achieving a number of goals on the sports level such as organizing the FIFA World Cup Qatar 2022™, thereby further transforming sport into a national activity that fosters the Qatari national identity. In addition, the state adopted "Sports Day" as a sports-focused national holiday that encourages the practice of sports as a lifestyle, and promotes the nation's interests in the field.

Challenges

Such a strategy benefits from the lessons and experience of the implementation of the first strategy and focuses on overcoming a series of main challenges. These challenges are related to Qatar National Vision 2030, and are the same adopted in the first strategy:

- Modernize while preserving traditions.
- Flow of foreign labor with its cultural challenges on the Qatari society.
- Guaranteeing the future generations' needs through satisfying the needs of the current generation.
- Achieving targeted growth and controlling undisciplined expansion.
- Balancing between economic and social development and preserving the environment.

The Strategy identified potential institutional challenges through the weakness of integration and sectoral coordination, which leads to the deceleration of the implementation of some projects. This is a result of the absence of the culture of planning and working as a team requiring the common work and coordination of efforts.

In addition to the main challenge on the level of economic development, the decrease of hydrocarbon income constitutes a big pressure on the expenditure capacity and requires reconsidering the priorities for the major development projects. Adding to that a major challenge which appeared during the crisis between the State of Qatar and the blockading countries, the imposed siege led to the reconsideration of many productive partnerships and commercial exchanges in order to preserve the developmental track identified for the state.

The same challenges apply as well to the sports and culture sectors, in order to achieve cultural enrichment and sporting distinction. The National Development Strategy emphasizes a group of challenges on various levels, aiming to activate the role of culture so that Qatari society preserves its identity and promotes its values. In fact, many concerns are related to the accelerated developmental pace and the welfare achieved due to the increase of the per capita income. Other challenges are related to the interaction with new cultural concepts, due to the flow of labor required for the development, and to the interaction with global issues through modern communication tools, especially social media.

Cultural and Sports Goals of the National Development Strategy 2018 - 2022

The strategy works on activating the participation of youth in the public sphere by creating communication means and recognizing their aspirations and needs and developing their personal and collective capacities and skills. In the sports field, it focuses on the distinction of the sports practice by discovering, supporting sports talents, developing the national sports skills, and helping them in achieving advanced results in different competitions.

This strategy considers youth as a sector in need of development, specifically as one that is relevant to the sports and cultural areas. This link was showcased after the Ministry of Culture and Arts was merged with the Ministry of Youth and Sports, under the umbrella of the Ministry of Culture and Sports.

Starting from the Qatar National Vision 2030, and from the lessons learned from the first National Development Strategy, the second Strategy establishes the general framework for the sports and culture sectors in order to reach a "creative and efficient youth, sports and cultural system supporting the Society in its action towards development preserving its values and constants". In the context of achieving such a strategic goal, the Strategy establishes a set of objectives to be reached in different fields as stated:

- Culture as a framework to maintain identity and promote citizenship and civilized communication:
  The Strategy seeks to ensure the development needs, while preserving the identity, society's values, and cultural heritage. This would be possible through plans to support the national cultural production, and by implementing attractive programs that help the promotion of Qatari values and citizenship, as well as the support of cultural exchange. The strategy also emphasizes the necessity of the interaction with incoming cultures, while enforcing the necessary mechanisms to protect and develop Qatari cultural heritage.

- A high level of community participation in culture and sports:
  The Strategy gives a significant importance to societal participation on the sports and cultural levels, encouraging youth and promoting their participation in the public interest. In such a context, the creation of a societal participation strategy ensures the participation of all society's classes as well as preparing the sports, cultural and youth facilities to be more attractive to the public. These initiatives aim to promote their benefits in society, through focusing on awareness campaigns and annual programs of cultural and awareness of varying subjects that further encourage the public to participate in cultural and sports activities and events.
- Distinct national sports and cultural talents:
  The Strategy assures the importance of discovering sports and cultural talents and developing them. Doing so will lead to the development of distinguished athletes and various participations and competitions that national teams of Qatar will have a representation in, through developing a national system that discovers and supports national creative talents.
- Regional and international cooperation that reflects the civilized image of the State:
  The Strategy stresses on promoting the regional and international cooperation and communication in a manner reflecting the civilized image of the State by benefitting from the membership of Qatar in international and regional organizations pertaining to the sports and cultural sectors, keeping in mind that the State of Qatar seeks to become an active member on the international level. In addition, the state has activated the bilateral agreements to further ensure that foreign participations support Qatar's strategy to achieve its goals.
- Culture and Sports as sources of national income:
  The State of Qatar faces significant challenges on the level of investment in culture and sports; in spite of the big expenditure

over such two sectors, the financial income does not satisfy the state's ambitions within these two fields. That is why the current strategy seeks to make a move in enabling both sectors to support the budget with a revenue that suits the volume of investment. By determining the productive components relying upon such sectors, the strategy emphasizes investing towards: enhancing participation, diversifying the income sources, and activating a strategic partnership with the private sector.

- Empowered and qualified youth for an Effective Role in the Society:
The strategy will work on the development of young people and their skills, to enable Qatari youth to play an efficient role in society and to participate in the development of the country. This would be achieved through implementing mechanisms to develop the knowledge and to enhance the voice of youth. In addition, the plan is to deliver programs and initiatives to support meeting the needs and aspirations of youth.

- High-Level of Sports:
The Strategy aims at improving the process of developing and managing sports talents by putting in place complete plans to develop such sports talents. These initiatives work towards increasing the number of Qatari professional athletes of different age categories, as well as the technical staff of the Qataris working in the sports sector.

- Effective cross-sector governance:
The Strategy stresses the necessity to create a comprehensive review of the legislations and policies related to the sector, to meet the challenges presented by the national and international development and changes. It will also ensure effective governance. The strategy will ensure promoting and activating partnerships among the sector's effective institutions. A sectoral knowledge structure should be established based on reliable and comprehensive database, information, and studies for monitoring the changes and help facing their challenges.

INTELLECTUAL AND RELIGIOUS APPROACH TO CULTURE

After discussing the objective approaches linked to the institutional methodology of the Ministry of Culture and Sports, which is in line with the Qatar National Vision, and the first and second National Development Strategies, it is necessary to examine the conceptual and values system adopted by the Ministry in its work in terms of the intellectual approach of this governmental entity.

Through the Wijdan Cultural Center, one of the Ministry's cultural centers affiliates, the Ministry of Culture and Sports has set intellectual approaches constituting a scientific measurement means for assessing the development progress of the state on a societal level. Through the values embedded within this center's mission and goals, they aim to observe the position of the Qatari society, setting development aims and producing practical plans for working towards sustainable development on a societal level.

Such initiatives introduced by the Ministry stem from its belief in the necessity of making a fundamental change to the level of the cultural structure of the Qatari society. By developing the society's view to a set of major cultural perceptions, these initiatives aim to achieve "an effective cultural renaissance based on an authentic value system that supports the society in achieving civilization progress" according to the public statement on their website.

Wijdan Cultural Center conducted several studies in this regard, using its results to further introduce a system to measure the Qatari societal development through key perceptions related to society culture and values. This initiative is studied in sociology through a theory known as "values orientation theory".

In fact, numerous research and studies tackle this theory, most notably the work of Kluckhohn and Strodtbeck (1961). Their work aims to demonstrate that society's development can be measured through a set of common values: "Value orientations are complex but definitely patterned principles, resulting from the transactional interplay of the three analytically distinguishable elements of the evaluation process-the cognitive, the affective, and the directive elements-which give order and direction to the ever-flowing stream of human acts and thoughts as these relate to the solution of common human problems."

In their research, the authors introduce an analytical method for societies depending on the value orientation and argue that most societies have the same main common issues, as they state: "the conceptual scheme used for the classification of the value orientation and the ranges of variations postulated for them rests upon these three major assumptions: (1) there is a limited of common human problems for which all peoples at all times must find formulae. (2) While variations in these formulae certainly exist, they are neither limitless nor random but are, instead, variations within a limited range of possible solutions. (3) All variants of recurring solutions are present in all cultures at all times but receive, from one society to another, or one subculture to another, varying degrees of emphasis. The five common human problems for which, thus far, ranges of solutions are postulated concern the nature of man itself, his reaction to nature and supernature, his place in the flow of time, the modality of human activity, and the relationship man has to his fellow human beings." (Kluckhohn, & Strodtbeck, 1961).

The Holy Quran Universal Solutions

These same human issues are also tackled in the Holy Quran. In fact, many studies have shown that the Holy Quran presented universal solutions to these problems, from the time it was introduced to humanity. Indeed, the system adopted by the Wijdan Cultural Center concerning those perspectives found in its pillars are derived from the Holy Quran. These values are firmly embodied in Muslim principles, as taught through the Holy Quran. They directly emerge from Muslim culture and values inherited throughout history. This brings to the fore the importance of this system's legitimacy, as it expresses the cultural environment to which Qatari society is compliant, complemented with the traditions and the values that the society promotes.

This is highlighted in the perspective levels through their connection with the Holy Quran, and the level of the reference made by the Holy Quran or the Hadith. Below are some examples of these statements.

Quran and the perspective of Nature

"And He has subjected to you whatever in the heavens and whatever is on the earth - all from Him. Indeed, in that are signs for a people who give thought." (Verse13 Al-Jathiyah, The Holy Quran)

In this verse the Holy Quran makes it clear that earth and heavens were available for humans to exploit. Especially "for a people who give thought". All that which is in the heavens such as spheres, impurities, anthroponomy, and everything on this earth such as trees, rocks and laws are subject to thinking. This is the key to the perspective of nature and its relation to humans. This perspective for nature encourages thinking in order to research and discover the secrets of the universe and make the benefits available for people.

"Indeed, in the creation of the heavens and earth, and the alternation of the night and the day, and the [great] ships which sail through the sea with that which benefits people, and what Allah has sent down from the heavens of rain, giving life thereby to the earth after its lifelessness and dispersing therein every [kind of] moving creature, and [His] directing of the winds and the clouds controlled between the heaven and the earth are signs for a people who use reasons." (Verse 164 Al-Baqarah, The Holy Quran).

Again, in this verse we notice the importance of "reason" and of thinking to the creation of the earth by God. Indeed, it is emphasized that nature is an integral part of creation for humans.

Quran and the perspective of Work

The Holy Quran also introduces the concept: *"Which of you is best in deed"* (Verse 2 Al-Mulk, The Holy Quran). For this reason, all work, plans and achievements are a reflection of this Quranic concept. Work competition is directly related to the nature of people who can achieve more work than others in a more efficient way. All of it serves the purpose of improvement of humans.

Also, in the Haddith text: *"Allah loves those who master their work."* It is a clear invitation for people to work efficiently and to master their work.

Quran and the Perspective of Others

The Holy Quran is also very clear in encouraging people to get to know each other, and respect each other: *"O mankind, indeed. We have created you from male and female and made you people and tribes that you may know one another. Indeed, the most noble of you in the sight of Allah is the most righteous of you. Indeed, Allah is Knowing and Acquainted"* (Verse 13, Al-Hujurat, The Holy Quran).

This also indicates that the origin of these relations is getting to know people despite differences between humans: *"And if your Lord had willed, He could have made mankind one community; but they will not cease to differ"* (Verse 118 Hud, The Holy Quran).

Quran and the perspective of Human Dignity

Since the dawn of the creation of humans, angels have seen a problem in the universe, as they said: *"Will You place upon it on who causes corruption therein and sheds blood"* (Verse 30, Al-Baqarah, The Holy Quran), *"and the Creator privileged him with the secret of knowledge "and He taught Adam the names – all of them"* (Verse 31, Al-Baqarah, The Holy Quran).

Therefore, with this knowledge, he was transformed into an honored Creator: *"and [mention] when We said to the angels, "prostrate before Adam"* so they prostrated, except Iblees" (verse 34, Al-Baqarah, The Holy Quran). His readiness to learn, gave him, thus, the power to choose and act, and this, indeed, shall be a kind of test: *"[He] who created death and life to test you [as to] which of you is best in deed – and He is the Exalted in Might, the Forgiving –"* (Verse 2, Al-Mulk, The Holy Quran), and to his guidance, he sent messengers and left the choice to him, *"Indeed, We guided him to the way, be he grateful or be he Ungrateful"* (Verse 3, Al-Insan, The Holy Quran).

This neutral nature: *"He has succeeded who purifies it, and he has failed who instills it [with corruption]"* (Verse 8,9, Ash-Shams, The Holy Quran). He was created in the best of stature *"we have certainly created man in the best of stature"* (Verse 4, At-Teen, The Holy Quran). When he shall feed his negative side, he shall become, *"Indeed, mankind is [generally] most unjust and ungrateful"* (Verse 34, Ibraheem, The Holy Quran). *"And ever has man been stingy"* (Verse 100, Al-Isra, The Holy Quran). *"Indeed, mankind is ungrateful"* (Verse 66, Al-Hajj, The Holy Quran).

Nonetheless, with his good and evil side, humans are honored: *"And We have certainly honored the children of Adam and carried them on the land and sea and provided for them of the good things and preferred them over much of what We have created, with [definite] preference."* (Verse 70 Al-Isra, The Holy Quran).

The realms of the universe are under his possession: *"Do you not see that Allah has made subject to you whatever is in the heavens and whatever is in the earth and amply bestowed upon you His favors, [both] apparent and unapparent?"* (Verse 20, Luqman, The Holy Quran). This made him a successor upon the earth: *"indeed, I will make upon the earth a successive authority"* (Verse 30, Al-Baqarah, The Holy Quran) and assigned him the mission of building it: "He has produced you from the earth and settled you in it"(Verse 61, Hud, The Holy Quran).

According to these verses we notice that the human being in the Holy Quran is honored. On this basis, nations that understand this idea turned existential human dignity into a concept that they adopt. Everything under this concept as for human rights shall become a title for the dignified human life, and this was reflected in its rules and regulations on the criminal, legal, social, economic, and political levels.

Quran and the perspective of Knowledge

When you read the Holy Quran, you will find several verses that talk about knowledge: *"And if Allah were to impose blame on the people for their wrongdoing, He would not have left upon the earth any creature, but He defers them for a specified term. And when their term has come, they will not remain behind an hour, nor will they precede [it]."*. (Verse 61, An-Nahl, The Holy Quran)

Then ordered him to read: *"Recite in the name of your Lord who created Created man from a clinging substance. Recite, and your Lord is the most Generous. Who taught by the pen"*. (Verse 1,2,3,4 Al-Alaq, The Holy Quran)

He made fear related to knowledge: *"Only those fear Allah, from among His servants, who have knowledge. Indeed, Allah is Exalted in Might and Forgiving"*, (Verse 28, Fatir, The Holy Quran). He made knowledge accessible: *"And mankind have not been given of knowledge expect a little"*, (Verse 85, Al-Isra, The Holy Quran).

Also, He made the demand of addition, a supplication: *"and say, "My Lord, increase me in knowledge"*. (Verse 114, Taa-Haa, The Holy Quran).

"O company of jinn and mankind, if you are able to pass beyond the regions of the heavens and the earth, then pass. You will not pass except by authority [from Allah]". (Verse 33, Ar-Rahman, The Holy Quran).

Based on this, the Holy Quran opens us up to all forms of knowledge that can enhance humanity and help progress society. Thus, this remains the most pivotal pillar of Wijdan Cultural Centre's approach to enhancing the growth and development of the Qatari Society.

Pillars of the Wijdan Cultural Center

Through their scientific research and based on the teachings of the Holy Quran such as the ones stated previously, Wijdan Cultural Centre adopted a set of perspectives that best exemplify the Qatari Society. These perspectives are centered on the 'Human', 'Nature', 'Science', 'Work', 'Time', 'Afterlife', 'Related Others', and 'Non-Related Others'.

The religious and scientific basis behind these perspectives encompass the intellectual pillars grounded in the work ethic of the Wijdan Centre and more importantly, the cultural growth of Qatari society. Similarly, the Ministry of Culture and Sports emphasizes the use and implementation of these perspectives and the value systems pertaining to them in their work within Qatar.

These perspectives are detailed below as stated by the Wijdan Cultural Center Website:

Perspective of Human

The first perspective addresses all that encompasses human nature and what it means to be human. The notion of human dignity is imbued in our understanding of humans, both as individuals and as a social being. Human dignity is composed of three concepts: freedom, fairness, and peace. Humans are granted existential human dignity upon creation. By exploring divine laws, and the characteristics of humans as revelation dictates, we can determine the human rights instruments that society should abide by.

The international instruments of human rights reinforce this concept. The fundamental freedoms of a human are guaranteed by the international laws, his/her right to total fairness is inherent and fundamental, and his/her protection from transgression is a universal human demand. Moreover, the instruments of human rights also refer to the concept of existential human dignity as a principle that is superior in nature, and an inherent right unconditionally available to us on the grounds of our humanity.

The concept of human dignity combines three important elements: law, politics, and ethics. These elements reflect the importance and relevance of human rights. For this reason, law guarantees penalties against any relevant transgression, where services and support are provided to sustain and uphold it, and its importance is emphasized in the way society is regulated by nations. Politics also informs human dignity as it stresses its importance in the establishment of the future of humans, and more importantly the future of the society to which they belong. Ethics as well as its related values, deepen our social presence and our sense of social belonging.

The behaviors and actions of people reflects their level of awareness and application of the values related to the elements that shape the perspective of the human in their lives. This may be noticed through the perception of people towards each other, their behaviors, the way they deal with the invoked laws, the services provided by establishments, and the values and concepts that govern relations between the members of the society. Thus, societies considered developed must adopt and uphold these values that shape humans and their dignities. With these values, members of the society can prolong and maintain the growth of society.

Perspective of Others

The perspective of others shapes our understanding of the development process of countries, populations, relations between populations, cultures, and different countries. This includes others close to us in our society to whom we are related through a common culture, and the different relations shared among different social groups within the borders of the country. This perspective is not only limited to the 'others' perceived within our society, but also includes 'others' far from us who belong to another country, who share a different language, culture, or understanding of society. The concept of the perspective of others may be determined by our perception of other populations, and the level of our feeling of the existence of a universal human identity that brings us together on a common level — without any harm to our local identity and our sense of belonging to it.

In this era of interconnectivity and openness, societies should not be isolated and withdrawn into themselves, and the geographic distance should not be an obstacle between cultures. The world nowadays can be characterized as cultural diversity mixed together and mingled. In addition, the openness to media and communication exposes the culture to channels of information, engagement with international cultures, and engagement in the news and politics that frame events globally.

The biggest and most important obstacle that the perspective of others may encounter is how to achieve a level of openness that can helps unite races, communities, and societies without compromising the national identity and the sense of cultural belonging. In this context, one should stress the fact that the values of meeting somebody, sharing experiences, and embodying the pillars that define humanity and our identity should function as a guiding manual for our relationship with others. Through the value of sharing, projects serving humanity should be established based on common interests, which in its turn and through the value of humanity can create a common culture that upholds humanity as the highest value.

This further introduces the concept of 'international identity' where important matters are raised about having a 'local identity', its conservation, as well as how identity fuels relations with others.

Indeed, the openness to others outside our culture must be corresponded with a sense of internal cohesion that we practice within our social contexts. Thus, it is important to identify the levels of internal cohesion when exploring other societies and contexts, as many societies continue to experience conflicts on the grounds of politics, ethnicity, race, and religious belief.

How we view others may be informed by the social fabric that we subscribe to. Interactions within and among societies are based on the respect and dignity shared between people to maintain a more cohesive and coherent social structure. By maintaining these factors, societies will indeed grow stronger.

Perspective of Nature

Conflicts that humans engage with can be described as power struggles to control, foster, and manage the sources of wealth that serve national and personal interests. Nature constituted, and still constitutes, the principal source of wealth, starting from the land areas and its resources, to the wealth it provides. We are currently living in a world in which the main interest is the maintaining of natural resources. Competition is not only about manufacturing and innovating; rather it includes the development of natural resources and attempts to find alternative energy sources which nature provides. This area remains one of the most important ones that fuel the competition between nations and is a way to gain power that grants nations international status. The resort to natural resources should embody the perspective of nature, which includes respecting nature, and undertaking research aimed at harnessing it. Caring for issues affecting nature such as energy, environment, animals, and climate is not only a matter of intellectual projection, but a matter that informs the needs for a human to have a better lifestyle—financially, psychologically, and most importantly, in terms of health. Thus, nations should compete to maintain these perspectives of nature.

Perspective of knowledge

The perspective of society regarding education diverges from the earlier perspectives. knowledge determines the growth of society in the future. Knowledge also engages the ability of those societies to respect the required values emerging from their economic and social structures. In return, through education one can achieve sustainable development of the society and ensure the prosperity of all its members. In fact, knowledge can be considered a life journey, and its tools include research and discovery; nonetheless, experience and mistakes inform it and provide education with a sense and a goal. Moreover, the outputs of knowledge should be a society able to create and innovate, in order to serve the needs of society and the country.

In addition, questions, criticism, creativity, and production are significant keys that initiate the process of learning.

The perspective of knowledge is related to the questions asked and to the questioning process. Questions lead to different answers, and having many answers requires a dialogue to achieve an understanding respecting or compromising between different points of views. Questions also shift our philosophy of knowledge from giving ready answers to understanding, participating, and having a constructive dialogue.

Perspective of Work

The perspective of work is connected to several concepts and values. The development and prosperity of society is bound by the respect of these concepts and values, and the quality of the work of its members and their overall efforts. Some essential concepts may be defined as follows:

- Human value and human dignity are important elements that shape a person's improvement and contributions within the workspace. Any accomplishments that embody these values directly aid the growth and development of society. Human value is not related to origin or nationality, it shall rather be his / her work, achievement, and role in helping to develop society.
- Empowering to reach our aims. Those aims make the most difference amongst societies, and shape the level of growth, intellectual development, and productivity of societies. The higher the social expectations are on what is considered as "the best", the better the work of its members will be.

- Each member of society, no matter how small his/her role is and regardless of his/her abilities and skills, should contribute to the improvement and the development of his/her country. Contributions refer to giving ideas and working within a specific role. These collective contributions constitute a national project aimed at growth and productivity.

Perspective of Time

Time is important as it connects a human to his / her reality and future. It is considered the measurement and the core of one's existence. Without perceiving time, a human is lost in an unlimited space, further making him / her lose the ability to organize things, ideas and plans. Time is a natural wealth, one that is as vital and as important as natural resources.

It is crucial to understand the importance of time, and to have a firm conviction about the necessity of saving time, and then take a positive position concerning this conviction.

By wasting time, a person is wasting the most important natural wealth available to individuals and societies. All values of things float in the space of time and wasting time will lead to mismanagement of all sources of wealth and its loss. The importance of time amongst societies comes from the firm conviction of its importance, and the necessity to spend it in the best way. Culture embodies a main challenge concerning the perspective of time. Thus, we consider the spread, embodiment, and value of time and how we spend it as a requirement and an essential element of culture.

These intellectual pillars developed by the Wijdan Cultural Center, in addition to the principles we previously presented, constitutes the intellectual pillars for the Ministry of Culture and Sports.

The ministry relies on these intellectual principles, on the Qatar National Vision, and on the National Development Strategy to formulate its strategy. The aim of this strategy is to achieve the ministry's vision and mission to help create a common society culture based on these intellectual foundations, moving thereby towards achieving sustainable development goals at the state level.

MINISTRY OF CULTURE AND SPORTS STRATEGY AND PLAN

The strategy of the Ministry of Culture and Sports is a combination between the requirements of both the Qatar National Vision and the Strategies of National Development and the intellectual principles that the Ministry wishes to achieve. It has also set the essential results through the achievement of several goals set by dozens of programs to be implemented directly or through partnerships operating in the sector.

According to the official website of the ministry: "The Ministry of Culture and Sports uses a guiding paradigm to implement its vision of achieving the social renaissance. The table is based on a series of directions in the creation of cultural products, where the guides are major perceptions that lie in the depth of thinking and determine the deep identity of the individual and the community, while cultural products from clothing, language, food, architecture and other artistic cultural expressions are the superficial part of this identity".

Integrating society and values

The Ministry of Culture and Sport embodies this intellectual perception of change in the iceberg model, in which the great concepts occupy the hidden and largest part mainly in:
- Promoting citizenship as a condition of progress.
- Increased community solidarity and dialogue with each other in and outside society.
- Enhancing the value, mastery, and non-exclusion of work on one side without the other.

- To increase the value of science and scientific research, to acquire technology and to expand sources of income.
- Taking time into consideration as the most important resource for the future generations to inspire optimism.

The strategy of the Ministry of Culture and Sports from 2018-2022 meets these principles, in the framework of ensuring the balance between the accelerated efforts of the State in achieving development, promoting a value system that reflects society and its cultural heritage. The key Goal of its strategy reflects the orientation towards "an active action related to culture, sports and youth based on an authentic values system that supports the society in achieving the progress of human civilization". This is achieved through enriching the cultural scene by influencing national production to support national identity, establishing a strong basis for different cultural industries, in addition to creating a stimulating environment for sports and the participation of society, and working to empower youth in building the country.

In this regard, the Ministry of Culture and Sports seeks to provide an encouraging environment, for the potential of Qatari society in all its components to be achieved within a national project that would lead to a transition to the status of being a developed country.

With a view to achieve a balance between modernization and the preservation of the values system of society, the Ministry of Culture and Sports aims to accomplish an effective cultural renaissance. The framework embodying this culture should respect an authentic values system that helps society in achieving progress through enriching the cultural scene with a distinguished national production, and establishing a strong basis for the different cultural industries.

It also helps in creating an environment for sports, ensuring societal participation at large scale, as well as working to empower youth in supporting their contribution to national sporting development.

Results that reflect the strategy

In this context, the Ministry uses its updated operational system that emphasizes its role as an organizing and sponsoring body for sports and culture. This entails reviewing and modernizing the legislative structure and developing general policies for the State in the three fields of the sector and fostering the efficiency of institutional work. The ministry will encourage its different executive bodies, as the centers of culture and youth, and the sport clubs, as well as the group of partners in the sector to execute the policies, and to carry them out under the oversight and the follow up of the relevant administrations. According to the Strategy of the Ministry of Culture and Sports Strategy, these results were demonstrated in four dimensions (Ministry of Culture & Sports, Ministry's strategy 2018-2022):

- The first objective the strategy has determined is to "identity as a framework for preserving culture, promoting citizenship and civilized communication". Therefore, the Ministry has a goal to foster cultural industry that aims at cultivating national identity through developing appealing cultural events that raise the level of societal participation. In addition, it also aims to discover and sponsor cultural talents, as well as increasing the cultural industry that supports the identity and organizing events that contribute to raising the cultural communication with the residing expatriates. All of these efforts are in line with the strategy to strengthen the cultural position of Qatar regionally and internationally.
- The second objective for the strategy affirmed "a sport with a distinguished level". This is showcased by the continued efforts of the ministry to enable a motivating environment for members of society to practice sports and physical activity through making sports facilities of the Ministry more attractive to the public and to eventually create a more active society. Furthermore, it also aims at supporting the social and cultural

role of sports clubs to become more active in addition to discovering and sponsoring talented people in different games in order to create sports groups that achieve sports excellence for the country. The Ministry established the Qatar Sports For All Federation in 2015 to support sports and embed it as part of daily culture and lifestyle. The Federation has contributed with the Ministry to seek to meet the needs of Qatari society, in all its age ranges, when it comes to the different sports programs. It plans to supervise its organization in a way that suits the nature of the members of society, and uses the different sports facilities and resources in the country in the best possible way, as well as setting programs that support the activities and plans made to engage with all the groups in Qatari society.

- The third objective emphasized the idea of "the qualified and empowered youth to play an active role in the society" by empowering youth to have an active role in the development of the country, through strengthening the concepts of citizenship and national values. It also focused on increasing their life skills and leadership capacities and encouraging their creativity and innovation. To achieve this result, the Ministry through its strategy, empowers youth, extends their choices and listens to their voice that reflects their hopes and aims in order to raise their motivation and their sense of entrepreneurship by means of a system of programs and events. In this framework, youth must participate in decision-making on the level of the sectors of sports and youth and set the required administrative arrangements and organizational structures that allow them to participate. In addition, the necessary measures to achieve equal job opportunities for young women and men shall also be guaranteed through providing the required conditions to perform their national duties.

- The fourth objective aims at "an efficient institutional performance that accomplishes professionalism and administrative excellence". The Ministry aims to develop and foster the efficiency of the institutions performance by activating its organizational structure, ensuring its accomplishment of the Ministry's vision, and strengthening its leadership in the sports and cultural work in the country and its role in supporting the society in accomplishing the vision of transition to the status of a developed country.

Culture and Sports as Means of Communication:

The Ministry of Sports and Culture strives with the relevant centers and bodies to implement its strategy that serves the intended goals through the programs and events it organizes in addition to the awareness campaigns it launches on social media. The Ministry is also making use of the communication tools it has, particularly on the level of the different arts as well as the youth and cultural centers. Below are some examples showing how the Ministry of Sports and Culture use the communication tools at their disposal to create change in society.

Doha International Book Fair

The Doha International Book Fair between 2018 and 2020 (noting that the fair was not held in 2019 after changing its date from November to January) is an excellent case study. In fact, the Ministry set specific goals to be achieved while organizing the fair and those goals were directly related to the perspectives adopted by the Ministry.

In 2019, the theme of the fair was "Doha of knowledge and conscience" which reflects the importance of Doha as a place for experience and expertise exchange to develop knowledge and conscience. Furthermore, the Doha International Book Fair was not only a market to sell and trade in books, but also created a space to exchange cultures and circulate knowledge. It is therefore a renewed call for dialogue, especially in matters related to the book industry.

The Doha International Book Fair established its particular vision for knowledge as an adventure in discovering the unknown, liberation of the energies of creativity, and a precious value. The book fair was in fact an occasion to express that reading is a sign of love of human existence and in relation with fellow human beings (Doha Book Fair, 2019).

In 2020, the theme of the fair was "seeking knowledge" associated with a confirmation of the value of education and knowledge in the life of humans, by emphasizing the importance of questions, research, and discovery.

"Life changes and human takes his adventure in existence by seeking knowledge, so the world will be its open book and life will be a space of knowledge, which make him understand different cultures, languages, and races. The story of the human started with science and continued its cycle with the renewed calling for reading, so that science is the basis of human dignity and the mark that Allah has given him upon all his creatures and made him worthy of prostrating" (Doha Book Fair, 2020).

The Ministry of Culture and Sports insisted, by organizing the Doha International Book Fair, on creating a space for the knowledge exchange, as the fair is not a market to sell books only. It is, thus, a cultural demonstration that includes hundreds of workshops, seminars, conferences, and panel discussions. In addition to that, the fair was also a supporter of a cultural renaissance in Qatar, particularly because of the conviction of the organizers that the development of countries is measured by its capacity to produce knowledge.

Movement of Theater

The Ministry of Culture and Sports has also organized efforts to empower the theater industry, due to the importance of the theatrical arts in addressing the audience and its impact. The most important area of support may be the financial support that it provides to some theater performances, which correspond to the Ministry's general framework for changing the perceptions of people and tackling the social concerns that audiences are interested in.

The Theater Affairs Center of the Ministry of Culture and Sports evaluate the plays that may receive financial support in accordance with the appropriateness of the performances. For this purpose, a special committee was founded to evaluate the scripts that should receive support. The "Committee of evaluation of theater plays" has a specific role to evaluate the plays for the theater season with regards to production. Indeed, this committee specializes in evaluating the theater plays and performances happening during the theater season in order to announce the winning play or performance in the theater season and the relevant awards. Awards are also granted to the best performance or play for the relevant season of theatre for both adults and children.

The ministry of culture and sports promote a free theatrical movement, while supporting financially the plays in lines with the ministry's intellectual framework.

National Sports Day

With regards to sports, the Ministry of Culture and Sports also aims to achieve its goals on the basis of its vision and values system. In this framework, a healthy society is the Ministry's primary goal, which is why the idea of National Sports Day was created for the occasion.

National Sports Day is an annual national holiday, declared by virtue of a decree by H.H. the Amir in 2011, stating that the second Tuesday of February of every year will be National Sports Day. Everyone is encouraged to participate in sports activities with their family members and colleagues. The first National Sports Day in the State of Qatar was organized in 2012.

The main goal of the National Sports Day is to promote sports and inform the local community of ways that reduce health risks related to a sedentary lifestyle, such as cardio-vascular diseases and diabetes. A number of ministries and private companies organize several sports events for their employees and the general public on this day. It is seen as an opportunity to bond with different parts of society through sports, based on the principles of building team spirit, unity, inclusion, participation and fitness, as well as health. In addition to the several sports activities around the country, National Sports Day also focuses on Qatari Culture through traditional championships which are a reminder of Qatar's sports heritage and its role in the development of the country.

Qatar Sports for All Federation

The Qatar Sports for All Federation of the Ministry of Culture and Sports also aims to promote awareness of the importance of sports, in addition to helping expand the scope of practicing sports in the country and particularly in achieving the following:

- Spreading the culture of sports in general, affirming the concept of Sports For All and the continuity in practicing sports on a regular basis for all age ranges, and increasing awareness on the importance of sports for its economic, mental, social and health impacts on members of society and the country.
- Raising the number of people, regardless of age and gender, practicing physical activities by setting programs for Sports activities, supervising the organization of those programs, and following up through their evaluation.
- Supporting and encouraging sports activities and programs for everyone to better meet the needs of the body in terms of exercising and improving fitness and health.
- Providing all the means and possibilities for everyone to practice sports in a way that ensures participation of all and that is accessible for everyone in accordance with the concept and philosophy of Sports for All. (MCS Website, Sports for All).

The important role that Qatar Sports for All Federation plays will lead to more people adopting sports as a lifestyle and an essential manner to build a healthy society with a healthy body without illnesses. This applies especially to those health issues that can be avoided or reduced by practicing sports on a regular basis.

Awareness Campaigns

Awareness campaigns are one of the most popular direct means of communication adopted by the Ministry of Culture and Sports to communicate with the general public regarding a specific subject in order to have an impact when it comes to changing particular lifestyles.

These campaigns are within the value system adopted by the Ministry that accomplishes its vision and strategy. The relevant administrations in the Ministry are responsible for managing the communication process of the campaigns, especially when it comes to managing public relations and announcements. For instance, the modern and traditional awareness campaigns on a media level help to strengthen the value of work in people, to motivate the idea of considering the work of a human being as part of his dignity.

The campaigns promote the perceptions and values adopted by the Ministry. In fact, these campaigns cover a wide range of issues like encouraging youth participation in public affairs, performing better at work, and many other issues aligned with the Ministry's strategy, vision, and intellectual pillars.

CONCLUSION

The Ministry of Culture and Sports is assuming a major responsibility by aiming to achieve a social transformation that enables supporting the new status of the state. The role of the Ministry of Culture and Sports is essential in aligning the activities it holds and its strategies with the overall strategy and vision of the Qatar National Vision 2030.

- On a national level, it is working to establish a way of communication and new cultural activities, including society as a whole to improve it and move forward with the plans established.

However, within the diversity of the Ministry's plan, is it also making sure to preserve the values of the Qatari citizens, in addition to strengthening the foundations of cultural diversity, in terms of creating an intellectual and value framework allowing its growth and consolidation at the community level. This is also translating with tangible results when activating several activities and events in a way that allows its development.

Internationally, the Ministry is also working through a developed approach regarding cultural exchange, between countries and societies as this aspect constitutes a basic pillar in achieving openness to other cultures and acceptance through convergence of what is common, for a more prosperous future for everyone.

Cultural change in societies requires a lot of effort, and despite the Ministry's success in various areas, it still needs to push for change, to be more profound in its impact, and more rapid to spread awareness. In fact, the Ministry's direct implementation of their strategies and planning have just started and still have a long way to go as it is a process under development to achieve the desired results.

The main challenges facing the Ministry is related to duplications of competences with other institutions working actively at the cultural, sports, and youth sectors. These intuitions enjoy great independence in developing and implementing its plans, which makes it even more important to implement one clear strategy.

In addition, the need for a highly qualified and professional human resources has shown to be crucial, which is why it currently aims to attract the most experienced staff.

The role of the Ministry of Culture and Sports remains important in setting the general framework for the country's communication strategy approach at an external level. In addition, it is a key partner in creating and developing Qatar's brand, to guarantee an advanced position for the State of Qatar among nations.

There is no doubt that culture is a particularly important pillar in moving forward with Qatar's development. Strategies and policies stressing the importance of culture in general, and the role it plays in reducing distances are all indications of the state's continued investment in culture and sports as an essential element of its communication strategies.

REFERENCES

Doha Book Fair (2019):
> https://29.dohabookfair.qa/%d8%a7%d9%84%d9%85%d8%b9%d8%b1%d8%b6/%d9%85%d9%86-%d9%86%d8%ad%d9%86/%d9%83%d9%84%d9%85%d8%a9_%d8%a7%d9%84%d8%af%d9%88%d8%b1%d8%a9_29/

Doha Book Fair (2020):
> https://30.dohabookfair.qa/%d8%a7%d9%84%d9%85%d8%b9%d8%b1%d8%b6/%d9%85%d9%86-%d9%86%d8%ad%d9%86/%d9%82%d8%b5%d8%a9-%d8%a7%d9%84%d8%b4%d8%b9%d8%a7%d8%b1/

Intellectual Principles. (n.d.). https://www.mcs.gov.qa/en/intellectuals-principle/

Kluckhohn, F. R., & Strodtbeck, F. L. (1961). *Variations in value orientations Florence R.Kluckhohn ; Fred L. Strodtbeck.* Evanston, IL: Row, Peterson.

Ministry Of Culture & Sports About us. (n.d.) https://www.mcs.gov.qa/en/about-us/.

Ministry Of Culture & Sports, Ministry`s strategy (2018-2022) https://www.mcs.gov.qa/%d8%b9%d9%86-%d8%a7%d9%84%d9%88%d8%b2%d8%a7%d8%b1%d8%a9/%d8%a7%d8%b3%d8%aa%d8%b1%d8%a7%d8%aa%d9%8a%d8%ac%d9%8a%d8%a9-%d8%a7%d9%84%d9%88%d8%b2%d8%a7%d8%b1%d8%a9/

National Development Strategy for the State of Qatar 2011-2016, March 2011 https://planipolis.iiep.unesco.org/sites/planipolis/files/ressources/qatar_national_development_strategy_2011-2016.pdf

Pillars and Visions, Wijdan Cultural Center. http://wijdancenter.net/%d8%a7%d9%84%d9%82%d9%8a%d9%85-%d9%88%d8%a7%d9%84%d9%85%d9%86%d8%a7%d8%b8%d9%8a%d8%b1-%d8%a7%d9%84%d8%ab%d9%85%d8%a7%d9%86%d9%8a%d8%a9/

Qatar National Vision 2030, July 2008
https://www.psa.gov.qa/en/qnv1/Documents/QNV2030_English_v2.pdf

Qatar Second National Development Strategy 2018-2022
https://www.psa.gov.qa/en/knowledge/Documents/NDS2Final.pdf

Strategy of the Ministry of Sports and Culture 2018-2022.
https://www.psa.gov.qa/en/knowledge/Documents/NDS2Final.pdf

Sports Strategy (n.d.). from https://www.mcs.gov.qa/en/sports/

The Strategic Orientations in the Field of Youth
https://www.mcs.gov.qa/en/youth/

Tāriq, '., & Gilani, Z. A. (1966). *The holy Quran*. Lahore: M. Siraj-ud-Din.

CHAPTER FIVE

Qatar's Communication Strategy: New Approaches to Enhancing Qatar's Branding

The technological development the world witnessed for more than a century has accelerated economic growth, bridged the gaps between societies and countries, and imposed new specializations on governments. The role of public authorities has become more complex and more engaged in emerging fields. These developments imposed new patterns of work in the government's relations with its citizens from inside the state, and with the recipients of governmental policies from outside the state. Strengthening communications with internal and external audiences has become important to explain public policies and seek to positively impact public opinion. The feedback received from the public helps the government to implement policies more effectively, and serve the society and the state. Governments should work on strategic communications to communicate clearly, concisely, openly, and proactively, thereby ensuring proactive public participation in policy implementation.

Communication strategies have become a necessity for governments, especially when dealing with external audiences. On a global level, a country's self-image, and self-representation further influence how it is perceived internationally, and how it becomes represented by different global entities. On a social level, a country's image, vision, and values play a significant role in the development of its relations with different societies. Thus, in a world where information is easily accessible, governments need to develop their own communication strategies by relying on strategic communication grounded in statistics and facts. This helps to ease the modes of tackling specific issues in society, and helps the government communicate its position toward any such issues.

Countries need to strengthen their images and enhance their identities. This must be done with the aim of bringing countries and people closer together. The approach between peoples and communities contributes to enhancing inter-cultural communication, as a means of reducing misunderstandings and problems that could potentially arise between people and their governments. Governments rely heavily on communication strategies and public relations plans to reflect their cultural image. This helps countries to show the real image, away from any preconceived ideas that are often wrong.

There are several objectives that fall under rapprochement between people. The primary is enhancing understanding. Here, governments develop specific communication strategies as means of reducing the gaps existing between communities—on a cultural, religious, social, and even linguistic level. Secondly, rapprochement plays a significant role in helping the sectors that are essential for intercultural understanding, such as the tourism sector and the financial sector. With the growth of these sectors, governments utilize communication strategies and their brand image as the necessary tools for economic development.

Communication strategies help the government connect to the public and achieve their public policy goals. They directly serve the marketing objectives of governments and provide a soft power tool to market governmental policies and the country's image and identity. These strategies subtly embed the brand of the state through language, advertisements, and other policies. This can be understood as soft power, or a governmental tool that relies on cultural, social, symbolic, and linguistic forces as ways of relaying the state's national image and identity. Governments rely on their own agencies to develop and implement these communication strategies on a domestic level. They also depend on global agencies specialized in the field to develop those strategies. The work of global agencies acts as complementary to the work of the governmental agencies.

On 16 June 2015, Qatar established the Government Communication Office (GCO), which falls under the direct jurisdiction of the H.E. the Prime Minister. The GCO is tasked to coordinate communications across governmental and public sector funded agencies: "The GCO communicates the priorities of the Government of the State of Qatar, works with ministries and other key organizations to tell Qatar's story and supports government entities in responding to media enquiries in a timely manner." (Qatari Government: Office of Communications, 2015).

The GCO is a valuable partner of the local, regional, and international media outlets, interest groups, the public, and others who seeks to learn more about Qatar. The GCO's objectives are clearly stated on their website, with five main objectives to consider:

- Be the principle source of news and information related to the government of Qatar.
- Present an accurate image of Qatar to the world, through clarifying facts and showcasing the contributions of Qatar in various fields.
- Showcase the government's vision, policies, and programs.
- Provide communications support to the Government of Qatar and other entities.
- Engage with local and international media outlets and respond to media enquiries through the GCO or by referring them to other government entities.

The GCO played an important role in crisis management, especially in containing the problems that stemmed from the blockade on Qatar in 2017, and the spread of the novel Covid-19 pandemic in 2019. Additionally, the GCO plays a major role managing media relations and media responses toward many important issues in Qatar, including but not limited to: labor rights, FIFA World Cup Qatar 2022™, the Gulf crisis and many more issues. The role of the GCO varies, but overall the GCO determines the validity of knowledge sourced from the media, and carefully presents the narratives that are the most accurate and the closest to the state's national identity.

The focus of the GCO is placed on an external and proactive communication strategy to serve the pillars of Qatar Vision 2030, and Qatar's National Development Strategy 2018-2022. The GCO leads the efforts behind the creation and implementation of such strategies in coordination with all respective governmental and semi-governmental entities. It sets in place standard follow-up processes to ensure the successful and effective implementation of this strategy.

NATION BRANDING

Early studies of branding and its importance in marketing date back to the sixteenth and seventeenth centuries. However, more specialized, and focused research about branding appeared at the beginning of the twentieth century. At that time, definitions did not differentiate between "brand" and "trademark". More in-depth studies were published at the end of the twentieth century and the beginning of the twenty-first century, identifying clearer and more specific definitions of both concepts (Bastos & Levy, 2012).

Branding is the backbone of marketing and carries a commercial character par excellence. However, with the development of means of communication and the challenges facing countries and governmental agencies, it was necessary to consider marketing concepts within governmental communication strategies. In a short period, approaches to branding have evolved from image to reputation to values. Notably, it was in the twentieth century that brand, "an entity that until then had mostly been acted on by its immediate creators, became more democratic and absorbed inputs from a large array of actors" (Bastos & Levy, 2012).

There is no single comprehensive definition for branding but checking different definitions can help us to understand the concept. One source identifies a brand as "a name, term, design, symbol or any other feature that identifies one seller's good or service as distinct from those of other sellers" (American Marketing Association, 2020). Another attempt to define branding considers it as "a set of tangible and intangible attributes designed to create awareness and identity, and to build the reputation of a product, service, person, place, or organization. The holistic perspective of branding as a long-term strategy includes a wide set of activities ranging from product innovation to marketing communications" (Sammut-Bonnici, 2015).

A strong, developed brand should represent the organization's personality, identity, and portrays its reputation. To stakeholders, a successful and distinguished brand brings quality and elicits trust. With that comes loyalty. Additionally, an organization's brand should evolve and adapt to organizational and environmental changes ("Report of the sixty-seventh plenary session of the Conference of European Statisticians", 2019).

These definitions directly focus on the relation between consumers and products in the commercial sense. However, nation branding includes various activities related to the nation — ranging from the country's name and the country flag's shape and color, to a more sophisticated branding campaigns: "Nation branding is a managed process of building the brand identity, image, and reputation. Nations put efforts into nation branding with the help of various branding techniques" (Lee, 2009). Countries and governments began to create their own image and create symbols to signify it before the academic foundations of the field of communication were laid, even before defining branding as a concept.

Governments are facing strong competition to ensure economic growth and sustainable development. It is even more crucial in this age of globalization to attract foreign currency through investors, tourists, and qualified labor force to increase competitive advantages. Governments work on mobilizing all of their resources to secure new markets and lay down the necessary foundations for sustainable development.

Governments now use different means to convey their position and explain their policies. Often, they develop commercial marketing techniques into communication strategies to help boosting the nation's brand.

Perhaps the most evident indication of this is the state's flag, which is raised to indicate the uniqueness of each country. The flag is the brand symbol of countries, and it has long preceded the definition of what brand means. The flag becomes the sign by which we connect our relationship with nations. The flag is not just a piece of cloth, or a drawing to differentiate between states. Rather, it is a symbol of perceptions, concepts, values, and cultural norms that distinguish one country from another. The flag is the link of the perceptions or ideas formed about a country and the thoughts and immediate awareness of its nationhood.

The nation uses its thoughts, perceptions and patterns as the primary messages that are linked to specific symbolic images. This helps them in the process of storing these symbols and evoking them when needed.

In this era, governments are counting more on nation branding to create real connection with different countries. It is important to win the hearts and minds of foreign people to ensure deeper connections and facilitate the cash flow to the country through different means and across different sectors. Nation brands are developed to portray the values, identity, and perceptions of the people and the government. They are tailored to portray the image and the identity of the country through strong messaging, symbols, and tools. That was the case, for example, for the successful nation brand creation for Estonia (Kentie, 2020).

Many countries owe part of their successful development to their nation brand, entitling them to more advantages in comparison to other countries. In one report prepared by Brand Finance (Brand Directory, 2020), the importance of the relation of nation brand with economic power is displayed, including the development of tourism based on number of arrivals. In fact, the top ten ranked countries in nation branding hold the most economic power, compared to those with weak nation branding. Also, eight of the top ten ranked countries in nation brand have the highest numbers of arrivals.

Any successful nation's brand should follow a roadmap to achieve four main objectives:
- To promote the nation's brand for others to know the main characteristics of the nation.
- To ensure a connection with other people through a deep understanding of these characteristics.
- To create a positive interaction that serves the interests of the nation at many levels.
- To guarantee an advocacy role from others in favors of the nation's brand and interests.

A nation's brand is not a one-way process, where one nation promotes its strategy and expects others to blindly follow its perspective. Rather, it is a proactive approach that is continuously developing through interaction with other countries' perspectives, interests, and needs. It requires a thorough follow-up process and regular updates to adapt to the necessary changes and modify a country's goals and objectives.

QATAR BRANDING

Many players and factors influence the development of nation brand positively or negatively. Those include the use of a long-term effective tool — the media, which nowadays is best exemplified through social media platforms, and promotion tactics.

Nations who are attempting to create a national brand face many challenges, especially when their image and position is negative in the world. Nation branding requires more effort from those nations to reverse the damage to the nation's brand and create strategies to ensure a good positioning.

Our study here examines how a new brand for Qatar can boost the nation's global and regional positioning and the positive sentiment toward it. Achieving these two major goals will boost the nation's competitiveness in attracting more investors and tourists, which will further steer the state towards the diversification of the economy. To achieve that, it is important to study the challenges that Qatar faces regarding its brand and the key element of that brand, especially Qatar's image.

Qatar faces many challenges on different dimensions when it comes to nation branding. The nation brand is not well established, or at least it is not clear for the public. In the previous chapter, we reviewed the Ministry of Culture and Sports and their work towards creating cultural change in an effort to produce new perspectives, whilst adopting universal human perceptions and values. A potential challenge may be that many entities are working independently to create the positive image of Qatar and promote it to the external public. A unified strategy on how to approach this matter is vital, in order to enhance coordination between those entities to agree on the main goals and create a plan to achieve those goals.

Another major challenge that Qatar faces is the ineffective media presence in international outlets and the negative labeling or politicized journalism targeting Qatar. In most cases the media time is more reactive and less proactive. Qatar is labelled negatively when it comes to workers' welfare regardless of the immense progress in preserving workers' rights. Another issue that negatively affects Qatar's image in the media is the alleged connections to and the financing of terrorist groups, especially the intensive accusations from countries in conflict with Qatar during the blockade. In addition, Qatar's wealth is labeled negatively sometimes. It is perceived as purchasing power, where anything can be bought without giving the necessary weight to the cultural or investment aspects of the deal.

On the other hand, Qatar enjoys many advantages that can enable and influence the nation brand positively. A key factor to understand these elements and utilize them better lies in the creation of a comprehensive communication plan to promote the nation brand and achieve the communication strategy goals.

By the end of 20th century and the beginning of the 21st century, Qatar's branding image was created through three major pillars: the media through Aljazeera Network, Qatar's mediator role in regional conflicts, and its position as a key host of international sports championships and events.

Qatar has used media diplomacy for years to advance its nation brand. Al Jazeera Media Network was established in 1996 to cover news and political events, and to help express Qatar's point of view and political positions. All of this was done while ensuring an objective approach and coverage of the political events in the region and the world (Sultan, 2011). Another media outlet focused on sports was developed, as beIN Sports was launched in 2014. The network is a rebrand of Al Jazeera Sports, which was established in 2003. beIN Sports is an essential part of Qatar's new branding strategy as host of mega sport events (beIN Media Group, 2020).

Al Jazeera network is a key pillar for Qatar's public diplomacy. Al Jazeera helped Qatar to reach out to Arabic language speaking audience at the first stage and to English speaking audiences at a later stage. The role of Al Jazeera was effective at certain levels and challenging on many others. Although it cannot be denied that Aljazeera has helped create a Qatari media presence and positioned Qatar in the region and the world, at the same time it has created many challenges because of an editorial line that is not welcomed by many countries.

Another key element to Qatar's image is its active role in political mediations and by extension an agreements brokering role. Qatar has developed and maintained many political relationships regionally, internationally, and sub-nationally with many political players in many states. This has allowed Qatar to play a successful mediator role in many regional conflicts and enabled its role as a broker of many political deals for different countries. That role was effective to reach deals between Lebanese factions in 2008, and to resolve the Darfur long-term conflict. In his chapter "Qatar's Resilience Strategy and Implications for State–Society Relations," Abdullah Baabood affirms this by mentioning:

> The image that Qatar was able to achieve has given it a recognized status within the international community as a country that promotes peace and stability. As such it has occasionally been called upon by global powers to help in resolving other conflicts such as those in Afghanistan, Israel–Palestine and Yemen, thereby building goodwill, diplomatic relationships and alliances that add a further dimension to its security and the resilience of the state (Baabood, 2017).

In the sports scene, Qatar consistently played a key role in hosting sports tournaments and championships since the early 1990's. Up to 2020, more than 30 international sports events, and many regional and domestic sports championships were hosted by Qatar on a yearly basis (Baabood, 2017). Qatar's advanced development, organizational and managerial skills, along with its hospitality and welcoming values helped in hosting those events. These events successfully created a positive image of Qatar as a hosting country that is capable of delivering major sports projects and events.

At this stage, Qatar is living a new era in nation branding and image creation. New developments on many levels and sectors have helped to tailor a new brand that serves positioning Qatar positively, and ensuring a proactive role of Qatar on the international scene.

Sports events are still a major sector for Qatar's branding. Many events will be hosted by Qatar such as the FIFA World Cup Qatar™, which is one of the most important global sports events.

Qatar has a long history of hosting major events in sports. The quantity of tournaments expresses the high confidence of the international sports community in the capabilities of Qatar in organizing and managing such tournaments.

Hosting these events helped Qatar develop the necessary infrastructure, especially in terms of the unique sports facilities. Qatar continuously aims to achieve the highest levels of creativity and the best quality standards when hosting major events. These facilities are a major investment for the state, which benefit the local community and the international community. Hosting mega sport events helps shape Qatar's brand as a key international organizer and host.

Hosting sports events is not only a sports achievement. In fact, it is an opportunity for cultural interaction and exchange between different countries and people. It is an opportunity for rapprochement between people, despite their differences, and contributes to strengthening ties between them. These tournaments create opportunities to get to know Qatar as a center for dialogue, and exchange of ideas.

The cultural interaction resulting from hosting sports event is a key pillar to creating Qatar's national brand. Visitors are exposed to a rich cultural experience when they interact with the different aspects of the Qatari local culture. They get the chance to understand the values and perceptions of the Qatari society, focusing on the main common human values.

In addition to sports and culture, education plays a great role in shaping Qatar's image as a center for education and development in the region. Qatar Foundation plays a critical role because of its global initiatives that created international connections and active engagement of the Qatari state on a global level over the past two decades.

Qatar Foundation is an organization working in education, research, and community development. More than 50 entities supported by partnerships with leading international institutions address the most recent challenges to create global opportunities, and empower people to shape the present and the future (Qatar Foundation, 2020).

Meanwhile, Qatar Airways, the Qatari flagship airlines, played a great role in promoting Qatar. It flies Qatar's name all over the world and has sponsored one of the most famous football clubs in the world named FC Barcelona, in addition to developing a portfolio of football club sponsorships around the world and being a sponsor of FIFA tournaments. Qatar Airways will always be a key communication tool to promote Qatar's branding and image.

The most prevalent challenge in creating Qatar's nation branding emerges in the tourism sector. Major changes hit this sector so quickly after the blockade in 2017, which enforced a need for quick adaptations and variations in these sectors. Tourism authorities focused initially on portraying Qatar as a destination for family tourism with tourists and visitors from the GCC region as its main target. However, after the blockade everything changed drastically, as the flow of visitors from the GCC stopped completely, and new markets were needed to jump-start the sector again.

We believe that these four sectors are essential in creating Qatar's branding. In addition, external messaging should include the well-developed infrastructure sector, helping to shape Qatar's branding. Legislations are being modernized to meet investment needs, to allow faster processing for new investments, and especially to allow foreign investors to easily access the Qatari Market. Infrastructure development is taking place at a fast pace; the transportation sector reached a well-developed level in the past years through an international award-winning airport, the Hamad International Airport, which is one of the best airports in the world, and through the opening of Hamad Port. Equally the new well-maintained network of roads and the state-of-the-art Doha Metro have added new transportation options for Qatar. Services are meeting the highest standards, especially in the communications, information, and technology sectors.

In writing down Qatar's nation branding, communication strategists need to evaluate Qatar's interests and asses the advantages and risks to tailor a better branding strategy that effectively serves the interests of the state. By clearly identifying Qatar's nation brand vision, nation brand goals, nation brand strategy, and the nation brand operation, the result will be a well-developed nation branding plan.

CULTURAL DIVERSITY SHAPING QATAR'S BRANDING

Cultural diversity refers to the plurality and the presence of different cultural backgrounds among members of the same community. The relationships between individuals from diverse cultures should be based on respect and tolerance, in addition to enjoying equal rights.

Cultural diversity is a debatable concept, as it generally refers to a reality of coexistence of different cultures in the same society or country. Regardless of the approach taken to define cultural diversity, "the core theme of discussing it always is equity and justice, whose meanings vary widely, ranging from showing equal respect for all cultures to maintaining cultural diversity, to recognizing all identities associated with cultures, and to transforming social systems." (Lin, 2020, p.4).

Qatar is a great example of a diverse community. In 2020, Qatar's population was just over 2.7 million people (Qatari Planning and Statistics Authority, 2020).

There is no official data available regarding exact percentage of different nationalities, but Snoj, Jure, (2019), present a comprehensive report, stating that expatriates come from over 94 different nationalities. The majority of the population residing in Qatar is Muslim. In addition, there are large groups of Hindus and Christians, with smaller groups of Buddhist and those who believe in other religions.

The different cultures, languages, and nationalities coexisting in the Qatari society have represented a driving force for the development of Qatar in all fields and have influenced its local culture. Qatari society is unique in its openness to the different cultures of the world, and is rich with the plurality of cultures and the diversity of its residents. This diversity helps in categorizing Qatar as an open and cohesive nation.

Promoting cultural diversity contributes to building sustainable relations between people and nations based on acceptance of others and mutual respect. Respect for cultural diversity is key to building peace between countries, and a pre-condition for achieving domestic stability.

The main challenge that any forward-thinking nation faces, including Qatar, is the dilemma of the preservation of national identity while remaining open to interact with other cultures and identities. Qatar has acknowledged preserving national identity as a challenge of development. In the National Development Strategy 2018 – 2022 report it is mentioned that:

> "Modernization while preserving traditions comes on top of these challenges. The ever-increasing inflows of culturally and linguistically diverse expatriate workers and their dependents may potentially affect traditional Qatari and Islamic cultural values and identity" (NDS-2 2018-2022).

Qatar approaches its national identity with an open mind. As discussed earlier in Chapter Four, major progress is underway on societal perceptions and value levels. Efforts were made to enforce a new approach of national identity that promotes Qatari society's interest in fostering common human values. This open approach to national identity and societal values will allow a more open society, made stronger by its values that embrace ideals of justice, fairness, and human dignity.

New legislations were issued to guarantee equal rights for all people residing in Qatar, especially the rights of workers to guarantee quality life and employment rights. In addition to that, Qatar has canceled the Kafala system which restricted employees from freely change employers.

Qatar understands the importance of culture as a tool of soft power, and an effective communications channel. Major efforts were made in the past two decades on many levels to ensure an effective cultural infrastructure that allowed for the co-existence of all cultures in the society in an equal and just manner.

Qatar believes that supporting cultural diversity is a way to achieve peace in the world. In addition to being a resource to enable human creativity in various fields, Qatar considered cultural diversity as part of the objectives it seeks to achieve. The Qatar National Vision 2030 and the National Development Strategy 2018-2022 both emphasize achieving three goals in this area (NDS-2 (2018-2022)):

- Intensify and promote cultural exchange with the Arab peoples and other peoples in general.
- Foster and support dialogue among civilizations and coexistence among different religions and cultures.
- Contribute to realizing international peace and security through political initiatives and development and humanitarian aid.

Qatar created many initiatives to encourage cultural diversity and promote it both internally and externally. This includes dialogue of civilizations, cultural years, and translation, as we will see in the following sections.

Dialogue of Civilizations

Qatar expressed its belief in promoting dialogue, especially dialogue between religions. The Doha International Centre for Interfaith Dialogue was established in 2010 aiming at "supporting, strengthening, developing, and spreading the principle of dialogue between religions and the peaceful co-existence between religious followers and all humanity, as well as promoting religious values for healing human issues and problems" (Qatari Emiri Decree No. 20, Article 3, 2010).

The center was established by an Amiri Decree. H.H. the Amir stated that the center's aim is: "to contribute to enriching the culture of peaceful co-existence and acceptance, and to promoting the role of religious values in healing human issues and problems, and to expanding the dialogue to include all aspects of life in relation to religion" (Qatari Amiri Decree No. 20, Preamble, 2010).

Despite the fact that the establishment decree was issued in 2010, conferences following the same theme were conducted as early as 2003 under the title "Freedom of Religion." This was followed by a second conference in 2004 entitled "Building Bridges". A third conference was held in 2005 entitled "The role of religions in building human civilization".

Intellectuals and representatives of major religions (Islam, Christianity and Judaism), as well as a select group of religious scholars, academics and heads of interfaith dialogue centers from around the world attended the forums. Those conferences allow those who are interested in interfaith and intercultural dialogue to address issues of concern to their societies. In addition, they discuss challenges of peaceful coexistence between different religions and cultures; and foster a culture of peace among human beings (Doha International Center for Interfaith Dialogue, 2020).

The center grants an award called "The Doha International Religious Dialogue Award." The award encourages the efforts and initiatives of individuals and institutions that have had a significant impact in promoting dialogue and fostering a culture of peace.

Another initiative to promote "Dialogue of Civilizations" is the Qatari Committee for the Alliance of Civilizations, established by the Council of Ministers' resolution No. (8) of 2010. The committee works to achieve the human goal of peaceful coexistence, acceptance of others, and respect for different peoples and cultures. It seeks to achieve closer cooperation between races, religions, and cultures by laying the foundations of solidarity and the exchange of experiences based on the values of truth, justice, and equality ("Qatari Committee for the Alliance of Civilizations", 2019).

An additional initiative to promote openness and rapprochement between societies and people is the "Qatar International Prize for Dialogue of Civilizations." In 2018, the Committee's collaboration with ICESCO (the Islamic World Educational, Scientific and Cultural Organization), and the College of Sharia and Islamic Studies at Qatar University resulted in the launch of this prize.

Years of Culture

The "Years of Culture" is an annual initiative for cultural exchange between Qatar and other cultures. Qatar began organizing the Years of Culture in 2012 with the cooperation with Japan. Since then, the initiative has become an opportunity to exchange knowledge, ideas, values, and customs. Over the past years, Qatar has cooperated with different countries including Brazil (2014), Turkey (2015), China (2016), Germany (2017), Russia (2018), India (2019), France (2020), and the USA (2021).

Each year of culture runs a cultural exchange program that "aims to convey Qatar to an international audience through a variety of exhibitions, festivals, competitions and events. The programs promote mutual understanding, recognition, and appreciation between countries. They invite people to explore their cultural similarities, as well as their differences" (Qatar Museums, 2020). In fact, the overall impact of the years of culture varies according to the legacy of each program, and the initiatives that are created between entities from Qatar and other countries.

For Qatar Museums, the Years of Culture form a fundamental pillar of cultural diplomacy. Through this mechanism Qatar invites people to explore cultural similarities and differences. It allows the exchange of ideas, art, information, and dialogue among peoples towards broader cooperation and mutual understanding between countries (Al-Sharq News, 2018).

The Years of Culture initiative was successful in introducing the world to Qatari culture more widely, while also allowing Qatar citizens and residents to learn more about other cultures. It has encouraged dialogue through cross-border cultural exchange. The initiative also facilitates understanding of the values of Qatari society and conveying Qatar's voice to different cultural discussions.

The Years of Culture encourages the use of all cultural forms to challenge stereotypes, overcome cultural barriers, and open intellectual horizons on both sides. In addition, it promotes mutual understanding, recognition, and appreciation between the two countries concerned, through projects conducted throughout each cultural year.

Cultural Diversity Activities

Qatar is a culturally rich country with a wide variety of cultural activities. These activities are great opportunities for people in Qatar to interact with different cultures and get to know each other. Many cultural diversity events are organized annually, which provides open cultural spaces for residents and citizens to interact and learn about different cultures.

The Cultural Village Foundation, Katara, is a great example of a cultural space that promotes cultural diversity. The Cultural Village Foundation provide opportunities for human interaction through art and cultural exchange.

Katara Cultural Village is a place where people come together to experience the cultures of the world. With its beautiful theatres, concert halls, exhibition galleries and cutting-edge facilities, Katara aims to become a world leader for multi-cultural activities (Katara, 2020). It also keeps pace with the different global and cultural trends that emphasize the importance of diversity in human development.

This project was made possible thanks to the vision of H.H. Sheikh Hamad Bin Khalifa Al Thani, the Father Amir of the State of Qatar (Katara, 2020).

Katara, in addition to many projects and initiatives, organizes "The Cultural Diversity Festival" to introduce the world's cultures and the artistic and folkloric heritage of other countries. In the first three editions, the festival has presented performances that reflect on the cultures and arts of different countries in the world. This festival confirms Katara's keenness to maintain cultural interaction and human openness to connect people from different backgrounds.

Furthermore, the Ministry of Culture and Sports continues to organize the Francophone Days in cooperation with the Embassy of France, and other French-speaking embassies. This event increases the opportunities for cultural dialogue and builds a bridge of communication between Qatar and France.

Different institutions organize activities and events that support the promotion of cultural understanding. One example is the Communities Music Festival, where music plays a major role in bringing people closer and spreading common human values.

Translation

Translation plays an important role in cultural exchange and bridging the gaps between different societies and people. Translation helps in expanding the fields of dialogue and promotes diversity and pluralism. Qatar has undertaken several official and private initiatives to promote cultural exchange through translation.

Perhaps the most prominent initiative is the Sheikh Hamad Award for Translation and International Understanding, founded in 2015. This award is important and foundational in promoting language and understanding as:

The Award seeks to honor translators and acknowledge their role in strengthening the bonds of friendship and cooperation amongst peoples and nations of the world. It hopes to reward merit and excellence, encourage creativity, uphold the highest moral and ethical standards, and spread the values of diversity, pluralism, and openness. The Award also aspires to inculcate a culture of knowledge and dialogue, promote Arab and Islamic culture, develop international understanding, and encourage mature cross-cultural interaction between Arabic and other world languages through the medium of translation (Hamad Awards, 2020).

The Ministry of Culture and Sports also emphasizes translation as a major factor in cultural diversity. The translation of international literary and intellectual works into Arabic, and the translation of Qatari literature into foreign languages, helps to improve understanding with other cultures.

Expat Communities Radio Stations

The Ministry of Culture and Sports supported different expatriate communities to create and run radio stations. These radio stations help communities to feel at home in Qatar and play an important role in creating opportunities for cultural dialogue.

There is a long list of cultural diversity projects and initiatives that help create, promote, and sustain Qatar's branding. It portrays Qatar as a nation that is embracing cultural diversity through active work, which is important to make a great use of the country's cultural diversity characteristic as part of nation branding.

Having cultural diversity as a key pillar of Qatar's branding will require a deep understanding of developing effective cultural diversity initiatives and programs by key stakeholders. Most importantly, the stakeholders need to have a deeper understanding of proactive promotion of those programs as a part of the national strategy to enforce Qatar's image and create a positive perception of the country.

FIFA WORLD CUP QATAR 2022™ AND QATAR'S BRANDING

Over the past years, Qatar has hosted a series of prestigious sporting mega events. These mega-events create developments opportunities for the host country on many levels, including its economy and infrastructure. Furthermore, it boosts the host nation's branding and communication strategies.

The Chief Executive of the South African World Cup 2010 Organizing Committee, Danny Jordaan, stated: "[The World Cup] is about nation building, it's about infrastructure improvement, it's about country branding, it's about repositioning, it's about improving the image of our country, and it's about tourism promotion. It's also about return on investment, job creation and legacy. These are the things that drive not only our nation but the nations of the world." (Allmers & Maennig, 2009). Sports mega-events present nation branding opportunities for nations lacking nation branding, facing an image crisis, or aiming to promote a rebrand or image change.

Media Exposure

Hosting sports events attracts media outlets from around the world, especially the top-tier global media including broadcast (TV and Radio), written press, digital and social media.

Media coverage follows two paths: the first is through mainstream media outlets, and the second is through social media platforms.

Media professionals in general and social media influencers in specific play a significant role in engaging audiences as part of covering those sports events.

The FIFA World Cup Qatar 2022™ is a golden opportunity for Qatar to promote its branding through a well-tailored communications strategy. A key factor for Qatar is the ownership of beIN sports, a world class sports channel covering major worldwide sports events like Olympics and FIFA World Cup tournaments, with exclusive rights in the MENA region (Middle East and North Africa area).

beIN Sports has exclusive rights for the FIFA World Cup Qatar 2022™ in the MENA region, with shared rights in different countries like France with TF1 (FIFA, 2016).

What beIN Sports has to offer to Qatar is totally different than any other host country. beIN Sports is a Qatari media outlet that offers a great leverage for Qatar in promoting the country's branding. Television is still the main media outlet to cover sports events, but in recent years online platforms have provided an extensive coverage of sports events, especially the social developments around the event itself. With billions of users around the world, social media platforms provide a new media tool that is independent from the mainstream media. The case study of the FIFA World Cup Brazil 2014™ proves the importance of utilizing social media platforms to cover sports events. The World Cup was the "Top Global Topic" on Facebook and the "most talked about global moment" on Twitter (Finn, 2014). Visitors could become brand ambassadors for the host country. Thus, special attention should be given to social media coverage and the utilizations of these platforms to serve the host country's interests.

New Image Opportunity

Hosting a sports mega-event requires the commitment of the host government to take all necessary actions to meet the expectations and develop necessary infrastructure. At the same time, a lot of effort is required to design the right branding to successfully promote the event. Many entities are required to work together to secure a successful nation brand, help create a positive image, and influence the economic growth through the development of different sectors.

Qatar needs to maintain the momentum of hosting the FIFA World Cup™ by laying down a clear brand with specific targets, maximizing the benefits of organizing the tournament, and increasing the global recognition of Qatar's nation brands.

The GCO (Government Communication Office) role in this matter is crucial. The Office is charged with leading the process of brand creation and maximizing the positive effect of the FIFA World Cup™ moment.

Public Diplomacy

Hosting a sports mega-event is a public diplomacy moment in which the host countries is able to gain global recognition by organizing such events. Most countries count on soft power in addition to hard power to advocate for their policies on an international level, and to promote their approaches to local and international matters: "'Soft power' provides a useful lens through which to capture the motives of advanced capitalist states and, increasingly, 'emerging' states, for bidding for and hosting sports 'mega events', it tells us little about the mechanisms used to leverage such events for social, economic or reputational benefits" (Grix, 2013). Thus, hosting the FIFA World Cup™ in 2022 provides Qatar with a great advantage to boost its new branding with a more positive image internationally.

In fact, this moment is not related to the event only. It is a process that starts by bidding to host such an event and continues for a time after the tournament is hosted. Qatar is already using this event and sports events as means of leverage and a means of creating a positive image of Qatar as a welcoming host, key organizer on the international scale, and a country that is capable to receive millions of tourists.

Having this important hosting opportunity does not guarantee a positive image of the host country because it needs great attention in tailoring the nation brand and the image that needs to be promoted. This will be achieved through making the best possible impression on media and creating a plan for long-term image management and a brand maintenance strategy.

Engagement and Loyalty

The FIFA World Cup Qatar 2022™ presents a great chance for engagement with global audiences and creates a connection to form a certain degree of positive sentiment and loyalty toward the host country. One highly unique aspect of a sport mega-event is: "the emotional appeal, connection and degree of attachment that the event creates with its global audiences. The FIFA World Cup was described as an event with a large global appeal. It is hard to find other examples of events or occurrences that capture the attention of the global audience combined with the shared emotional attachment of passion that transcends many global divisions such as language, race, religion, and nationality" (Knott, Fyall, & Jones, 2017). This would be an opportunity for multi-platforms engagement activities and initiatives to connect with the audience in Qatar and worldwide.

This event can transform Qatar into an unforgettable experience destination through a wide range of programs, leveraging the opportunity of having all the games easily accessible within a short distance from each other by Doha Metro. In addition, special online promotion programs allow for engaging connections with audiences around the globe.

EDUCATION AND RESEARCH: GLOBAL APPROACH FOR A BETTER FUTURE

Qatar has shown a great interest in investing in education and research over the past decades, with a significant focus on education for building a better future. Qatar National Vison 2030 and the National Development Strategies nurture a culture of education and local knowledge production. Extensive development plans and initiatives were put into action on the local and external level. It is therefore important for us to shed a light on the role Qatar Foundation plays in creating and sustaining Qatar's nation branding.

For over 20 years, Qatar Foundation, under the leadership of H.H. Sheikha Moza bint Nasser, has worked to drive regional innovation and entrepreneurship and fostered a culture of lifelong learning and development.

Education City is an educational hub with branch campuses of some of the world's most reputable educational institutes. It is home to eight branches of American, British, and French universities, along with Hamad Bin Khalifa University, the home-grown Qatari university. This collective institution presents a unique model of education in the region, aiming to benefit Qatar and the rest of the world (Qatar Foundation, 2020).

Qatar Foundation and its higher education facilities present a comprehensive Education City ranging from the school system and the pre-university education to the university education. Thirteen schools covering all regions of Qatar provide high standard education by offering primary and secondary education through schools operated by Qatar Foundation. Students have the chance to take advantage of many pre-university programs, from IB-accredited school systems to specialized schools (Qatar Foundation, 2020).

Qatar Foundation believes in making Qatar a leading hub for research and innovation. It is home to a dozen research centers that serve Qatar and the world through innovation: "The Research, Development, and Innovation (RDI) ecosystem of Qatar Foundation was created to place Qatar at the forefront of scientific research and technological advancement, addressing national needs while generating global impact" (Qatar Science & Technology Park, 2020).

Qatar Foundation's core mission is creating an ecosystem for national and international students and entrepreneurs. Students who are passionate about technology can finish their school, and follow their college specialization at Carnegie Mellon University at Qatar Foundation. In addition, they can conclude their research at Qatar Computing Research Institute (QCRI) which focuses on tackling large-scale computing challenges (Qatar Foundation, 2020). They can also launch their startup at Qatar Science and Technology Park (QSTP), which is a hub for applied research, technology innovation, incubation, and entrepreneurship (Qatar Foundation, 2020).

A similar path is set for students pursuing a career in medicine. They can finish their studies at Weill Cornell Medicine-Qatar, then finalize their research at many institutions including Qatar Biobank, Qatar Genome Programme, and Qatar Biomedical Research Institute (Qatar Foundation, 2020). They can also practice medicine at Sidra Medicine, which provides children, women, and young people with healthcare services in an innovative and ultra-modern facility, especially designed to promote recovery (Sidra Medicine, 2020).

Qatar Foundation is a local foundation with global aspirations. It is a great educational pillar in the region that provides a well-maintained ecosystem. One of Qatar Foundation's most reputable educational initiatives on the global scale is World Innovation Summit for Education (WISE).

WISE was launched in 2009, with a biennial summit organized in Doha, and different initiatives around the year. WISE is an international, multi-sectoral platform for creative thinking, debate, and purposeful action, and aims to promote innovation and build the future of education through collaboration (WISE, 2020).

Since 2009, WISE gathered opinions from leaders, decision-makers, and practitioners from around the world at the Summit in Doha, Qatar to explore innovative solutions and initiatives aspiring to aid the development of education worldwide.

An important initiative launched by WISE is the "WISE Prize for

Education". The prize was established in 2011 to recognize an individual or a team for an outstanding, world-class contribution to education. The WISE Prize for Education raises the status of education by giving it similar prestige to other areas for which international prizes exist – such as literature, peace, and economics (WISE, 2020). WISE is a key international platform for education and is bringing new innovative approaches for education, and most definitely is not the only international educational initiative launched by Qatar.

In 2012, H.H. Sheikha Moza bint Nasser founded Education Above All (EAA). The organization aims to contribute to human, social, and economic development through the provision of quality education. The organization shares a particular focus on those affected by poverty, conflict, and disaster (Education Above All, 2020).

Educate a Child (EAC) is the key program which aims to significantly reduce the numbers of children worldwide who are deprived from exercising their right to education (Education Above All, 2020). Four key programs help achieve EAC's mission to ensure inclusive and equitable quality education for vulnerable and marginalized people, especially in the developing world. Since its inception, the Educate A Child initiative has implemented 74 projects in 51 countries. To date, EAC's actual enrolment surpasses more than 10.4 million out of school children, and enrollment commitments with excess of 12.8 million. (Education Above All, 2022.

Reach Out to Asia (ROTA) is another initiative by EAA that works to bring about a world where every young person has a sense of belonging to a common humanity. Together with its partners, volunteers, and local communities, ROTA works to ensure that young people across Asia, and around the world have access to the training they need to make a positive difference in their own lives and in the lives of their communities (Education Above All, 2020).

Protect Education in Insecurity and Conflict (PEIC) is another initiative that promotes and protects the right to education. Whether through death and injury, damaged buildings, disruption, fear or migration, times of unrest have a profound effect on learning (Education Above All, 2020).

Al Fakhoora launched its first projects, as a response to the conflict in Gaza that destroyed numerous schools and universities. Following the higher education and empowerment scholarship program in Gaza, Al Fakhoora has begun replicating this approach on a multi-country scale. Dynamic Futures has expanded to six new regions to support Palestinians in the West Bank, and Syrian IDP's and refugees in Syria, Turkey, Lebanon, Jordan, and Iraq (Education Above All, 2020).

Under the vision and leadership of H.H. Sheikha Moza bint Nasser, Qatar's high investment in education is paying off in a significant way by achieving long-term educational goals.

Qatar demonstrated a strong commitment to provide new educational opportunities and to enhance the existing ones in Qatar and worldwide. This role is attributed to Qatar's commitment to human common principles, where knowledge and science are key factors to national development and to secure peace worldwide.

This important role based on common values, is being employed as another pillar of Qatar's nation branding. This helps to enforce Qatar's civilized image and creates more positive sentiments about the country.

TOURISM: PROMOTING UNFORGETTABLE EXPERIENCES IN QATAR

Developing the tourism sector is a key pillar to diversifying the economy. This requires extensive work on two levels: the first through creating a definition for the tourism sector and growing it, and the second by developing a communication strategy supported by a strong marketing plan to attract tourists. It is important to understand what we are promoting, and for whom. Instead of a destination promotion, the most successful campaigns are centered around an experience promotion. Tourists are looking for an authentic experience. They want to live joyful moments, which would eventually transform into unforgettable memories. Travels and tourism are sources for happy moments, which constitute a life-long collective memory of our happiness. People travel to experience new places and cultures as a means for them to experience fulfilment and happiness.

Every tourist has a unique taste and preference. Some search for a different experience to feed their senses or mind, while others aim for a balance between their senses and their mind. Tourism is a journey in time, taste, and one's own soul. Tourists search for experiences to learn, develop, and enjoy the world around them. They work to make connections through history and heritage to understand the world around them and reflect on their own views of it. They analyze the present through associations and simulations with the past. This happens through archeological site visits and museum discoveries. They dig into other people's perceptions and values, compare it to their own, and conclude with a better vision of the world and themselves.

This is what tourists look for, and these kinds of experiences should be guaranteed for tourists visiting Qatar. Qatar is not merely a destination; Qatar is an experience, one that is never lived or experienced at any other destination.

Qatar also faces challenges in the tourism sector, and the most important challenge is related to Qatar's nation branding. Many challenges arose in the past years, mainly since the blockade in 2017. Before 2017, most tourists came from Saudi Arabia (more than 30%) and the GCC for family tourism (Qatar Tourism Authority). Qatar was promoted in the region as a family-friendly destination, especially for conservative families in comparison to the lavish touristic experience in the neighboring UAE. After 2017, everything changed for the tourism sector. The focus is shifting from being a family hub in the region to being a touristic center for the world.

Another challenge is concerned with creating a unique tourism experience. A question that arises is: what would be the nature of this tourism experience in the future? Should it be leisure and entertainment, business events, sports and recreation, culture and heritage, or health and wellness, or a mix of all these experiences? And what would make the Qatar tourism experience so special, for those who have chosen it as a touristic destination on their 'bucket list'?

Another challenge may be the society's welcoming nature and acceptance of others from different backgrounds and cultures. Qatar has made a great progress in this area, and Qatari society is becoming more open and welcoming to others while preserving the core values of society. Generally, Qatari people are known to be very hospitable because the diversity of cultures in Qatar has helped in enforcing this characteristic of society.

Knowing these challenges will help Qatar work on ways to overcome them and move towards a more developed tourism sector. Qatar enjoys a variety of touristic characteristics and resources that are utilized in the main branches of Qatar's tourism sector. The conventional '3S's', which refer to "Sun, Sand, Sea", would always be relevant for Qatar, especially for tourists who needs to escape the coldness of the winter and enjoy the beautiful, moderate winter climate in Qatar. The country will always be a beach destination for sea lovers, but these same destinations needs to adjust to meet a new range of touristic expectations. New and innovative tourism attractions, services and facilities are being offered to remain competitive to avoid stagnation or decline (Giampiccoli, & Mtapuri, 2015).

Another new branch developed in the past decade would be MICE, or "Meetings, Incentives, Conferences, Exhibitions" aspect of tourism. The potential challenges would be how to transform these business encounters to real touristic opportunities. Culture is always the key attraction for tourists, including festivals, heritage, history, arts and more. Qatar offers a wide range of attractions including museums, galleries, and archaeological sites (Al Zubarah has been listed as a UNESCO World Heritage Site), forts and towers that can be used for interesting city tours.

Nature is another unique feature of Qatar. Many tourism projects have been developed to benefit from the desert and the coastline for many activities including diving, truffle picking, swimming, and hunting. Significantly, Qatar has the largest gathering of whale sharks in the world, and a gathering of over 100 Dugongs in the North- West of Qatar's sea (Engle, 2018). The biodiversity in Qatari beaches should be utilized to encourage tourism.

Sports are a key factor to attract tourism and promote Qatar. Organizing sports events, especially mega-events, boosts Qatar's image, and creates opportunities to attract visitors, as well as promotion across numerous media and digital channels. Special landmarks are key attractions too, which include the Msheireb district, the traditional Souqs (Souq Waqif and Souq Al Wakrah), and the new Lusail city. A simple marketing strategy to promote all these features will not guarantee the flow of tourists. Thus, it has been essential to create a detailed strategy in order to create an AUP experiences for tourists: where AUP means authentic, unique, and personalized. Tourists search for unforgettable memories, through different unique experiences, meeting their personal aspirations and perceptions. In order to boost Qatar's AUP tourism experiences, the country is developing bold new approaches, and dreaming big for more attractive initiatives and projects.

Qatar has always been adventurous and continues to dream big. This is primarily what the tourism sector needs.

QATAR'S EXTERNAL COMMUNICATION STRATEGY OUTLINE

After reviewing the key pillars for Qatar's branding, we will outline a communication strategy that uses this branding framework and serves it at the same time. Qatar's Government Communications Office (GCO) is the authorized institution to outline Qatar's external communications strategy and coordinate the implementation with different stakeholders. The GCO played a significant role in containing two major crises: (1) an external one –the blockade that has started in 2017; and (2) an internal one—the COVID 19 pandemic that emerged in the beginning of 2020. The GCO also coordinates the key media interviews of high-level Qatari officials including their Excellencies the Ministers and CEO's of main Qatari entities, especially when it is related to foreign media interviews, foreign media releases about Qatar, and responses to these releases if needed.

By taking a more proactive approach an external communications strategy serves Qatar's main goals as indicated in Qatar National Vision 2030 and Qatar National development Strategy 2018-2022. This strategy has to outline the key goals and follow that up with implementation. The execution plan would be clear and include cross-sectorial coordination procedures to achieve optimal results.

According to *The FAO Foundations of Communication Strategy Design* handbook, a Strategy can be defined as a set of structured procedures, which combine various means and methods in order to achieve a change or a main objective through the use of available resources in a specific period of time (Mefalopulos & Kamlongera, 2004).

Similarly, a communication strategy is a well-planned series of actions taken by one party aimed at achieving a change in the behavior or thoughts of a second party. In other terms, a communication strategy is a plan for communicating information related to a specific issue, event, situation, or audience.

Communication strategies serve as the blueprints for communicating with the public, stakeholders, or even colleagues (United States Environmental Protection Agency, n.d.).

Many researchers and communication strategists use different principles for effective communication. A large group of communication strategists insist on using the five "C's", but there remains no consensus on the meaning of all the five "C's". We agree much more with the five "C's" stated by the Berghof Foundation for effective communication:
- Credible: not to undermine credibility. Facts, statistics, and other data presented should be always correct.
- Comprehensive: cover all aspects of the matters in place. Have at least one document that provides background details and a comprehensive picture of the conflict.
- Consistent: the core messages and information disseminated should be consistent, although the delivery channels might differ depending on the audience.
- Continuous: frequent and continuous outreach is important.
- Collaborative: while respecting the independence of the media and other societal stakeholders, operate in a collaborative manner, establishing professional relationships and permanent contacts that will result in respect and empathy.

(Berghof Foundation, 2014).

The communication strategy should be short, precise and must include the following sections:
1. Background and Strategic Overview
2. Goals and Objectives
3. Target Groups of Audiences
4. Tailoring Key Messages
5. Communication Channels and Activities
6. Implementation Timeline
7. Budget and Human Resources
8. Evaluation

Background and Strategic Overview

Qatar is a small country in terms of space and is located in a region that is relatively unstable politically. The conflicts on a regional and international level may directly threaten Qatar's stability. Qatar's geopolitical location makes it vulnerable to tensions in the region, which was evident during the blockade which started in 2017. Thus, it needed an intense diplomatic campaign to limit the dramatic repercussions of the blockade.

Additionally, Qatar faces various economic challenges despite its strong economic performance. The high national income is threatened by fluctuations in oil and gas prices. Economic diversification projects are promising, but their results are not significantly influential at this stage. The dependency on the carbohydrate sector is strong. The desert nature of Qatar makes food security a permanent threat. In response to this problem, Qatar has sought to produce its food locally and through cooperation with foreign partners. These projects were accelerated after the 2017 blockade, where new routes were initiated, and many agricultural and livestock projects were developed in Qatar and abroad. Hassad Food is leading these projects, especially in Australia, Oman, and Qatar (Hassad Food, 2020). In addition, Qatar is seeking to move towards a knowledge-based society where knowledge and science are the main drivers of societal and national growth, despite its aims to preserve traditions as seen in the work of the Ministry of Culture and Sports.

These and other challenges make it necessary for Qatar to work on multiple fronts to diversify the economy by strengthening its diplomatic network and ties with many friendly countries. The challenges mentioned above, in addition to many others, were tackled in Qatar's National Vison 2030. Plans are underway to overcome these challenges. The key answer for all these challenges is sustainable development and introducing a holistic communications strategy to aid the development plan. Communication channels need to be constantly utilized to deliver the necessary messages to a targeted audience for greater impact.

Goals and Objectives

Qatar's National Vision 2030 did set the goal of sustainable development by highlighting development in four key sectors, namely the economic, social, human, and environmental areas. To achieve economic development, plans are focused on diversifying the economy by developing non-oil sectors and the carbohydrate sector. The main sectors of focus are the following:
- Knowledge-based Economy
- Tourism
- Transportation
- Industry: clean energy, food, steel
- Business and Financial Services

Based on Qatar National Vision's goals, the goal of achieving sustainable development is addressed through focusing on economic diversification to guarantee the sustainable well-being of citizens. The detailed plans of the 2030 Vision that is included in the National Development Strategy, would suggest a focus on the following three strategic goals for Qatar's external communication strategy:
- Promotion for the State of Qatar's culture and hospitality to attract tourists.
- Promotion of the State of Qatar's economic openness to attract foreign investments.
- Promoting Qatar's nation branding to enhance Qatar's national image and create a positive sentiment toward the state.

The first goal is concerned with tourism promotion. The promotion of a tourism experience in the State of Qatar can be done by presenting the elements of the experience. This includes cultural monuments, especially archaeological ones, and artistic, sports and cultural events, by focusing on an enriching experience for tourists that adds unforgettable memories to their tourist experiences.

As for the second goal, this entails a promotion of the general development that the country is experiencing. In particular, the state-specific features that attract investments on two main levels. The first level is concerned with the infrastructure including transportation, communications, and other similar sectors. The second is promoting investment opportunities.

Regarding the promotion of a positive image of the State of Qatar, it can be done by adopting Qatar's nation branding and promoting it. It should aim to strengthen cultural, political and economic ties with different countries to serve the state's position, its foreign relations, and its strategic interests.

These are the three strategic goals for a communication strategy. However, the goals cannot be achieved without the coordination among different stakeholders, and the specification of agreed sectorial objectives and roles. For example, in the cultural sector, the specific objectives could be the following:
- Develop cultural exchange by establishing strong cultural partnerships.
- Enforce cultural diversity initiatives and promoting it.
- Promote the cultural progress of the State of Qatar in various fields.
- Achieve cultural rapprochement with other nations and people.

Achieving these cultural sectorial objectives would serve the strategic goals mentioned earlier.

Target Groups of Audiences

In tailoring an audience map for Qatar's external communication strategy, we need to differentiate between two types of targeted audience and the nature of communication that suits that nature:
- Official communication of governments and government entities with their counterparts or with regional or international organizations
- Public communication when using communications channels to directly communicate with foreign people.

Also, another grouping of audience would be done based on sectors. This means targeting audience with specific sectorial interests. For Qatar's strategy, the sectors could be the following:
- Tourists
- Investors
- General public

Grouping the audience into segments is essential to ease communication with the targeted countries and the targeted audiences of those countries.

Tailoring Key Messages

In content, messages are an elaboration of Qatar's nation branding. Delivering the right message can be challenging, in terms of prioritizing the key messaging. What could be the focus?

Communication strategists needs to find the shortest and most effective messaging to introduce Qatar, win the hearts and minds of the audience, and at a final stage transform the audience to become potential advocates for Qatar. A slogan can be chosen by answering the following questions: Who is Qatar? What sector can deliver the messages? Reviewing the main four sectors would help communication strategists in deciding which sector should lead the external communication messaging. Is it the culture sector? The tourism sector? The sports sector? The education sector? Or is it a combination of two or more of these sectors? In terms of style, messages need to be credible, creative, comprehensive, consistent, and adaptable for different communication channels.

Communication Channels and Activities

There is a correlation between the targeted audience and the channels used. Every group of audience would need a specific way of communication to deliver messages more effectively. Channels are either direct like media outlets, or indirect like events. Successful strategies use a combination of different channels. The harmony between the messages and the channels is crucial for better effect. Even when the channel is direct, the messaging still needs to be subtle and modest.

Qatar has strong communication tools including media outlets (TV channels and web platforms) with strong regional and international presence; key international activities like conferences (Doha Forum, WISE, WISH…etc); sports events (FIFA World Cup Qatar 2022™, Tennis championships, FIM MotoGP, FEI Equestrian Global Champion Tour); and cultural events (years of culture, Doha International Book Fair). Deciding on the channels would be related to the targeted audience and the messages that need to be delivered.

Implementation Timeline

Setting a timeline for the strategy does not confine the planning only for long-term or short-term. Timelines could be a long-term strategy executed throughout shorter-time benchmarks. The communication strategy and the execution timeline need to be flexible to reflect the changes and the occurrence of current events. A timeline is a necessity to show commitment towards specific goals, projects scheduling, events, and campaigns. Thus, Qatar's communication strategy could be conducted over a five-year period with a timeline that includes detailed plans for projects and events.

Budget and Human Resources

Budgets are a crucial element for the success of any communication strategy, especially to finance direct campaigns. Qatar could allocate a yearly budget for its external communication strategy, but most importantly it could utilize the available communication assets and activities and coordinate the process accordingly. It is important that Qatar's communication strategy should be led by the GCO. This allows the GCO to evaluate the available communication resources, and communication procedures, and conduct a cost-benefit analysis to find the best low-cost approach for the strategy.

Evaluation

Recurrent scheduled evaluation is important to understand the effects of the projects and campaigns implemented. Evaluations should be conducted every six months with a market study, and on a yearly basis to assess the effectiveness of the strategy. This evaluation will help in reassessing the effectiveness of the strategy and updating the plans to reflect any changes in direction or the tools used. A flexible strategy is needed to allow room for changes when needed.

CONCLUSION

As mentioned earlier, the GCO's proactive role is a necessity for Qatar's national brand creation and adoption. In addition, this role is significant for tailoring the necessary external communication strategy to promote the national brand with an effective marketing plan. It may be challenging to coordinate the procedure with all the stakeholders, because of the independency that each stakeholder enjoys when pursuing their mission.

Another important challenge for the communication strategy is agreeing on cross-sector communication goals and a framework. Cross-sector promotion is important to have a comprehensive context for branding. Communication strategists need to put down specific procedures to facilitate the cross-sectoral co-operation.

In order to push the cultural promotion needed during sports events, there would be special activities tailored for those events. Organizers could follow the directions set by the communication strategists for a better outcome of these events.

Creating Qatar's branding is the cornerstone to promoting Qatar. Branding should relate to the receiving audience's experiences as a way to meet their expectations. The messages should be tailored carefully to match these expectations. We believe that branding should focus mainly on the cultural and touristic experiences, while creating special supportive aspects of branding through sports and education. This can be done by creating different cultural experiences for different audience segments to match tourist expectations and experiences in Qatar.

Culture is expressed in many ways including heritage, education, and sports. Heritage tell the story of a people, of a community; a story of the people's daily lives, movements, transportation, needs and much more. Most importantly, it tells a story of their values. Heritage is a value vessel; it is a time machine for values. Heritage brings people together, builds bridges, and lets people understand each other, and connect to each other. Sports is a key feature of any society and the societal perceptions of it can explain the degree of development of this society. Therefore, sports events would always be a key marketing tool in any host nation's history, but it only lasts for a moment that will eventually pass. The legacy left by organizing sports tournaments constitutes an opportunity for continuous communication with the fans of the sports and the public in general. Sports mega-events play a dual role in the nation branding. These events are part of the branding itself and are a communication tool to promote the nation's brand. Sports mega-events are a nation's effective marketing tool. It is important to have the marketing or promotion content ready, and the cornerstone for that is national branding. In addition, it is important to understand how to use this tool for an effective promotional campaign.

Education is a key in branding because it shows key values of the society in relation to knowledge and science. Societies believing in research and knowledge to find solutions to human and natural problems are usually open societies and share common values with other nations and societies. Education and sports should be promoted, but the key pillars for the branding creation of Qatar's identity could be culture and tourism.

Qatar has numerous well-developed sectors, and strong communication channels. Thus, it is essential to have a clear vision regarding how to promote the country, and where. The key questions that remain are: Who is Qatar? What is Qatar? Why is Qatar unique? These are the hardest questions for any nation to answer, but the answers help to give a clear direction to move forward as a nation and to attract tourists and investors.

REFERENCES

Al-Sharq News. (2018). Qatar's Participation in St. Petersbourgh Conference. Retrieved from https://al-sharq.com/article/14/11/2018/%D8%A7%D9%84%D9%85%D8%B4%D8%A7%D8%B1%D9%83%D8%A9-%D8%A7%D9%84%D9%82%D8%B7%D8%B1%D9%8A%D8%A9-%D9%81%D9%8A-%D9%85%D9%86%D8%AA%D8%AF%D9%89-%D8%B3%D8%A7%D9%86%D8%AA-%D8%A8%D8%B7%D8%B1%D8%B3%D8%A8%D9%88%D8%B1%D8%BA-%D8%AA%D8%B9%D8%B2%D8%B2-%D8%A7%D9%84%D8%AA%D8%A8%D8%A7%D8%AF%D9%84-%D8%A7%D9%84%D9%85%D8%B9%D8%B1%D9%81%D9%8A.

Allmers, Swantje & Maennig Wolfgang, (2009). Economic Impacts of the FIFA Soccer World Cups in France 1998, Germany 2006, and Outlook for South Africa 2010. *Eastern Economic Journal, 35*(4), 500–519. https://doi.org/10.1057/eej.2009.30

American Marketing Association. Branding. Retrieved from https://www.ama.org/topics/branding/

Baabood, A. (2017). Qatar's Resilience Strategy and Implications for State--Society Relations (pp. 1-22). Istituto Affari Internazionali (IAI).

Bastos, W., & Levy, S. (2012). A history of the concept of branding: practice and theory. *Journal of Historical Research in Marketing, 4*(3), 347–3.

Bein Media Group (2020), The Group. Retrieved from https://www.beinmediagroup.com/the-group/

Berghof Foundation. (2014). Designing Effective Communication Strategies. Retrieved from https://www.berghof-foundation.org/fileadmin/redaktion/Publications/Other_Resources/Strategic_Frameworks/Framework_Communication_Strategies_final.pdf

Brand Directory (2020). Global Soft Power Index. Retrieved from https://brandirectory.com/globalsoftpower/download/brand-finance-global-soft-power-index-2020.pdf.

Doha International Center for Interfaith Dialogue (2020). Annual Conferences. Retrieved from http://www.dicid.org/annnual_conferences_ar/.

Education Above All .(2020). Al FAKHOORA Program. Retrieved from https://educationaboveall.org/#!/programme/al-fakhoora.

Education Above All .(2020). Educate A Child Program. Retrieved fromhttps://educationaboveall.org/#!/programme/educate-a-child.

Education Above All .(2020). PROTECT EDUCATION IN INSECURITY AND CONFLICT. Retrieved from https://educationaboveall.org/#!/programme/peic.

Education Above All. (2022). About Education Above All. Retrieved from https://educationaboveall.org/about-eaa/who-we-are

Engel, Tilman. (2018). interview with Hassan Al-Ibrahim, Acting Qatar Tourism Authority Chairman. Retrieved from https://www.sbc-international.de/wp-content/uploads/2018/10/Qatar-Tourism-Strategy-World-Cup-2022.pdf.

FIFA (2016). FIFA grants media rights in France to TF1 and beIN SPORTS for major tournaments. Retrived from https://www.fifa.com/who-we-are/news/fifa-grants-media-rights-in-france-to-tf1-and-bein-sports-for-major-to-2755440.

Finn, Greg (2014). Twitter and Facebook launch their 2014 'Year in review' with top content, trends & more. Marketing Land. Retrieved from https://marketingland.com/twitter-facebook-launch-2014-year-review-top-content-trends-110643

Giampiccoli, Andrea & Mtapuri, Oliver.(2015). Tourism development in Qatar: towards a diversification strategy beyond the conventional 3 Ss. *African Journal of Hospitality, Tourism and Leisure, 4*(1).

Grix, J. (2013). "Image" leveraging and sports mega-events: Germany and the 2006 FIFA World Cup. *The Journal of Sport Tourism, 17*(4), 289–312. https://doi.org/10.1080/14775085.2012.760934

Hamad Awards (2020). About Sheikh Hamad Award for Translation and International Understanding. Retrieved from https://hta.qa/en/.

Hassad Food. (2020). About Hassad Food. Retrieved from https://www.hassad.com/English/Pages/OperationsPortfolio.aspx68. https://doi.org/10.1108/17557501211252934

Katara (2020). About Katara. Retrieved from https://www.katara.net/About-Katara.

Kentie, Peter (2020). A Story of a City and A Nation [PowerPoint Slides]. Retrieved from https://dkf1ato8y5dsg.cloudfront.net/uploads/14/57/1605-peter-kentie.pdf.

Knott, B., Fyall, A., & Jones, I. (2017). Sport mega-events and nation branding: Unique characteristics of the 2010 FIFA World Cup, South Africa. *International Journal of Contemporary Hospitality Management, 29*(3), 900–923. https://doi.org/10.1108/IJCHM-09-2015-0523

Lee, K. M. (2009). Nation branding and sustainable competitiveness of nations. *Unpublished PhD Thesis, University of Twente.*

Lin, C. (2020). Understanding Cultural Diversity and Diverse Identities. *Quality Education*, 929-938.

Mefalopulos, P., & Kamlongera, C. (2004). *Participatory communication strategy design: A handbook.* Food & Agriculture Organization.

Qatari Committee for the Alliance of Civilizations (QCAC). (2019). Retrieved 20 September 2020, from https://mofa.gov.qa/en/foreign-policy/international-cooperation/alliance-of-civilizations

Qatar Foundation (2020). About Qatar Foundation. Retrieved from https://www.qf.org.qa/about.

Qatar Museums (2020). Years of Culture. Retrieved from http://www.dicid.org/annnual_conferences_ar/.

Qatar Science & Technology Park (2020). About Qatar Science & Technology Park. Retrieved from https://qstp.org.qa/about/.

Qatari Emiri Decree No. 20 (2010).

Qatari Government . Office of Communication. (2015). Objectives and Mission. Retrieved from https://www.gco.gov.qa/en/about-the-gco/objective-and-mission/

Qatari Government. Planning and Statistics Authority. (2020). Monthly Figures on Total Population. Retrieved from https://www.psa.gov.qa/en/statistics1/statisticssite/pages/population.aspx.

Qatar Tourism Authority, Retrieved 25 September 2020 from: https://auth.qatartourism.gov.qa/binaries/content/assets/media/upload-file/en/tourism-investment/qta_investment-brochure_v2.pdf

Report of the sixty-seventh plenary session of the Conference of European Statisticians. (2019). Retrieved 12 September 2020, from https://www.unece.org/fileadmin/DAM/stats/documents/ece/ces/2019/7_Strategic_commmunication_framework_for_consultation.pdf

Sammut-Bonnici, T. (2015). Brand and branding. *Wiley Encyclopedia of Management.*

Snoj, Jure,(2019) "Population of Qatar by nationality - 2019 report", Population of Qatar by nationality in 2019 (priyadsouza.com)

Sidra Medicine (2020). About Sidra Medicine. Retrieved from https://www.sidra.org/.

Sultan, Nabil (2011). "Aljazeera: Media or Medium of Change in the Arab World?" Conference Paper at *Conference: Gulf Research Meeting At: Cambridge University (UK) July 2011.* Retrieved 18 September 2020 from https://www.researchgate.net/

publication/277770964_Aljazeera_Media_or_Medium_of_Change_in_the_Arab_World

United States Environmental Protection Agency. *GUIDANCE REGARDING COMMUNICATION STRATEGIES*. Retrieved 25 September 2020, from https://semspub.epa.gov/work/11/174743.pdf

WISE (2020). About WISE. Retrieved from https://www.sidra.org/.

CHAPTER SIX
Successful Communications Strategies: A win-win situation for all

Communication is the cornerstone in any connection we seek to make. It is the most important foundation of any project and is often something that needs to be learned and practiced over time and applied differently depending on the general context.

Experience has taught us that good communication is the essence behind any good business or relationship. In general, whenever a good communication strategy is implemented, we can expect a good workflow in any sector or field.

Strategic communication is the science and plan behind the tools of communications. It refers specifically to policymaking and guidance for consistent information activity within an organization, for better flow of business and between organizations for better transactions and business exchange.

Strategic communication management is essential as it is the area responsible to implement, plan and realize a good flow of communication, media development and image care in a strategic approach.

However, we have come to notice that not all communication strategies are effective if they are not based on a clear and objective analysis, or if they are not applied successfully. This is in addition to the compliance of the parties involved, which can cause many obstacles for a good communication plan to succeed. Establishing strategies is the first step, but taking action is the essential part of the plan that will drive business forward.

According to Dr. Shell (2017):

"Strategy and strategic are two of the most overused words in business today. Everything from hiring to purchasing to logistics is "strategic," and therefore, the term has lost some of its impact. In relation to business communications, however, strategy has a very specific meaning. A business communication is strategic when it considers the following key elements:

- Target audience(s)

A strategic communication is directed at a specific audience or set of audiences, within which there is typically a primary audience, a secondary audience and so on. They have different levels of knowledge on the subject at hand along with different priorities and concerns and have different degrees of trust in you and your organization.

- Context

Having clarified the audiences for your communication, it is important to define the context in which this communication will occur. This context defines your audiences' world, recent experiences, and reasonable expectations for the future.

- Intended outcomes

Every business communication has a set of specific purposes to achieve. One technique for defining outcomes is to consider "Head, Heart, and Hands"; that is, what do people need to know, believe, and do because of your communication? What is your call to action?

- Key messages

Once you've defined your purpose, construct messages that will resonate with your specific audience in the current context.

- Appropriate medium

The messages you communicate usually determine the most effective media to employ. Audiences respond differently to these choices of media, especially considering the context of the communication and the outcomes you are trying to achieve.

- Preferred messenger(s)

While you are the primary messenger for most of your business communications, you still must consider whether you will be the most effective messenger. The primary consideration in choosing a messenger is "Ethos," the credibility of the messenger with the audience. Factors that affect Ethos include:

Status and power: Many audiences have confidence in people with "big titles" (the CEO) or a clear position of influence in the organization.

Expertise: Other audiences prefer a messenger with demonstrated knowledge and experience in the subject area.

Relationship: A strong prior relationship with the audience can enhance a messenger's credibility."

Indeed, it is crucial to achieve a good communication strategy to convey the right message to the intended audience. Having the right audience is the most important step for communication to work. Whether it is the internal audience of the company or the external clientele audience.

Such communication strategies can be applied at small scale for small societies, businesses and companies, or at large scale for big organizations and governments. Each has a way of implementing these strategies, but all communication strategies have one common goal, which is to reach the right target audience with the right message to successfully drive their businesses or products and services forward.

GOVERNMENT COMMUNICATION STRATEGIES

Applying large-scale communication strategies by governments is no easy task and cannot be done overnight. It is a long process that needs to involve the right professionals and includes compliance of the people involved.

A government needs to have a trust foundation with its people, a well-established infrastructure for delivering information, and a solid plan of the right messages to be conveyed to its people.

Indeed, citizens have the right to know the policies and activities conducted by their governments and the information provided by government must be credible and timely, and most importantly transparent.

"To reach large numbers of the population, governments everywhere rely heavily on radio, television, magazines and newspapers. The media filters and analyses information from authorities to the citizens, and thus governments must take into account this "intermediary role" of the media when they seek to communicate with the population" (OECD, 1996).

We can also add to that the new social media channels on which many Governments and Government officials rely heavily to spread their messages and communicate with the population, as we have seen with the Gulf crisis sparked by the blockading nations.

Governments also need to have a clear and established external communication strategy with neighboring countries and foreign ones. While elaborating such strategies, many factors should be taken into consideration: culture, country's politics and general economic situation, previous friendly or hostile relationship and related statements.

If we take the Qatar example, we will notice that Qatari foreign policy is as much influenced by systemic regional factors, as it is the product of its political elite. In fact, regional order in the Middle East has been a mixture of hegemonic stability and a balance of power between regional states that oscillates between different coalitions and outside powers. Qatar has always tried to play a mediator role with every country involved in the Middle East conflicts and has built excellent relationships with European countries, including during the blockade.

PLANNING A GOOD GOVERNMENT COMMUNICATION STRATEGY

The business of governments has changed dramatically in recent years. Governments now have a crucial role in implementing transparent strategies towards their citizens. It is no surprise that the transformation of government operations, coupled with an unprecedented rise in citizen expectations, have created extraordinary demands on government communicators to implement successful communication strategies.

In order to do this, several steps need to be applied, from analysis to setting objectives, and to implement an action plan on an entire country and government scale. The relationship between people and their governments have changed a lot over the course of years. Nowadays, people have many expectations of their government and they want to pick and choose the information they consume. They have the power over how and when they receive their information and what they do with it.

This also means that governments should have several communication plans aligned to deal with any crisis that may arise. Successful and fast communication inspires confidence and helps keep things under control, which was exactly how the government of Qatar reacted towards the blockade.

So, what does this mean for a government wanting to communicate with their internal target audience effectively? The communication strategy needs to focus on what information your key audience wants and the best way to deliver it to them in a clear matter that will ensure compliance.

According to a Canadian study by Results Map in 2020, there are currently 8 best practices that governments should apply for their communication to flourish:

One Government One Voice:

The need for the government to always be united on the message it is conveying. The message needs to be strong and unified. Unity of a government is very important to convey a message of solidarity towards the population, showing them that the leaders responsible for the country have one message in common.

Audience Centric Communication:

Applied in a government context, this translates to citizen-centric communications, a model in which citizens can have a user-driven experience of accessing information.

For example, rather than sifting through several departmental websites, a citizen can access information that is relevant based on self-identified need, such as resources for seniors or information for small businesses.

Agile Communication Teams:

In an environment of digital communications and an unprecedented integration of channels, traditional soloed structures have been replaced with what's often referred to as a "trading floor" model, in which employees are deployed based on ability and area of interest, as opposed to rigid role structure. This involves deploying people based on skill, interest and initiative, as opposed to tenure or where one falls on an organization chart.

Digital and Open by Default:

Connected to *"digital* by default" is the focus on a government that is *"open* by default". This basic premise has been adopted by the Government of Canada (as formalized in the Ministerial Mandate Letters). This philosophy calls for a first assumption that information will be made publicly available in the interest of transparency, in contrast to historic approaches in which openness was an exception by conscious choice in particular circumstances.

Focus on Dialogue and Engagement:

This increased focus on dialogue and engagement is in part a result of the impact of social media in shifting expectations of communication as a conversation. Additionally, governments are now recognizing that trust is the necessary pre-condition of effective communication – and it requires new approaches to dialogue, engagement and openness.

Driven by Storylines:

One of the most significant trends in strategic communications and marketing in public sector institutions is the use of content strategies. This approach entails identifying priority themes and narratives that are brought to life through a concerted exercise of storytelling. This model is focused on "sense making" opportunities, in which a deliberate effort is made to create meaning for citizens by clustering various discrete elements of information into a coherent story.

Delivery:

Governments are now adopting "delivery" methodologies to ensure effective execution of priorities. The focus is on spear-heading government priorities through a repeatable cycle of identifying priorities, establishing accountabilities and metrics, monitoring operational performance, and reporting on progress. The delivery approach to government operations relies heavily on strategic communications as a key enabler, particularly with respect to operational and team communication.

Results Based:

The under-pinning of modern government operations is results-based management. From the United Nations to leading countries around the world and provincial / territorial and municipal governments in Canada, management by metrics has become the undisputed gold standard of operational delivery. This approach requires active, strategic involvement of communications on several levels: establishing the principle and communicating measurable goals, sharing success stories as well as lessons learned, and creating systems and processes for identifying, tracking and reporting on metrics.

As we conclude, governments have taken on a new role into being the model communicator with its people for all other things to fall into place. A good governmental communication drives the economic and political force of the country with the support of its people allowing it to develop and flourish.

QATAR'S 8 POINTS STRATEGY

Qatar implemented a good and proactive communication strategy that helped the government overcome the crisis in the right way, all while maintaining the trust of its people and the sympathy of major global partners.

In fact, the following eight points were applied by the Qatari Government in systematic ways, which greatly helped Qatar overcome the blockade:

1. One Government One Voice:

Indeed, one of the main things the Government of Qatar made sure to do was to keep the voice of the government united with few representatives who represented the entire government at the time of crisis. This included the Minister of Foreign Affairs, who was a main figure during the first days of the blockade and throughout the crisis.

2. Audience Centric Communication:

One of the main things that the Qatar government made sure to do was to maintain the calm and serenity of its people towards this unprecedented event. The government quickly established food and supplies channels from other neighboring countries, and always made sure to have an open communication with its people, making sure that their needs and concerns were a top priority.

3. Agile Communication Teams:

The Minister of Foreign Affairs and the Government Communication Office worked very hard to establish a good communication image for the government. H.H. the Amir also contributed significantly with his resilience and trust, portraying to the people that the Qatari government is strong and will not abandon them. A transparent communication line was maintained almost daily, informing the people of Qatar of all updates and news.

4. Digital and Open by Default:

As this was the first of its kind diplomatic crisis sparked by an online hacking incident, the effect of the blockade spread all over social media and especially on Twitter, a popular channel amongst Qatari people. Social Media helped increase the public's support of their Amir as the dust of the sudden blockade settled. The Qatari people began to introduce themselves on social media as descending from one tribe: Qatar. Twitter also played a big role in being an official communication channel for the government, on which they made sure to communicate all needed messages to their people.

5. Focus on Dialogue and Engagement:

Keeping the internal communication maintained on a daily basis reflected that the crisis management committee regarded people as the main priority in the crisis, and helped at calming their concerns and strengthening their trust in their leadership as they saw in the media continuously how the adopted policies had paid off instantly. The government kept open communication with the people, addressing all their needs and concerns.

6. Driven by Storylines:

Qatar really excelled in portraying the many problems that surfaced due to the sudden blockade. Stories of families that were shattered and could not be reunited, stories of businesses that faced many losses due to this crisis were shared on all media channels, including international ones.

7. Delivery:

It was clear that the communication strategists in Doha knew the significance of using various channels of media properly. Each medium functioned to target a specific audience (Social media to reach masses and the youth mainly, international TV channels to communicate with Western leaders and global public opinion). The swift and fruitful implementation of the management strategy made it clear that contingency plan had been set beforehand, and that the audience and delivery of the messages was well studied and established.

8. Results Based:

Many messages conveying care and concern had been carried through consistently; it was emphasized for example through Qatar's position towards its expatriates from the blockade countries, since they were given the choice to stay. Such a message portraying Qatar as the good and forbearing neighbor only adds to the desired image it aims to convey: the country's "grandeur" (Allagui, 2017).

DIRECT IMPACT OF A GOVERNMENT STRATEGY ON COMPANIES

Government policies play a big role in the good standing of the companies in the country. If a government facilitates the flow of businesses and investors, this will lead to a better development of companies and if the government imposes tough regulations and rules on companies, this will in parallel impact the establishment of companies in this country.

This is largely rolled out thanks to communication strategies. A good government communication strategy will allow rules and regulations to be transparent and for business to go smoothly, encouraging big companies and investors to invest and place big capitals in this country.

The main goal of government communications is to engage citizens and other stakeholders into processes regarding implementation of a policy. Their efficacy depends on circumstances of a given governmental activity – what kind of a policy is implemented and how much stakeholders are involved in the process. Unfortunately, despite the relatively large freedom of action and decision-making power, political factors can be a limitation of great importance if an initiative is too innovative or conceptually not close to the mainstream concepts. This also applies to communication management instruments (Liu, Horsley 2007).

Government Communication Impact on Public Sector

Since the turn of the 1980's and 1990's in many European countries there was a significant change in the approach to public sector management theory. It was caused by the creation of a new concept based on managerialism (van Duersen, Pieterson after Duivebon, Lips 2002).

In order to comply with new conditions in the first place, people usually try to adapt existing solutions. This is exactly how these models evolved into being applied to the public sectors. Since they were working in the private sector, governments decided to start applying such strategies into their own communications mediums and public institutions. Models born of needs from corporation management, primarily based on the theory of marketing, were used to describe reality of the public sector.

Strategic planning and marketing techniques were supposed to help in "selling" a government policy to citizens. They were seen as useful because researchers treated relationship between the state and taxpayers as a regular market exchange – citizens pay for some products and services provided by public sector directly (when they actually had to purchase and pay a price in conditions similar to market reality) or indirectly (through taxes) (Walsh, 1994).

The first ways of direct communication between the public and governments was the media. Indeed, the marriage of public sector and the media is nothing new.

Many journalists and media channels were used solely to inform the public of the government's news and decisions. It was a one-way communication stream that many people perceived as propaganda for the government. This ended up doing more harm than good in many situations since the media has two significant roles: either the government allies or intended to uncover scandals inside the government.

Indeed, public administration is used to one-way communications that is based on a simplified, one-sided vision of the environment, which in some situations may be more effective because it allows for a faster decision-making process and announcing decisions and critical information in such situations as an unforeseen crisis.

First guidelines for communication management in public sector that can be classified as a complete theoretical basis were presented by Hiebert (1981). Although they were named by the author as the government communication process model, they were more like a set of advice than a theory. Walsh (1994) pointed out the increasing role of marketing in the public sector.

Marketing short-term agenda was accurate for ad hoc promotional and informational needs of public entities. Newly born awareness of communication needs in public administration structures were explained by him because of consumerism that forced more sensitivity to citizen's wishes and decentralization of public tasks. It required public entities to expand the range of their services and improve the system.

In the 1990's, in the field of Public Relations, a two-way symmetrical model was presented by Grunig (2008). It conceptualized how to adapt organization's strategies to effectively address needs of its stakeholders – it was necessary to find a middle ground where a dialogue could be established between involved parties where each of them was a sender and receiver of a message, and their relationship was based on mutual consensus and satisfaction (Wojcik 2011). Grunig's excellent model became the flagship of American researchers in the field of communication, sometimes called mainstream. According to author's assumptions a two-way symmetrical model is excellent, so it can be used for all situations where communication processes are in progress.

Exchange with a multitude of customers is not possible for public administration to get in touch with each of them individually and negotiate separately terms of participation. So naturally there is a huge need for information to extend citizen's knowledge about public policies and programs. This is where the role of communication professionals has been useful in establishing new Communication Plans for governments.

When creating models of communication, all the limitations should be taken into consideration. An attempt to do so resulted in the creation of the government communications wheel model, that is based upon four coexisting, complementary microenvironments (Liu, Horsley 2007):

- multilevel, where two or more levels of administration collaborate on a single issue,
- intra-governmental, inside of an institution or agency,
- intergovernmental, where cooperate units of the same governmental level,
- external, where stakeholders are involved especially private sector and NGOs

In all four, micro-environments managers share expertise and resources as well as coordinate communication.

In each of them information can be exchanged through different channels directly (direct-to-public communication) or indirectly (mediated).

What we live in now, some researchers like to call an information society and a global village. The most important factor distorting foundations of the perfect competition theory is a lack of information about the market.

Information itself is a part of every production process, product or service. Nobody will be surprised to hear its quality, completeness, and speed of spreading across market participants is a base of competitive advantage for economic entities [Goliński 2005, p.11-15]. Information about products and services actually creates consumer's tastes and directly influences demand. Appropriate communication management is of key importance for rationalizing economic choices.

QATAR'S COMMUNICATION STRATEGY FOR BUSINESSES

Given the turbulent nature of Middle Eastern politics, it is not surprising that regional countries pursue self-surviving strategies trying to build their own resilience against rising political, economic and social challenges and threats. Building successful communication strategies between governments and its people is a big challenge in the Middle East due to many political concerns.

Many people find it hard to trust their governments and the messages they are conveying and many often find these messages as simply being a propaganda for their government's political agenda.

Qatar has also had its share of difficulties in establishing well-communicated messages to its people, especially during the recent blockade events. This example is vivid for testing the perseverance and resilience of the Qatar government.

Qatar has come a long way, evolving from a traditional society into a modern welfare state and, following a constitutional referendum in 2003, it aims to be a constitutional monarchy. Once one of the poorest Gulf states, Qatar has been transformed into one of the richest countries in the region, backed by the world's third-largest natural gas and oil reserves.

H.H. the Amir Sheikh Tamim bin Hamad Al Thani followed his father's policy and set the country on a development path with unprecedented financial investment, improving the domestic welfare of Qatari citizens and residents, including establishing advanced healthcare and education systems and expanding the country's infrastructure in anticipation of hosting the FIFA World Cup Qatar 2022™. The prospect of hosting the FIFA World Cup™ has prompted Qatar to invest significantly in stadia, transport links and other infrastructure. Residents are seeing the benefits of these projects, which include improvements to expressways and the opening of the Doha Metro. Government planners are also looking beyond the hosting of the event to ensure that it has a lasting economic legacy, by developing the project pipeline.

Qatar National Vision 2030 has created a blueprint for diversification to cushion the economy from future swings in demand for commodities.

New measures were taken in 2019 to encourage foreign direct investment, including legal changes to allow 100% foreign ownership of companies in most sectors, excluding financial services and insurance.

A new government body – the Investment Promotion Agency – was formed to streamline procedures for businesses interested in locating to the country. Qatar Financial Centre, an onshore hub with its own legal and regulatory framework, saw registered business numbers increase by one-third in 2019.

The same study indicates, that although Qatar faces the challenge of diversifying its economy, the country does not face the same levels of pressure to find work for its young nationals as some of its neighbors. The most recent PSA estimate of the population in the third quarter of 2019 was 2.77m and that of the economically active population was 2.06m. This was made up of 1.95m expatriates and 109,000 Qataris. The unemployment rate sat at just 0.1%, with the unemployment rate for Qataris at 0.2.

In January 2020 Qatar introduced new labor laws for expatriates, giving foreign workers the right to change jobs and allowing them to leave the country temporarily or permanently during their contract of employment. The law also gave workers a non-discriminatory minimum wage, which the UN described as a regional first. Qatar has been working with the International Labor Organization since 2017 to reform its employment laws.

"Qatar is changing," Sharan Burrow, General Secretary of the International Trade Union Confederation, said in a UN report. The new tranche of laws has removed the kafala (sponsorship) system and implemented modern industrial relations.

In a country with such a large proportion of expatriate workers, up-to-date information on the population is vital for economic planners. And this is exactly where a good communication plan implemented by the government comes in useful.

"In the 2015 census Qatar made use of a multi-modal approach to data collection with face-to-face interviews and the latest electronic devices, onto which geographical maps of each area covered by the researcher were downloaded," Saleh bin Mohamed Al Nabit, president of the PSA, told OBG. "Qatar has since experienced an increase in population, and the 2020 census will require the administrative records of various government agencies around the country." The aim of the new census was to create a high-quality central register of the population, with comprehensive coverage and a system for the continuous and simultaneous updating of this data. The final phase of the data collection was finalized in 2021.

With these new mediums in place and with a successful communication strategy put in place by the government that was able to divert the impact of the blockade on its economy, Qatar is surely headed to a bright economic future. The Qatari government has increasingly shifted its focus to small and medium-sized enterprises (SME's) and start-ups as it moves to expand economic diversification and non-oil growth in the state. Start-ups and entrepreneurs will benefit as a result, with the state launching new support mechanisms for the sector, including the recently established Qatar Business Incubation Centre (QBIC), the largest mixed-use incubator facility in the MENA region. Offering a series of targeted training programs, facilities and financial support, the 20,000-sq-metre QBIC will join existing programs offered by various stakeholders and government entities in nurturing growth through provision of facilities, training, low- or zero-interest loans and mentorship.

SUCCESSFUL COMMUNICATION STRATEGIES FOR PRIVATE BUSINESSES THAT WERE ALSO ADAPTED IN QATAR'S CRISIS COMMUNICATION STRATEGY

Communication is one of the most important factors for business success. Regardless of size and industry, organizations depend on effective communication. However, while it seems straightforward, the process of facilitating effective communication can be complex. Because communication promotes better teamwork and collaboration, it contributes to the successful completion of many types of projects and even an organization's overall goals.

Business communications is the process of sharing information between employees within and outside a company, in addition to establishing a good flow of communication channels between management and employees, between employees themselves and between the entire company and its external clientele.

Effective business communication is how employees and management interact among each other to reach organizational goals and be more aligned with the <u>core company values</u>. Its main purpose is to improve organizational practices, eliminate silos, keep employees informed and reduce errors.

Effective business communication is essential for success and growth of every organization. Unlike everyday communications, business communication is always goal oriented.

In fact, successful communication involves several components that take a message through the process from start to finish, including the following:

- **The sender:** This refers to people with an idea, request or information that they want to share. It is up to the sender to consider the audience and choose a method that conveys the information effectively. In Qatar's Gulf Crisis case, we can say that the sender was the Government communicating all the needed information through the Minister of Foreign Affairs.
- **The receiver:** The receiver is the person for whom the message is intended. These individuals are responsible for understanding and processing the information they are given. The receiver when it comes to the Qatar case is the people and citizens of Qatar who are the main receivers of the government's messages.
- **The message:** This refers to the content of the message that the sender wants the receiver to hear. There were many messages conveyed during the Qatar crisis, but the main message from the government was to keep unity, to have faith in government and in H.H. the Amir and most importantly to strengthen the nationalism and belonging to Qatar amongst people.
- **The medium:** The medium is the device or circumstances through which messages are transmitted. This could be a cellphone (text message) or a computer (instant messaging). The Qatar crisis communication was mainly digital and through social media, showing that the government understands its people and the best ways to reach them.
- **The feedback:** The communication process typically ends when the message leaves one person and successfully reaches

another individual or group. This involves transmitting, receiving and, most importantly, understanding. The receiver should also provide feedback that indicates comprehension when responding to the message.

We can positively conclude that the feedback received from the people for the messages of the government was very positive. People were extremely happy with the way H.H. the Amir Sheikh Tamim Bin Hamad Al Thani spoke and reassured his people, all while opening up new markets and new business opportunities in Qatar that did not exist before.

- **The external factors:** The communication process often goes awry, and external factors are usually the culprit. Examples include "noise" that disrupts transmission or something more complicated, such as lack of context. During the Gulf crisis, foreign people or entities were trying to disrupt the government and the decisions of H.H. the Amir through several means and most importantly through online bots and fake media channels that were spreading rumors to build a sense of instability amongst the people of Qatar.

WHAT ARE THE COMPONENTS OF A SUCCESSFUL COMMUNICATION STRATEGY AND HOW DID THE STATE OF QATAR IMPLEMENT THEM

There are several ways to encourage effective communication in the workplace, many of which involve working from the top down.

Define what appropriate communication is

The first step in establishing best practices for communication is deciding what is and is not acceptable. Entrepreneur notes that you can ask the following questions to get started: "To what extent should communication be formal, and when? Is casual communication encouraged and permitted, or do you require a business-only approach across the board? What is the proper way to address superiors, associates and customers?"

Eliminate weak language

One of the most important ways to establish effective communication strategies is to eliminate weak language. Business leaders should work to ensure they are conveying important points with clarity, and that starts with self-awareness and making subtle changes to your own speaking habits. One example is to avoid using the word "but" because "it can be interpreted to invalidate others' claims or ideas," Entrepreneur explains.

Focus on clarity in communication

It is also important to be precise in your language, always saying what you mean and asking the receiver if your message is clear. When your language is ambiguous, it's difficult to set clear expectations and work well with others on projects, presentations and more.

Be intentional with digital communication

As email and instant messaging become increasingly central to workplace communication, leaders should set expectations around how employees use these tools. Discuss what kinds of communication can be carried out digitally, such as quick questions or clarification, and what kinds of conversations require face-to-face interaction.

Other effective communication strategies include the following:

- Encourage the receiver to ask questions. This will allow the sender to ascertain whether the receiver has accurately interpreted the message and allows for any required clarification.

- Choose non-aggressive phrasing. When the sender gives feedback such as, "I'm not communicating well," vs. "You don't understand what I'm saying," it takes pressure off the receiver.
- Become hyper-aware of nonverbal cues. Tone and body language can disrupt a sender's message. Pay attention to how your body language may be contributing to poor communication outcomes, and work on appearing open and alert.
- Understand your audience. The terminology the sender uses should depend on the audience. A group of accountants might understand quarterly projections, while technology teams have a different body of knowledge.
- Taking steps like these to facilitate effective communication is critical for successful management, as well as career advancement. Business leaders and managers need strong oral and written communication skills that allow them to communicate with both employees and superiors

The Qatari government was quick to react after the blockade with a strong and determined tone of voice. Government officials showed a strict language that refused the actions taken against them by the blockading countries and refusing the 13 points, all while maintaining a message of hope, strength and empathy towards the people of Qatar. Communicating through social media and especially Twitter during the entire time of the blockade was also a big positive point for the government, as it was one of the best ways to directly reach its people, which in return reacted by filling twitter with hashtags and tweets about their love of Qatar.

Thanks to this successful communication strategy the government not only managed to keep the people of Qatar aligned, but also strengthened their patriotism and their love for the Amir during that difficult time.

EXAMPLES OF SUCCESSFUL MARKETING AND COMMUNICATIONS CAMPAIGNS

A marketing campaign is any action planned to achieve a marketing goal of a company. The goal could be increasing awareness for a product, service, business, or organization, drive new revenue, or help with turnaround.

From the Marlboro Man and the Nike's "Just do it" slogan to the "Got Milk" and the Old Spice's "Man your man could smell like", marketing campaigns have the power to reach innumerable audiences, create trends and needs and define the market.

Qatar's Internal Communication Success

Launching a new organizational communication initiative can be overwhelming, but the ROI of enhancing internal communications with new strategies and tools cannot be ignored. In fact, it has been proven that when companies start improving their internal communication this automatically translates into an improved public image and better performance overall.

Employees feel heard, and feedback is taken into consideration in improving all lines of work, this all translates into a positive work environment and thus better productivity.

The Holmes Report (2011), found that companies with strong internal communication strategies were able to give their shareholders 47% higher returns, while research from Smarp found that companies with high employee engagement are 22% more profitable. One study by the McKinsey Global Institute found that productivity rose by as much as 25% when employees used online social tools to collaborate. And companies with effective internal communications have more engaged employees and less employee turnover. But how can companies and governments follow some same strategies?

When Qatar was hit with the blockade crisis, the government used many internal communication tools to stay on top and in control of the situation.

In fact, the biggest companies in the world such as Amazon and Starbucks have recently adopted short, straightforward messaging inside the companies in addition to setting up their employees to the be their brand ambassadors. Indeed, such companies have realized that digital communication happens in real time, so it doesn't have to be as wordy as the memos of before, nor as complicated. Internal communication should be more like social media by distilling messages down so they contain only essential information. Starbucks even confirmed that the company's effective internal communication tools have ensured that employees and managers are all on the same page when it comes to the brand's key offerings and core values.

This is also what the government of Qatar did, as they rallied their people in their corner, helping gain the support and momentum needed to overcome the crisis. The messages shared with the people were strong, confident messages and most importantly clear ones that delivered the exact wording they were meant to deliver. As a reaction, the people of Qatar were very comprehensive and supportive of their government and did not hesitate to show their sympathy to their leaders all over social media.

Having internal assets in a company or within a country is the most important ally that will help overcome whatever crisis hits it. When people on the inside agree and understand the politics of its ruling entity, they become part of the communication process and thereby transform them into active ambassadors of this entity.

Qatar's External Communication Success

An external communication campaign is generally designed to attract customers to the company and to its products. As opposed to internal communications, external communications are used to transmit information from the company to its audience.

It is important to have the right tools such as a good website, a clear message content and other communication channels all aligned and conveying the right message for the target clients.

The past 20 years have seen an evolution in the way brands approach communication, with the introduction of social media placing a greater emphasis on the role of the consumer's voice.

External communication is about connecting with anyone outside of your business. This means that while they include things like social media marketing and video content, they also refer to presentations for shareholders, or investor campaigns.

Companies such as Red Bull quickly understood that the best way to market their product was by creating a full image and story behind the product. Thanks to their sports investments on so many levels, the company managed to demonstrate that there is more to the drink than meets the eye. In fact, in 2012, Red Bull Stratos launched a helium balloon from which Austrian skydiver Felix Baumgartner jumped 127,852 feet. He became the first person to break the sound barrier in freefall. The event was watched live by 8.3 million people on YouTube. According to Smart Insights, Red Bull sales increased 7% in the six months after the campaign, generating $1.6 billion.

The government of Qatar was also quick in applying some of these goals, thanks to its many investments in the fields of business and sports around the world. Indeed, Qatar's growing wealth within a volatile region led Qatar to put in place an ambitious plan for the future of the country via the enhancement of the nation's soft power assets and public diplomacy initiatives. The vision that emerged viewed the country as a multi-layered international hub, which would, in turn, attract investors, scholars, professionals, activists, artists, and tourists alike. In a 2014 interview with Charlie Rose, Qatar's former Prime Minister, H.E. Sheikh Hamad Bin Jassim Al Thani, who is considered one of the key architects of Qatar's drive for regional influence, confirmed that the chief motivation of the Qatari leadership was to position the country as a leading power in the region regardless of its small size (Rose 2014). According to academic Kristian Coates Ulrichsen (2014), Qatar's brand consists of promoting the country "as a neutral and progressive leader within the Arab and Islamic world, and to garner the support of the wider Arab region in addition to the broader international community" (Cherkaoui, 2018).

One of the critical steps initiated in this regard consisted of transforming Qatar into a knowledge hub in the Middle East via a multitude of educational, scientific, and cultural projects led by the Qatar Foundation. Another goal consisted of establishing Doha as a hub within global air transportation networks by launching Qatar Airways in 1997. The latter was intended to become a leader in the airline industry. The Qatari leadership also envisioned the country's international airport as a connector between long–haul and regional flights. The rise of Qatar Airways (and other Gulf airlines) constitutes a direct competition with European airlines and their respective hubs, which were traditionally the recipient of traffic flows between East and West (Delfmann et al. 2005).

In fact, these achievements came to aid Qatar in its time of need. The large diplomatic network that Doha built across the business, media, academic, and cultural spheres demonstrated its usefulness in times of need. Organizations such as QNHRC, the Qatar Foundation, and Qatar Museums to name just a few, mobilized their connections to spread awareness about the blockade faced by the country, which was a success for Qatar's image.

CONCLUSION

A good communication plan goes a long way to achieving successful outcomes, whether on a government level or on a private organization level. And once this communication plan is established, the flow will automatically lead to better performance and improvement. What leaders communicate and how they communicate will affect the way in which people prioritize and organize and mobilize themselves into action. In the organizational context, effective communication with stakeholders is a pre-requisite to ensure that the aspired mobilization around and prioritization of an organization's specific project or goal takes place.

In fact, for or an effective and efficient organizational performance, management and governments must both embrace; more clarity of ideas before communicating; better understanding of the physical and human environment when communicating; purpose of communication must be thoroughly analyzed; when planning communication, consultation should both be top down and bottom up. Being prepared to face and manage a crisis thanks to a well-established communication plan on a company or government level can be very beneficial and even save the company or country from many other mishaps.

And today more than ever, communication plans are taking on a whole new level with the presence of social media, Artificial Intelligence, and new monitoring systems. The technological development in the world of communication added many independent players in the process of transferring information and bridged the distance between people and center of events. Therefore, governments need new strategies, plans, and technologies to clarify their vision, directions and policies. The war today is a war of ideas, words, rumors and piracies all happening in the digital world.

This is exactly what happened with the state of Qatar during the blockade crisis. As we have seen throughout our chapters, the country was suddenly hit by the neighboring countries, considered as brothers, but it managed to stand on its own feet and to survive the hardships. While the blockade was supposed to make the country kneel and succumb to the conditions of the blockading countries, Qatar adapted, re-tooled its economy and foreign relations in ways that could re-shape the strategic layout of the Arabian Gulf. It also enhanced its ties with neighbors such as Iran and Turkey and improved foreign relationships with European countries, gaining the sympathy of many of them. There was also an improvement in its economy with additional manufacturing, farming and technology helping Qatar to become fully independent. Qatar reacted with a well-established communication crisis plan internally and externally.

Organizations and governments that use communication effectively during a crisis to authentically connect with stakeholders and their people have the best opportunity for long-term success. When they communicate with authenticity, transparency, and clarity, they build trust and confidence in their actions. People who trust organizations or their government are more likely to support and advocate for it. Strategic communication in a crisis gives these entities the confidence to advance their plans and progress in meaningful ways.

The bet on the field of communication is a bet on the future. The development that has been witnessed in this field gives it great importance in the work of governments to communicate its message to the internal audience in the State, and the external audience, outside the State. Therefore, the next time you are faced with a crisis, know that a well-established communication plan is the key to get you out of it. After all, there is no better example than this: the Qatar case study transforming a sudden blockade into an opportunity, thanks to a very successful crisis communications strategy.

REFERENCES

Abdin, MD. Joynal, The Impact of Government Policies & World Order on Business (April 7, 2009). Available at SSRN: https://ssrn.com/abstract=1138213 or http://dx.doi.org/10.2139/ssrn.1138213

Cherkaoui, T., 2018. Qatar's public diplomacy, international broadcasting, and the Gulf Crisis. https://risingpowersproject.com/quarterly/qatars-public-diplomacy-international-broadcasting-and-the-gulf-crisis/

Delfmann, Werner & Baum, Herbert & Auerbach, Stefan & Albers, Sascha. (2005). Strategic Management in the Aviation Industry.

Successful Communication Strategy: Five Elements. (2017, July 14). Glasscock School of Continuing Studies.

https://glasscock.rice.edu/blog/successful-communication-strategy-five-elements

OECD. (1996, January 1). *OECD iLibrary | Effective Communications Between the Public Service and the Media.* https://www.oecd-ilibrary.org/governance/effective-communications-between-the-public-service-and-the-media_5kml6g6m8zjl-en;jsessionid=3qPC5VS2qRg24baJmoMeOIQv.ip-10-240-5-150

8 Best Practices in Government Communications – Results Map®. (2020). ResultsMap. https://www.resultsmap.com/blog/8-best-practices-in-government-communications/

Report, H. (2016, April 29). *The Cost Of Poor Communications.* Provok. https://www.provokemedia.com/latest/article/the-cost-of-poor-communications

Chui, M., Manyika, J., Bughin, J., Dobbs, R., Roxburgh, C., Sarrazin, H., Sands, G., & Westergren, M. (2019, February 13). *The social economy: Unlocking value and productivity through social technologies.* McKinsey & Company. https://www.mckinsey.com/industries/technology-media-and-telecommunications/our-insights/the-social-economy

Liu, B. F., & Horsley, J. S. (2007). The Government Communication Decision Wheel: Toward a Public Relations Model for the Public Sector. *Journal of Public Relations Research, 19*(4), 377–393. https://doi.org/10.1080/10627260701402473

11 Reasons Why Business Communication is Critical to Your Company's Success. (2020). SMARP. https://blog.smarp.com/11-reasons-why-business-communication-is-crucial-for-companys-success

20 Best PR Campaigns. (2018). PR Week. https://www.prweek.com/article/1493241/20-best-pr-campaigns-past-two-decades

Qatar's diversification strategy supports economic development. (2020, December 24). Oxford Business Group. https://oxfordbusinessgroup.com/overview/steady-course-strong-fundamentals-and-robust-diversification-strategy-support-continued-economic

Walsh, A. J. (1994, June 1). *Meaningful Work as a Distributive Good.* Wiley Online Library. https://onlinelibrary.wiley.com/doi/abs/10.1111/j.2041-6962.1994.tb00713.x

Grunig, J. E. (2001). *Excellence Theory in Public Relations: Past, Present, and Future.* SpringerLink. https://link.springer.com/chapter/10.1007/978-3-531-90918-9_22

FULL BOOK REFERENCES

- *11 Reasons Why Business Communication is Critical to Your Company's Success.* (2020). SMARP. https://blog.smarp.com/11-reasons-why-business-communication-is-crucial-for-companys-success
- *20 Best PR Campaigns.* (2018). PR Week. https://www.prweek.com/article/1493241/20-best-pr-campaigns-past-two-decades
- *8 Best Practices in Government Communications – Results Map®.* (2020). Results Map. https://www.resultsmap.com/blog/8-best-practices-in-government-communications/
- Abdin, MD. Joynal, The Impact of Government Policies & World Order on Business (April 7, 2009). Available at SSRN: https://ssrn.com/abstract=1138213 or http://dx.doi.org/10.2139/ssrn.1138213
- Adreas Krieg (2019), Divided Gulf, The Anatomy Of A Crisis https://newbooksnetwork.com/andreas-krieg-divided-gulf-the-anatomy-of-a-crisis-palgrave-2019/
- AFP, 2017, Qatar's Foreign Minister Calls in Press Conference for the Blockade to be lifted Retrieved from: https://www.france24.com/en/20170619-qatar-demands-blockade-lifted-before- gulf-crisis-talks
- Ahmad el Rawi 2019, Cyberconflict, Online Political Jamming, and Hacking in the Gulf Retrieved From Cooperation Council International Journal of Communication, https://ijoc.org/index.php/ijoc/article/view/8989/2600
- Al Araby 2019, Two years on, Qatar has beaten the Saudi-led

- blockade (2019). Retrieved from: https://www.alaraby.co.uk/english/indepth/2019/6/5/two-years-on-qatar-has-beaten-the-saudi-led-blockade
- Al Jazeera (2017) Arab States issue 13 Demands to end Qatar-Gulf Crisis. Al Jazeera. Retrieved from https://www.aljazeera.com/news/2017/06/arab-states-issue-list-demands-qatar-crisis-170623022133024.html
- Al Jazeera (2017) Qatar donates 30m to help Harvey victims in Texas. Al Jazeera. Retrieved from https://www.aljazeera.com/news/2017/09/qatar-donates-30m-harvey-victims-texas-170908042945728.html
- Al Jazeera 2017, Qatar Foreign Minister Interview: Qatar Not Ready to Surrender. Retrieved from: https://www.aljazeera.com/news/2017/06/qatar-fm-ready-surrender-170608142453812.html
- Al Jazeera 2019, Emir Qatar Overcame Obstacles Gulf Blockade. Retrieved from https://www.aljazeera.com/news/2019/11/emir-qatar-overcome-obstacles-gulf-blockade-191105075057081.html
- Al Jazeera 2019, Fake Twitter Accounts Influencing Qatar Crisis. Retrieved from: https://www.aljazeera.com/news/2019/07/fake-twitter-accounts-influencing-gulf-crisis-190717052607770.html
- Al Jazeera English (2018, Feb 15) Qatar: Beyond the Blockade. [Video File] Retrieved from https://www.youtube.com/watch?v=Dc6n31wIuHI
- Al Jazeera June 2017, Turkish Parliament approve of Turkish Troops Deployment in Qatar. Retrieved from: https://www.aljazeera.com/news/2017/06/turkey-fast-track-troops-deployment-qatar-170607151127104.html
- Allmers, Swantje & Maennig Wolfgang, (2009). Economic Impacts of the FIFA Soccer World Cups in France 1998, Germany 2006, and Outlook for South Africa 2010. *Eastern Economic Journal*, *35*(4), 500–519. https://doi.org/10.1057/eej.2009.30
- Alshabnan, Ali (2018), The Politicization of Arab Gulf Media Outlets in the Gulf Crisis, Global Media Journal. http://www.

globalmediajournal.com/open-access/the-politicization-of-arab-gulf-media-outlets-in-the-gulf-crisis-a-content-analysis.php?aid=86958

- Al-Sharq News. (2018). Qatar's Participation in St. Petersbourgh Conference. Retrieved from https://al-sharq.com/article/14/11/2018/%D8%A7%D9%84%D9%85%D8%B4%D8%A7%D8%B1%D9%83%D8%A9-%D8%A7%D9%84%D9%82%D8%B7%D8%B1%D9%8A%D8%A9-%D9%81%D9%8A-%D9%85%D9%86%D8%AA%D8%AF%D9%89-%D8%B3%D8%A7%D9%86%D8%AA-%D8%A8%D8%B7%D8%B1%D8%B3%D8%A8%D9%88%D8%B1%D8%BA-%D8%AA%D8%B9%D8%B2%D8%B2-%D8%A7%D9%84%D8%AA%D8%A8%D8%A7%D8%AF%D9%84-%D8%A7%D9%84%D9%84%D9%85%D8%B9%D8%B1%D9%81%D9%8A
- American Marketing Association. Branding. Retrieved from https://www.ama.org/topics/branding/
- Anderson, M., & Anderson, S. L. (2007). *Machine Ethics: Creating an Ethical Intelligent Agent.* AI Magazine. https://doi.org/10.1609/aimag.v28i4.2065 .
- *Artificial Neural Network.* Artificial Neural Network - an overview | ScienceDirect Topics. (2015). https://www.sciencedirect.com/topics/earth-and-planetary-sciences/artificial-neural-network
- Baabood, A. (2017). Qatar's Resilience Strategy and Implications for State-Society Relations (pp. 1-22). Istituto Affari Internazionali (IAI).
- Banu Akdenizli & Ilhem Allagui1 (2019), The Gulf Information War and the Role of Media and Communication Technologies https://ijoc.org/index.php/ijoc/article/view/8988
- Bastos, W., & Levy, S. (2012). A history of the concept of branding: practice and theory. *Journal of Historical Research in Marketing, 4*(3), 347–3.
- BBC (2017) Qatar camels caught up in Gulf crisis. BBC. Retrieved from http://www.bbc.com/news/world-middle-east-40346329

- BBC (2017) Qatar Crisis: What you Need to Know. BBC. Retrieved from http://www.bbc.com/news/world-middle-east-40173757
- BBC, (2017) Middle East News Qatar says state news agency hacked after report cites Emir criticizing US https://www.bbc.com/news/world-middle-east-40026822
- BBVA (2013) The Impact of the Internet on Society. Retrieved from:https://www.bbvaopenmind.com/en/articles/the-impact-of-the-internet-on-society-a-global-perspective/
- BBVA (2019) The Past Decade and Future of Political Media: The Ascendance of Social Media, retrieved from: https://www.bbvaopenmind.com/en/articles/the-past-decade-and-future-of-political-media-the-ascendance-of-social-media/
- BBVA Dentzel Z, (2013) How the Internet Changed Everyday Life.
- Bein Media Group (2020), The Group. Retrieved from https://www.beinmediagroup.com/the-group/
- Benedictus, L. (2013) Qatar: 12 things you need to know. The Guardian. Retrieved from https://www.theguardian.com/global/2013/jun/25/qatar-12-things-you-need-to-know
- Bennett, L. (2006) "Communicating Global Activism: Strength and Vulnerabilities of Networked Politics." In Cyberprotest: New Media, Citizens and Social Movements, ed. van de Donk, W., Loader, B. D., Nixon, P. G., Rucht, D. London: Routledge.
- Berghof Foundation. (2014). Designing Effective Communication Strategies. Retrieved from https://www.berghof-foundation.org/fileadmin/redaktion/Publications/Other_Resources/Strategic_Frameworks/Framework_Communication_Strategies_final.pdf
- Biance W. (2020) Middle East Digital Transformation retrieved from:https://www.cio.com/article/3513416/middle-easts-digital-transformation-laggard-status-may-be-a-benefit.html
- Boyd, Danah M., and Nicole B. Ellison (2007)
- Brand Directory (2020). Global Soft Power Index. Retrieved from https://brandirectory.com/globalsoftpower/download/brand-finance-global-soft-power-index-2020.pdf.

- Brown, Tom B.& Mann, Benjamin & Ryder, Nick & Subbiah, Melanie (2020), Language Models are Few-shot learners. https://www.thetalkingmachines.com/sites/default/files/2020-12/neurips-2020-language-models-are-few-shot-learners-paper.pdf
- Camelia.P (2010) The Role of Mass Media in Modern Democracy, retrieved from: http://management.ucdc.ro/revista/full%20text%202010/Full%20text-15.pdf
- Cheng, B., & Titterington, D. M. (1994). Neural Networks: A Review from a Statistical Perspective.
- Cherkaoui, T., 2018. Qatar's public diplomacy, international broadcasting, and the Gulf Crisis. https://risingpowersproject.com/quarterly/qatars-public-diplomacy-international-broadcasting-and-the-gulf-crisis/
- Chui, M., Manyika, J., Bughin, J., Dobbs, R., Roxburgh, C., Sarrazin, H., Sands, G., & Westergren, M. (2019, February 13). *The social economy: Unlocking value and productivity through social technologies.* McKinsey & Company. https://www.mckinsey.com/industries/technology-media-and-telecommunications/our-insights/the-social-economy
- Cinzia Bianco and Gareth Stansfield, 2018, The intra-GCC crises: mapping GCC fragmentation https://www.chathamhouse.org/publication/ia/intra-gcc-crises-mapping-gcc-fragmentation-after-2011
- CNBC (2018) What is Fintech retrieved from: https://www.cnbc.com/video/2018/06/07/what-is-fintech.html
- CNBC International (2017, Jun 29) What does Qatar own around the world? CNBC Explains. [Video File]. Retrieved from https://www.youtube.com/watch?v=8mZl9AePmHs
- Copeland, B. J. (2020, August 11). *Artificial intelligence.* https://www.britannica.com/technology/artificial-intelligence .
- CPD Blog 2017, Qatar's Crisis Management Comms Plan. Retrieved from: https://www.uscpublicdiplomacy.org/blog/qatar%E2%80%99s-crisis-management-comms-game-plan

- Delfmann, Werner & Baum, Herbert & Auerbach, Stefan & Albers, Sascha. (2005). Strategic Management in the Aviation Industry.

- Deloitte (2017), National Transformation in the Middle East Report, retrieved from: https://www2.deloitte.com/content/dam/Deloitte/xe/Documents/technology-media-telecommunications/dtme_tmt_national-transformation-in-the-middleeast/National%20Transformation%20in%20the%20Middle%20East%20-%20A%20Digital%20Journey.pdf

- Desoukie, B. O. A. (2019, August 13). *How Artificial Intelligence Changes Media In The Middle East.* Communicate Online | Regional Edition | Advertising, marketing, public relations and media in the Arab world and beyond. https://www.communicateonline.me/digital/how-artificial-intelligence-changes-media-in-the-middle-east/ .

- Destiny J, (2017) How did the Obama Administration Use Social Media in 2012, retrieved from: https://www.destinyjackson.org/blogs/articles-essays/how-did-the-obama-administration-use-social-media-to-win-the-2012-elections

- Doha Book Fair (2019), https://29.dohabookfair.qa/%d8%a7%d9%84%d9%85%d8%b9%d8%b1%d8%b6/%d9%85%d9%86-%d9%86%d8%ad%d9%86/%d9%83%d9%84%d9%85%d8%a9_%d8%a7%d9%84%d8%af%d9%88%d8%b1%d8%a9_29/

- Doha Book Fair (2020), https://30.dohabookfair.qa/%d8%a7%d9%84%d9%85%d8%b9%d8%b1%d8%b6/%d9%85%d9%86-%d9%86%d8%ad%d9%86/%d9%82%d8%b5%d8%a9-%d8%a7%d9%84%d8%b4%d8%b9%d8%a7%d8%b1/

- Doha International Center for Interfaith Dialogue (2020). Annual Conferences. Retrieved from http://www.dicid.org/annnual_conferences_ar/.

- Ebrar Sahika Kucukasci 2019, The Saudi Led Blockade Won't End Anytime Soon, but Qatar has moved on. Retrieved from:

- https://www.trtworld.com/opinion/the-saudi-led-blockade-won-t-end-anytime-soon-but-qatar-has-moved-on-26803
- Education Above All .(2020). Al FAKHOORA Program. Retrieved from https://educationaboveall.org/#!/programme/al-fakhoora.
- Education Above All .(2020). Educate A Child Program. Retrieved from https://educationaboveall.org/#!/programme/educate-a-child.
- Education Above All .(2020). PROTECT EDUCATION IN INSECURITY AND CONFLICT. Retrieved from https://educationaboveall.org/#!/programme/peic.
- Education Above All. (2020). About Education Above All. Retrieved from https://educationaboveall.org/#!/about/1.
- Egypt Today 2017, What does Qatari Emir's Speech Mean. Retrieved from: https://www.egypttoday.com/Article/2/13184/What-does-Qatari-emir%E2%80%99s-speech-mean
- Engel, Tilman. (2018). interview with Hassan Al-Ibrahim, Acting Qatar Tourism Authority Chairman. Retrieved from https://www.sbc-international.de/wp-content/uploads/2018/10/Qatar-Tourism-Strategy-World-Cup-2022.pdf.
- EPRS, E. P. R. S. (2020). The ethics of artificial intelligence: Issues and initiatives, Study, Panel for the Future of Science and Technology EPRS, European Parliamentary Research Service Scientific Foresight Unit (STOA) – March 2020.
- FIFA (2016). FIFA grants media rights in France to TF1 and beIN SPORTS for major tournaments. Retrived from https://www.fifa.com/who-we-are/news/fifa-grants-media-rights-in-france-to-tf1-and-bein-sports-for-major-to-2755440.
- Finn, Greg (2014). Twitter and Facebook launch their 2014 'Year in review' with top content, trends & more. Marketing Land. Retrieved from https://marketingland.com/twitter-facebook-launch-2014-year-review-top-content-trends-110643
- Gabriel Collins, J.D., Baker Institute (2018), "Anti-Qatar Embargo

- Grinds Toward Strategic Failure" https://www.bakerinstitute. org/media/files/files/7299ac91/bi-brief-012218-ces-qatarembargo.pdf
- Gamal Gasim (2018), The Qatari Crisis and Al Jazeera's Coverage of the War in Yemen https://www.arabmediasociety.com/the-qatari-crisis-and-al-jazeeras-coverage-of-the-war-in-yemen/
- Ghahramani, Zoubin, "An introduction to Hidden Markov Models and Bayesian Networks", International Journal of Pattern Recognition and Artificial Intelligence, Hidden Markov Models, Applications in Computer Vision, Edited By: Horst Bunke (University of Bern, Switzerland) and Terry Caelli (University of Alberta, Canada), volume 45, June 2001. https://doi.org/10.1142/4648
- Giampiccoli, Andrea & Mtapuri, Oliver.(2015). Tourism development in Qatar: towards a diversification strategy beyond the conventional 3 Ss. *African Journal of Hospitality, Tourism and Leisure, 4*(1).
- Global Union, U. N. I. (2018). Top 10 Principles for Ethical Artificial Intelligence.
- Google. *Speech-to-Text: Automatic Speech Recognition | Google Cloud.* Google. https://cloud.google.com/speech-to-text/?utm_campaign=emea-emea-all-en-dr-bkws-all-all-trial-e-gcp-1009139.
- Grix, J. (2013). "Image" leveraging and sports mega-events: Germany and the 2006 FIFA World Cup. *The Journal of Sport Tourism, 17*(4), 289–312. https://doi.org/10.1080/14775085.2012.760934
- Grunig, J. E. (2001). *Excellence Theory in Public Relations: Past, Present, and Future.* SpringerLink. https://link.springer.com/chapter/10.1007/978-3-531-90918-9_22
- Guan, Z.-H., Hu, B., & Shen, X. (2019). Hybrid Intelligent Networks. *Introduction to Hybrid Intelligent Networks*, 1–26. https://doi.org/10.1007/978-3-030-02161-0_1

- Gulf Times (2020), Qatar Encourages Digital Transformation in Commercial Transactions, retrieved from: https://www.gulf-times.com/story/663161/Qatar-encourages-digital-transformation-in-commerc
- H.O.R (2020), House Of Representatives, H.R. 6216 To establish the National Artificial Intelligence Initiative, and for other purposes. House of Representatives, United States.
- Hamad Awards (2020). About Sheikh Hamad Award for Translation and International Understanding. Retrieved from https://hta.qa/en/.
- Hamilton, Eric, (2018) — Last Updated: 27 Dec'18 2018-12-27T08:37:12 00:00, & Name*. (2018, December 27). *What is Edge Computing: The Network Edge Explained.* Cloudwards. https://www.cloudwards.net/what-is-edge-computing/.
- Hassad Food. (2020). About Hassad Food. Retrieved from https://www.hassad.com/English/Pages/OperationsPortfolio.aspx
- Sports Strategy (n.d.). from https://www.mcs.gov.qa/en/sports/
- *Hybrid Intelligent Systems*. (2019). Lecture.
- IAStube (2017, Jun 24) 2017 Qatar Crisis Explained. [Video File]. Retrieved from https://www.youtube.com/watch?v=zHI5DcZWhSw
- *IEEE SA - Artificial Intelligence Systems (AIS)*. IEEE SA - The IEEE Standards Association - Home. https://standards.ieee.org/initiatives/artificial-intelligence-systems/index1.html?utm_expid=.qavZBKmuRnmUw2AK_BZo7g.1.
- Intellectual Principles. (n.d.). https://www.mcs.gov.qa/en/intellectuals-principle/
- Jake F. (2019) Virtual Currency retrieved from: https://www.investopedia.com/terms/v/virtual-currency.asp
- Jurafsky, D., & H. Martin, J. (2019). *Speech and Language Processing.* https://web.stanford.edu/~jurafsky/slp3/A.pdf.
- Katara (2020). About Katara. Retrieved from https://www.katara.net/About-Katara.
- Kaushik, A. (2017, November 6). *Artificial Intelligence:*

Implications On Marketing, Analytics, And You. https://www.kaushik.net/avinash/artificial-intelligence-machine-learning-implications-marketing-analytics/.
- Kentie, Peter (2020). A Story of a City and A Nation [PowerPoint Slides]. Retrieved from https://dkf1ato8y5dsg.cloudfront.net/uploads/14/57/1605-peter-kentie.pdf.
- Kluckhohn, F. R., & Strodtbeck, F. L. (1961). *Variations in value orientations Florence R.Kluckhohn ; Fred L. Strodtbeck.* Evanston, IL: Row, Peterson.
- Knott, B., Fyall, A., & Jones, I. (2017). Sport mega-events and nation branding: Unique characteristics of the 2010 FIFA World Cup, South Africa. *International Journal of Contemporary Hospitality Management, 29*(3), 900–923. https://doi.org/10.1108/IJCHM-09-2015-0523
- Krafft, P. M., Young, M., Katell, M., Huang, K., & Bugingo, G. (2020). Defining AI in Policy versus Practice. *Proceedings of the AAAI/ACM Conference on AI, Ethics, and Society.* https://doi.org/10.1145/3375627.3375835
- Kristian C. Ulrichsen* (2017), Lessons and Legacies of the Blockade of Qatar
  https://www.insightturkey.com/commentaries/lessons-and-legacies-of-the-blockade-of-qatar
- KWANCHAI RUNGFAPAISARN (2019) The impact of digital technology having on media organization Retrieved from: https://www.nationthailand.com/business/30375461
- Lea Hickert (2019), Qatar Crisis Blockade Embargo, Fair Observer Retrieved from https://www.fairobserver.com/region/middle_east_north_africa/qatar-crisis-blockade-embargo-saudi-arabia-uae-gulf-news-khaleej-38004/
- Lee, K. M. (2009). Nation branding and sustainable competitiveness of nations. *Unpublished PhD Thesis, University of Twente.*
- Li, Eldon Y. (1994). "Artificial neural networks and their business

applications", Institute of Information Management, National Chung Cheng University, http://eli.johogo.com/pdf/neural.pdf
- Lin, C. (2020). Understanding Cultural Diversity and Diverse Identities. *Quality Education*, 929-938.
- Liu, B. F., & Horsley, J. S. (2007). The Government Communication Decision Wheel: Toward a Public Relations Model for the Public Sector. *Journal of Public Relations Research*, *19*(4), 377–393. https://doi.org/10.1080/10627260701402473
- Lobelog (2017), Was Emir Tamim's Speech A Turning Point In The Qatar Crisis? Retrieved from https://lobelog.com/was-emir-tamims-speech-a-turning-point-in-the-qatar-crisis/
- MARC OWEN JONES 2019, Propaganda, Fake News, and Fake Trends: The Weaponization of Twitter Bots in the Gulf Crisis file:///C:/Users/maya.ghorayeb/Downloads/8994-37168-1-PB.pdf
- Mariam I. Al Hammadi – 2018, Presentation of Qatari Identity at National Museum of Qatar: Between Imagination and Reality https://www.jcms-journal.com/articles/10.5334/jcms.171/
- Mark I. Wilson and Kenneth E. Corey (2012), The Role of ICT in Arab Spring Movements retrieved from: https://journals.openedition.org/netcom/1064?lang=en
- McFarland, M. (2019, April 17). *Elon Musk: 'With artificial intelligence we are summoning the demon.'*. The Washington Post. https://www.washingtonpost.com/news/innovations/wp/2014/10/24/elon-musk-with-artificial-intelligence-we-are-summoning-the-demon/.
- Mefalopulos, P., & Kamlongera, C. (2004). *Participatory communication strategy design: A handbook*. Food & Agriculture Organization.
- Mehr, H., Ash, H. and Fellow, D., (2017). "*Artificial intelligence for Citizen Services and Government*", Ash Cent. Democr. Gov. Innov. Harvard Kennedy School, August 2017.
- Memri Staff- May 25, 2017, Uproar In The Gulf Following Alleged Statements By Qatari Emir Condemning Gulf States,

Praising Iran, Hizbullah, Muslim Brotherhood And Hamas https://www.memri.org/reports/uproar-gulf-following-alleged-statements-qatari-emir-condemning-gulf-states-praising-iran

- Ministry Of Culture & Sports About us. (n.d.) https://www.mcs.gov.qa/en/about-us/.
- Ministry Of Culture & Sports, Ministry`s strategy (2018-2022) https://www.mcs.gov.qa/%d8%b9%d9%86-%d8%a7%d9%84%d9%88%d8%b2%d8%a7%d8%b1%d8%a9/%d8%a7%d8%b3%d8%aa%d8%b1%d8%a7%d8%aa%d9%8a%d8%ac%d9%8a%d8%a9-%d8%a7%d9%84%d9%88%d8%b2%d8%a7%d8%b1%d8%a9/
- Mirela Atanasiu, 2017, Book: Qatar Crisis In The Recent Security Context Of The Middle East.
- Mitchel, T. (2006). The discipline of Machine Learning. Pittsburg; School of Computer Science, Carnegie Mellon University.
- Mitchel, J., & Lapata, M. (2009). Language Models Based on Semantic Composition.
- Mohammed Ahmad Naheem, June 2017 The dramatic rift and crisis between Qatar and the Gulf Cooperation Council (GCC). https://www.researchgate.net/publication/319693755_The_dramatic_rift_and_crisis_between_Qatar_and_the_Gulf_Cooperation_Council_GCC_of_June_2017
- Monett, D., Lewis, C. W. P., Thórisson, K. R., Bach, J., Baldassarre, G., Granato, G., ... Winfield, A. (2020). Special Issue "On Defining Artificial Intelligence"—Commentaries and Author's Response. *Journal of Artificial General Intelligence*, *11*(2), 1–100. https://doi.org/10.2478/jagi-2020-0003
- Mostafa, H. (2017) إدارة الازمة الخليجية... نموذج قطر الناجح. Alaraby Aljadeed. Retrieved from https://www.alaraby.co.uk/opinion/2017/9/7/إدارة-الأزمة-الخليجية-نموذج-قطر-الناجح-1
- Mouchantaf, C. (2017) A Huge Military Buildup is Underway in Qatar. But who will man the systems. Defense News. Retrieved from https://www.defensenews.com/global/mideast-africa/2017/

12/15/a-huge-military-buildup-is-underway-in-qatar-but-who-will-man-the-systems/
- National Development Strategy for the State of Qatar 2011-2016, March 2011 https://planipolis.iiep.unesco.org/sites/planipolis/files/ressources/qatar_national_development_strategy_2011-2016.pdf
- Noor Odeh, 2018, The artist behind Tamim Al Majd portrait. Retrieved from: https://www.qatarliving.com/forum/welcome-qatar/posts/artist-behind-tamim-al-majd-portrait
- NDS-2 (2018-2022). Qatar Second National Development Strategy 2018-2020 (pp. 1-337). Retrieved from https://www.psa.gov.qa/en/knowledge/Documents/NDS2Final.pdf.
- OECD. (1996, January 1). *OECD iLibrary | Effective Communications Between the Public Service and the Media*. https://www.oecd-ilibrary.org/governance/effective-communications-between-the-public-service-and-the-media_5kml6g6m8zjl-en;jsessionid=3qPC5VS2qRg24baJmoMeOIQv.ip-10-240-5-150
- Organisation, O. E. C. D. (2019). *Recommendation of the Council on Artificial Intelligence*. OECD Legal Instruments. https://legalinstruments.oecd.org/en/instruments/oecd-legal-0449.
- Ouissal, Said, (2020)" what is Edge computing?", https://www.quora.com/What-is-edge-computing/answer/Said-Ouissal-1
- Papazian , S., Risl, M., Bohsali, S., & Matar, A. (2017). *Empowering the GCC digital workforce Building adaptable skills in the digital era*. https://www.strategyand.pwc.com. https://www.strategyand.pwc.com/m1/en/reports/empowering-the-gcc-digital-workforce-full-report.pdf.
- Patricia M. West, Patrick L. Brockett and Linda L. Golden (1997), *"A Comparative Analysis of Neural Networks and Statistical Methods for Predicting Consumer Choice"*, Marketing Science, 1997, Vol. 16, No. 4 (1997).
- Pew Research Center (2009), The Internet's Role in Campaign 2008, retrieved from: https://www.pewresearch.org/internet/2009/04/15/the-internets-role-in-campaign-2008/

- Pillars and Visions, Wijdan Cultural Center. http://wijdancenter.net/%d8%a7%d9%84%d9%82%d9%8a%d9%85-%d9%88%d8%a7%d9%84%d9%85%d9%86%d8%a7%d8%b8%d9%8a%d8%b1-%d8%a7%d9%84%d8%ab%d9%85%d8%a7%d9%86%d9%8a%d8%a9/
- Pressform (June 2017), *Qatar Crisis Turns Hostile on Social Media*, Retrieved from https://pressfrom.info/us/news/world/-58344-qatar-crisis-turns-hostile-on-social-media.html
- Qatar Foundation (2020). About Qatar Foundation. Retrieved from https://www.qf.org.qa/about.
- Qatar Museums (2020). Years of Culture. Retrieved from http://www.dicid.org/annnual_conferences_ar/.
- Qatar National Development Strategy (2018) Retrieved from: https://www.psa.gov.qa/en/knowledge/Documents/NDS2Final.pdf
- Qatar National Vision 2030, July 2008 https://www.psa.gov.qa/en/qnv1/Documents/QNV2030_English_v2.pdf
- Qatar Science & Technology Park (2020). About Qatar Science & Technology Park. Retrieved from https://qstp.org.qa/about/.
- Qatar Second National Development Strategy 2018-2022 https://www.psa.gov.qa/en/knowledge/Documents/NDS2Final.pdf
- Qatar Tourism Authority, Retrieved 25 September 2020 from: https://auth.qatartourism.gov.qa/binaries/content/assets/media/upload-file/en/tourism-investment/qta_investment-brochure_v2.pdf
- *Qatar's diversification strategy supports economic development.* (2020, December 24). Oxford Business Group. https://oxfordbusinessgroup.com/overview/steady-course-strong-fundamentals-and-robust-diversification-strategy-support-continued-economic

- Qatari Committee for the Alliance of Civilizations (QCAC). (2019). Retrieved 20 September 2020, from https://mofa.gov.qa/en/foreign-policy/international-cooperation/alliance-of-civilizations
- Qatari Emiri Decree No. 20 (2010).
- Qatari Government. Office of Communication. (2015). Objectives and Mission. Retrieved from https://www.gco.gov.qa/en/about-the-gco/objective-and-mission/
- Qatari Government. Planning and Statistics Authority. (2020). Monthly Figures on Total Population. Retrieved from https://www.psa.gov.qa/en/statistics1/statisticssite/pages/population.aspx.
- QCAI, National Artificial Intelligence Strategy Qatar (2019). https://www.motc.gov.qa/sites/default/files/national_ai_strategy_-_english_0.pdf
- Report of the sixty-seventh plenary session of the Conference of European Statisticians. (2019). Retrieved 12 September 2020, from https://www.unece.org/fileadmin/DAM/stats/documents/ece/ces/2019/7_Strategic_commmunication_framework_for_consultation.pdf
- Report, H. (2016, April 29). *The Cost Of Poor Communications*. Provok.https://www.provokemedia.com/latest/article/the-cost-of-poor-communications
- Reuter, 2017, Qatar deposited over $10 bln in banks to offset crisis outflows Retrieved from: https://www.reuters.com/article/qatar-banks-deposits-idUSL5N1KI3X6
- Rondeau, T. W., & Bostian, C. W. (2009). *Artificial intelligence in wireless communications*. Artech House.
- Rumelhart, D. E., Widrow, B., & Lehr, M. A. (1994). The basic ideas in neural networks. *Communications of the ACM, 37*(3), 87–92. https://doi.org/10.1145/175247.175256
- Russel B (2017), Social Media New Technologies and Middle East, retrieved from:

- https://www.hoover.org/research/social-media-new-technologies-and-middle-east
- Sammut-Bonnici, T. (2015). Brand and branding. *Wiley Encyclopedia of Management*.
- Sandra WK (2018) Ecommerce Shopping Experience, retrieved from: https://securionpay.com/blog/ecommerce-shopping-experience/
- SAS. (2020). *What is Natural Language Processing?* https://www.sas.com/en_us/insights/analytics/what-is-natural-language-processing-nlp.html.
- Seabrook, J. (2019). *"Can a Machine Learn to Write for The New Yorker?"*, The New Yorker. https://www.newyorker.com/magazine/2019/10/14/can-a-machine-learn-to-write-for-the-new-yorker.
- Serrano, W. (2018, September 6). *The Random Neural Network and Web Search: Survey Paper*. SpringerLink. https://link.springer.com/chapter/10.1007/978-3-030-01054-6_51.
- Sheila S. (2007), Book: An Introduction to Communication Studies.
- Sidra Medicine (2020). About Sidra Medicine. Retrieved from https://www.sidra.org/.
- Siv R. (2017) The Impact of Technology in Healthcare, retrieved from: https://www.elcom.com.au/resources/blog/the-impact-of-technology-in-healthcare-trends-benefits-examples
- Snoj, Jure,(2019) "Population of Qatar by nationality - 2019 report", Population of Qatar by nationality in 2019 (priyadsouza.com)
- Social Network Sites: Definition, History, and Scholarship. Journal of Computer-Mediated Communication 13.
- Steve. C (2009) The Impact of Technology on Political Communication, retrieved from: https://observer.com/2009/06/the-impact-of-technology-on-political-communication/
- Stewart, D. (2017) Qatar's resilience – a lesson to all on how to respond positively to a crisis. Gulf Times. Retrieved from http://www.gulf-times.com/story/566847/Qatar-s-resilience-a-lesson-for-all-on-how-to-resp

- Straccia, Umberto (2014), Foundations of Fuzzy logic and Semantic Web Languages. Boca Raton: Chapman and Hall. 2014.
- Strategy of the Ministry of Sports and Culture 2018-2022.
- *Successful Communication Strategy: Five Elements*. (2017, July 14). Glasscock School of Continuing Studies. https://glasscock.rice.edu/blog/successful-communication-strategy-five-elements
- Sultan, Nabil (2011). "Aljazeera: Media or Medium of Change in the Arab World?" Conference Paper at *Conference: Gulf Research Meeting At: Cambridge University (UK) •July 2011.* Retrieved 18 September 2020 from https://www.researchgate.net/publication/277770964_Aljazeera_Media_or_Medium_of_Change_in_the_Arab_World
- Tāriq, '., & Gilani, Z. A. (1966). *The holy Quran*. Lahore: M. Siraj-ud-Din.
- Tefas, Anastasios, Iosifidis, Alexandros, and Pitas, Ioannis (2013), "*Neural Networks for Digital Media Analysis and Description*", Engineering Applications of Neural Networks, Springer, 2013
- The Africa Report.Com. Saudi Arabia ends its Qatar blockade, but dispute is not over. (2021, January 7). https://www.theafricareport.com/57423/saudi-arabia-ends-its-qatar-blockade-but-dispute-is-not-over/
- The GCC Crisis at One Year, 2018, Al Ansari, Baaboud et Al. Retrieved from: http://arabcenterdc.org/wp-content/uploads/2019/05/The-GCC-Crisis-at-One-Year.pdf
- The New York Times 2017, Countries That Broke Ties With Qatar Indicate Some Flexibility on Demands. Retrieved from: https://www.nytimes.com/2017/07/18/world/middleeast/qatar-crisis-demands-saudi-arabia-tillerson.html?rref=collection%2Fsectioncollection%2Fmiddleeast&_r=0
- The Qatar Crisis, its Regional Implications, 2018, and the US National Interest

https://smallwarsjournal.com/jrnl/art/qatar-crisis-its-regional-implications-and-us-national-interest

- The Strategic Orientations in the Field of Youth https://www.mcs.gov.qa/en/youth/
- United States Environmental Protection Agency. *GUIDANCE REGARDING COMMUNICATION STRATEGIES.* Retrieved 25 September 2020, from https://semspub.epa.gov/work/11/174743.pdf
- Vesna K. (2018) How Social Media Has Transformed Politics, retrieved from:

   https://strategicsocialmedialab.com/how-social-media-has-transformed-politics/
- Virginia, D. (2018). Responsible Artificial Intelligence: Designing AI for Human Values".
- Vladimir. R (2010) The Role of Information and Communication Technologies in Diplomacy and Diplomatic Services. Retrieved from:

   https://www.diplomacy.edu/sites/default/files/30112010141720%20Radunovic%20%28Library%29.pdf
- Walsh, A. J. (1994, June 1). *Meaningful Work as a Distributive Good.* Wiley Online Library. https://onlinelibrary.wiley.com/doi/abs/10.1111/j.2041-6962.1994.tb00713.x
- Wang, P. (2019). On Defining Artificial Intelligence. *Journal of Artificial General Intelligence*, *10*(2), 1–37. https://doi.org/10.2478/jagi-2019-0002
- Washington Post 2017, UAE Hacked Qatari Government sites https://www.washingtonpost.com/world/national-security/uae-hacked-qatari-government-sites-sparking-regional-upheaval-according-to-us-intelligence-officials/2017/07/16/00c46e54-698f-11e7-8eb5-cbccc2e7bfbf_story.html

- Webster, M. *Artificial Intelligence*. https://www.merriamwebster.com/dictionary/artificial intelligence
- Wheeler, T. (2020, May 6). *History's message about regulating AI*. Brookings.https://www.brookings.edu/research/historys-message-about-regulating-ai/.
- Wikstrom, C. (2017) Glorious Tamim: 'you won and you were silent'. Aljazeera. Retrieved from https://www.aljazeera.com/indepth/features/2017/07/glorious-tamim-won-silent-170718093327234.html
- WISE (2020). About WISE. Retrieved from https://www.sidra.org/.
- Yu, H., Shen, Z., Miao, C., Leung, C., Lesser, V. R., & Yang, Q. (2018). Building Ethics into Artificial Intelligence. *Proceedings of the Twenty-Seventh International Joint Conference on Artificial Intelligence*. https://doi.org/10.24963/ijcai.2018/779